TV creators

D1642892

The Television Series | Robert J. Thompson, Series Editor

Producer's seminar. Left to right: Robert Batscha (pres., MTR), Marshall
Herskovitz, Steven Bochco, Dick Wolf, David Kelley, Tom Fontana, Ed Zwick.

PHOTOGRAPHER, JAY BRADY. COURTESY OF THE MUSEUM OF TELEVISION AND RADIO.

TV Creators

CONVERSATIONS WITH AMERICA'S TOP PRODUCERS OF TELEVISION DRAMA

James L. Longworth, Jr.

Syracuse University Press

00   01   02   03   04   05   6   5   4   3   2   1

The paper used in this publication meets the mini-
mum requirements of American National Standard for
Information Sciences—Permanence of Paper for Printed
Library Materials, ANSI Z39.48-1984. ∞ ™

Library of Congress Cataloging-in-Publication Data

Longworth, James L., 1954–
    TV creators : conversations with America's top
producers of television drama / James L. Longworth,
Jr.— 1st ed.
        p. cm. — (The Television series)
    Includes bibliographical references and index.
    ISBN 0-8156-2874-9 (alk. paper) —
    ISBN 0-8156-0652-4 (pbk.: alk. paper)
    1. Motion picture producers and directors—
United States—Interviews. I. Series.

PN1998.2 .L64 2000
791.45'0232'092273—dc21

00-039476

Manufactured in the United States of America

TO our adopted dogs Scruff, Daisy, Parker, Blondie, Brunt, and to our horses Susie, Honey, Lady, Pal, Gigi, and Hank. They provided me with pleasant diversions during writing breaks (if you can call shoveling manure "pleasant"). Unconditional love is important when you're on deadline.

BOrn on March 11, 1954, in Winston-Salem, North Carolina, Jim Long-worth displayed an early talent for writing and broadcasting. As a student at R. J. Reynolds High School, he became one of the youngest announcers for WSJS Radio, and while attending the University of North Carolina at Greens-boro, Longworth learned all facets of television production at the campus stu-dio. After graduating, he followed a career path in television that included jobs ranging from camera operator to hosting and producing a live, daily talk show.

In 1980 Longworth and his wife, Joanne, founded a television production company that, today, specializes in production and distribution of documen-taries and public-affairs programming. During the past two years, Longworth has revived his writing career with articles that have appeared in *TV Guide*, *Western Clippings*, and *Columbia House RE-TV*.

Jim is a voting member of the Academy of Television Arts and Sciences, is president of Longworth Communications, Inc., and serves as publisher/ editor of *On Call*, a magazine devoted to the golden age of MTM studios with a particular emphasis on *St. Elsewhere*. Longworth has produced and directed a number of public-service television spots, including one that helped win passage of the nation's first significant handgun legislation. In 1999 he pro-duced and served as on-camera talent for a Public-Service announcement that documented the link between animal abuse by children and the violent crimes they commit as adults.

contents

Illustrations

Preface

Like the Martin Tupper character from *Dream On*, I was practically born in front of a television set. The year was 1954, and, according to R. D. Heldenfels, it was "television's greatest." A year later, Americans with TV sets first saw Marshal Matt Dillon walk and talk at the same time, a phenomenon not unlike that experienced by my parents as they witnessed the development of my motor skills.

In the mid-1950s, television and a boxer dog named Lady were my two best friends. This was nearly forty years before computer games were invented, and Blockbuster video rental stores opened, so I was pretty much left to my own devices when it came to entertainment. That resulted in much acting and pretending as I re-created scenes (and feats) from my favorite TV shows.

I drank milk from an opaque-looking Hopalong Cassidy mug, and pretended it was chuck wagon coffee. I brandished an official Zorro sword proudly, and took aim with a Davy Crockett musket, which, by the way, had a secret compartment for storing either gunpowder or bubblegum, whichever was more readily available. I also draped a bath towel over my shoulders and rivaled George Reeves's best take-off maneuvers. My launch pad was the living room sofa.

My parents and my big sister, Linda, were, I'm told, quite amused by my antics. Their favorite was my Alfred Hitchcock impersonation. Every week or so, I would walk out the back door to our one-story house on Oakalina Avenue and wait for the sun to find its mark. Then, as if cued by a stage manager, I extended my belly, puffed out my cheeks, and walked "into the shot," projecting my profile against the shadowed white siding of the house. "Gooood evvvening," I would say, in a staid, combination British and Southern accent. Suddenly, I *was* Alfred Hitchcock!

I was what you might call an "interactive viewer" decades before the term was coined. I suppose it was inevitable, though, that, with all of my jumping and leaping and swordplay, I was bound to sustain an injury or two. When only eighteen months old, I was rushed to the hospital for a hernia operation. The cause? "Superman, the Infant of Steel" had tried to lift the sofa.

In time, I got over the hernia, but not for my love of television. Then it happened. One day I began limping around the house. It was a pronounced and painful-looking limp. The affliction continued for several days, but each time my parents tried to ascertain the origin of the injury, I refused to speak. Worried, my mom and dad took me to see several doctors, none of whom was successful in diagnosing the problem. Finally, one of the specialists was somehow able to bring me out of my shell. "Jimmy," he asked, "why are you limping?" I responded with one word: "Chester." The doctor was still baffled, but my parents laughed with relief. They knew immediately what I meant. I had been impersonating Dennis Weaver's character, Chester Goode, from *Gunsmoke.*

It was a defining moment in my life. Unlike Chester, I didn't really limp. I wasn't even injured. I did suffer, however, from "televisionitis."

Looking back on it, I cannot "blame" Dennis Weaver for the medical bills my parents incurred, or George Reeves for my hernia. I realized later that the real "blame" lay with the writers and producers who created the on-camera personae of Superman and Chester. Just who are these powerful men and women who can have such an impact on the lives of millions of Americans? I was too young to read the credits then, but later I started to keep a close watch for these behind-the-scenes perpetrators.

Then an interesting thing happened. As I got older, and spent nearly all of my adult life producing television programs and documentaries, I came to realize that creators, writers, and producers of TV drama never really were the cause of my hernia or my limp. Instead, these people simply take us on wonderful excursions. They allow us to meet fascinating characters. They help us understand ourselves and those around us. They even teach us how to deal with issues that affect our lives.

As an adult, I no longer act out scenes from TV dramas but I do *re*act to them. At the end of the 1998–99 season, I remember watching the finale of *NYPD Blue* and I shed a tear when Andy and "Upstairs" John embraced. As I was writing this preface, I took a break to watch an early episode of *ER,* and was deeply moved when Carol blew marijuana smoke into an incapacitated man's mouth so that he could endure the ravages of pain and nausea.

I count myself as fortunate to have spent time getting to know twelve of the men and women whose creations have meant so much to me and to millions of others. Their dramatic programs also continue to initiate dialogue between parents and children, between blacks and whites, and between men and women.

These are the "above the line" folks who toil day in and day out to enrich our lives, and I am grateful they would spend time sharing their thoughts and feelings about television in particular and life in general.

In reading this book, you'll understand what drives John Wells at a pace not unlike that of *ER* and *Third Watch*, and you'll find out how religious disciplines helped Tom Fontana take us all to *Oz*.

You'll be touched by John Masius's journey to *Providence*, and fascinated by the origins of David Chase's ability to create *The Sopranos*.

You'll understand how Ed Zwick's and Marshall Herskovitz's life experiences helped redefine America's "fortysomething" generation in *Once and Again*.

You'll cheer for Brenda Hampton and Nancy Miller as they redefine the role of working women in Hollywood, while, at the same time, giving us *7th Heaven* and *Any Day Now* as springboards for better communication in our society.

You'll read about a Pulitzer Prize-winning mentor who helped David Milch learn how to write stories such as *N.Y.P.D. Blue*, and make them much more than just shows about cops and robbers.

You'll find out why Dick Wolf thinks that New York City is the best place to enforce *Law & Order*.

You'll also come to realize just how much of an influence Barry Levinson and Steven Bochco have had on shaping the television industry.

Former NBC executive and television legend Don Ohlmeyer, commenting on our twelve *Above the Line* producers, told me,

> When you look at the work these guys and gals have done that have emotionally touched tens of millions of people on a regular basis, it really is extraordinary. When you think of the greatest writers [in literature] of all time, they didn't touch as many lives as have the folks you are writing about. They've made audiences laugh, they've made them cry, they've made them question their lives, and brought up issues that the viewer had never confronted before. These are extraordinarily sensitive and talented people . . . the emotionality of Dick Wolf is different from that of Marshall and Ed, or Fontana or Masius—they have totally different frames of references in their lives, which is why there's great variety in the work they do. But that's what they have in common. The people that you've chosen to write about not only have had success, but they've done things that are about something, and it's not just about great storytelling—they've done things that were about the human condition.

Now, as you've probably already surmised, this is not a coffee-table book, nor is it about pop culture. It is not just for academicians or television insiders. And unlike many books about TV that often fail to include original interviews, *TV Creators* gives our interviewees an extended and unrehearsed forum. I believe this book will give scholars and fans alike an interesting representation of the men and women profiled, and, as a result, provide an accurate historical record of their contributions and philosophies.

I can honestly say that, thanks to the introspections of our twelve guests, I learned not just about them and their work, but also about my own life. In that sense, preparing this book has been therapeutic.

In retrospect, I probably should have devoted additional space in this book to say more about these twelve outstanding persons. However, I just heard my wife calling me from downstairs, and I think she wants me to move the sofa for her. "Superman Chester" to the rescue! I feel a limp and a pull coming on. Damn those television producers!

Petersburg, Virginia   James L. Longworth, Jr.
December 1999

Acknowledgments

In 1976 I produced and hosted a half-hour telecast with Red Skelton as the sole guest. At one point, he explained to me the three stages of man: "Youth, middle age, and 'Gee, you look good'." I think I may be fast approaching that final stage. Not long ago, while conducting a television interview with a local physician, I learned that men my age can lose a hundred thousand brain cells per day. My wife told the doctor that, in my case, the loss was much more than that. At any rate, I'm sure that I will forget to thank some of the people who deserve to be recognized, so please accept my apologies in advance.

I am grateful to the twelve *Above the Line* folks who took time out of their jam-packed schedules to speak with me. They didn't have to participate nor did they need to. Still, it is most fortunate for fans and scholars alike that they did. Egotistical as I am, I doubt that anyone would want to read a book full of my questions without any of their answers.

Thanks are also in order to the dedicated assistants who keep track of our distinguished producers: Lydia Friedman (Wolf), Donna Lee Gerber (Levinson), Bernadette McNamara and Jennifer Freeland (Milch), Josh Gummersall (Herskovitz), Graham Larson (Zwick), Shelagh Mary O'Brien (Wells), Karen Hacker (Miller), Jodie Gold and Patty Holmes (Masius), Sunil Nayar, Shannon Logan-Torres, and Lisa Randolph (Fontana), Maureen Milligan (Bochco), Julie Ross (Chase), and Jonathan Cycmanick (Hampton). Besides performing five hundred different duties every day, these folks also had to endure numerous telephone calls from me, and not once did any of them use swear words.

I salute Bob Batscha, president of the Museum of Television and Radio, and his secret weapon, David Bushman. As a tandem force, they make the museum and its activities more meaningful. Also, by inviting me to attend a special seminar in May of 1999, they afforded me access to the participants, which was of tremendous value in the preparation of this book.

Thanks to Tom Fontana and Mark Tinker for getting the Television Academy to accept me as a voting member—something both men have since come to regret.

My appreciation to Dr. James McNeer, president of Richard Bland College of the College of William and Mary, who believes, as I do, that television is an art form, and should be studied as such. Jim's support assisted me in my travels and research.

To Bill and Bonnie Daniels, the only married couple to ever win Emmys on the same night for the same program (*St. Elsewhere*), I extend my thanks for their support and for making sure that I ate a good dinner after a long day of jet lag on one of my journeys to the left coast.

Thanks to Jayne Meadows, for her kind words of encouragement about my writing ability, and to Steve Allen for not disputing her opinion until after I had left the room. Seriously, though, Mr. Allen is not only my favorite comedian, but also one of my favorite authors. My literary work pales in comparison. Of course, I was pale *before* I started writing.

A tip of the hat to programming visionaries Don Ohlmeyer, Chris Albrecht, Matt Blank, and Dawn Tarnofsky-Ostroff, for their contributions to the television industry and for sharing both their time and their insights with me.

My regards to *TV Guide*'s Lisa Bernhard and Beth Arky, for helping legitimize my avocation.

Thanks also to Emmy historian Tom O'Neil, for telling me to persevere, and to Bob Thompson, for his prodding.

Finally, I want to thank my wife, Joanne, for the countless hours she spent in front of the computer. Without her love and support, this book wouldn't have been possible. She inspired me as I embarked upon a new, late-life career.

Introduction

In an article for *Rolling Stone*, Jay Martel wrote, "The more television expands into myriad cable channels, the more the major networks seem inclined to draw within themselves, growing smaller and smaller until, like a cartoon snake swallowing its tail, they completely disappear."

Martel's observation was made at the beginning of the 1990s, but it would have been just as valid at the end of the decade. Throughout the nineties, the big three (ABC, CBS, NBC) continued to lose audience share. According to Baker and Dessart in their book *Down the Tube,* the networks dominated household viewing as late as 1980, with nearly 98 percent of the audience, but by 1995, that percentage had dropped to 63. At the beginning of 1999, it looked as if the free fall would continue unabated.

The decline had occurred partly because of growing cable penetration and the fact that channels such as HBO and Showtime were staying ahead of the creative curve by offering informative, entertaining, and compelling programming. But the big three's shrinking numbers were also due to what they (and their affiliates) were *not* doing.

In the 1990s, while cable was gearing up for competition in a five hundred–channel universe, networks and their affiliates became bogged down with every social, political, creative, legal, and internal squabble that reared its head. Even worse, they never seemed able or willing to offer substantive solutions.

Compensation

For example, the networks fought with their affiliates over compensation. Local TV stations wanted more money to carry network programming, and the big three wanted to pay less. As that debate raged on, two things happened. First, the local affiliates, instead of trying to create more programming that would secure long-term viewer loyalty, became more and more reliant on network programs to shore up their own offerings, something that became increasingly important as TV stations poised themselves for purchase by large media conglomerates. To put it simply, as far as most local television stations were concerned, "if it's not from the network or King World, it doesn't exist." Second, to add insult to injury, as the affiliate reliance grew, network programming itself became less entertaining. So, affiliates, by demanding continued compensation from the big three, were essentially fighting for the right to be paid to carry, in many cases, an inferior product. Baker and Dessart say, "So long as the marketplace is limited to commercial enterprises, all of which are committed to the highest possible ratings in the service of ever-increasing short term profits, the so-called competition will more likely create not diversity . . . but mere imitative mediocrity." CBS chief Mel Karmazin must agree. In June 2000, he told affliates, "of all the networks, we suck less."

Direct Satellite Service

Another distraction for networks and their "dependents" came when direct-to-home satellite service entered the picture. Not only did the eighteen-inch dish bring hundreds of channels into living rooms, but it also offered signals from distant network affiliate stations. A dish owner in Richmond, Virginia, for example, could watch *Oprah* on a station from Los Angeles and, as a result, would not receive Richmond-area commercials. However, this phenomenon wasn't entirely new. More than twenty-five years earlier, cable companies fought for the right to carry TBS and WGN, while local TV stations sought relief to force cable companies into carrying local signals. In the 1990s, however, network audience share was dropping as fast as the quality of most prime-time programs, so several affiliates sued DirecTV, and were successful in halting (albeit temporarily) distant signal offerings. Congress worked out a compromise that forced satellite programmers to offer local signals, and the controversy began to subside.

Still, most everyone missed the point. Once again, affiliates were protecting local turf, but, at the same time, refusing to excel in local programming. Except for the six and eleven o'clock newscasts, virtually everything else was network or syndicated fare (in markets such as Seattle and Greensboro, TV stations still preempted the network with locally produced daily programs of one variety or another, but they were exceptions to the rule). A result of all the whining and turf protecting was a nation of homogenous local signals. It was like going to a McDonald's; no matter where you traveled, the food always looked the same. Tune in a local newscast in Cleveland and it will have the same look as a broadcast in Atlanta, and so on. Rather than creating original local programs that communities could identify with, affiliates were essentially fighting to keep a "distant" *Oprah* or a "distant" *Jenny Jones* or *Wheel of Fortune* out of their homogenous backyard. This was trickle-up buffoonery at its best, and the networks themselves were committing the same kind of mistakes. Year after year, the big three played it safe and maintained the status quo. It is ironic in an industry born of something called "the box" that most television executives couldn't seem to think outside of it.

High Definition Television (HDTV)

Then there was (and is) HDTV. The FCC and networks demanded that affiliates offer high definition television, regardless of the unrecoverable costs incurred. Clearly, HDTV is a superior technology, but two things are evident. First, very few consumers are going to pay five to ten thousand dollars for a television set, and second, no technology in the world can improve the quality of the content. So, in 1999, the big three were boasting that anyone who had a compatible set could be enthralled by the HDTV version of *Suddenly Susan* or *Veronica's Closet.* Unfortunately, those kinds of shows wouldn't be any better even if the networks broadcast them in three-D TV!

The Internet

Speaking of technology, as the century closed, about 40 percent of Americans were active on the Internet, and networks were capitalizing on the new trend. *Drew Carey* was the first to do a live show on TV and as a Webcast simultaneously. Industry experts say the *Drew Carey* experiment will soon be the norm, but history tells us that every technological advance usually needs time to take hold. Internet use will probably not approach 80 percent until 2010, but TV network integration will continue in the meantime.

Mergers

As if Satellite service, HDTV, and the Internet weren't enough to distract an already mediocre industry, the late-1990s also became television's decade of mergers. ABC joined Disney. NBC became part of the GE family. CBS married Viacom. Such corporate activity brought with it a whole new set of issues to consider, among them, caps on market penetration (station ownership) and effective use of vertical integration. The latter even manifested itself into a major, end-of-the-century flap between producer Steven Bochco and ABC when the network threatened to bump *N.Y.P.D. Blue* out of its regular time slot in favor of the new, Disney-owned drama *Once and Again*. Independent producer Stephen J. Cannell blamed the FCC and Congress for allowing these megamergers. From the Los Angeles Times/Washington Post News Service, September 19, 1999: "American viewers need to know this sorry group of shows this fall is the new look of network television thanks to the blockheads in Washington who allowed the networks to take control of production without the public ever knowing what was going on."

With all due respect to Mr. Cannell, the new dramas of the 1999–2000 season are anything but sorry. Still, his analysis is not totally without merit.

Violence and Morality

While tempers were flaring from Hollywood to Washington, real-life violence would consume the industry in 1999 as incidents of mass shootings, hate crimes, and road rage increased. A stockbroker in Atlanta opened fire on an office full of colleagues. In Fort Worth, seven people were gunned down while attending a worship service. Also in Texas, a black man was dragged to his death, chained to the back of a pickup truck. And in Virginia, a black man was beheaded by two white racists.

But the rise in indiscriminate school shootings most rocked the nation in the last years of the millennium. There had been incidents in several other communities the year before, but in 1999 high school students in Littleton, Colorado, were killed by two of their classmates. Suddenly, educators, politicians, and assorted lobbyists were "concerned." Delayed a reaction as it was, the concern was justified, but they began to blame television for the rise in violence, and that wasn't entirely justified. Networks were under pressure to be sensitive to the charges leveled against them. An episode of *Buffy the Vampire Slayer* was postponed because it was about killing vampires at the high school prom. Episodes of other programs, such as *Homicide*, were aired out of their original order because of violent themes.

Congress and the FCC had forced a new TV rating system on the television industry before the violence escalated, yet many activists weren't satisfied. They threatened to mobilize for change (translation, censorship).

Fueled by research from the Washington-based Center for Media and Public Affairs, which reported that, in 1999, viewers were subjected to a violent scene every four minutes, politicians went on the attack again. Sen. Joseph

Lieberman and former U.S. secretary of education William Bennett presented the "silver sewer" award to the Fox network for perpetrating a "cultural disgrace." Fox's 1999–2000 season was singled out for its "tireless, tasteless, and ongoing efforts to drag down network programming standards, and for its cutting edge contribution to the coarsening of our culture" (from *Broadcasting & Cable* magazine).

No doubt Fox has some poor programs, but Fox also gave us *The X-Files* and *The Simpsons*. Even if Lieberman and Bennett had a legitimate concern, they should have known that everything goes in cycles. By the end of the 1900s, many of the less original sitcoms on television were being thrashed by quality, adult dramas.

Meanwhile, Sen. Sam Brownback, who had earlier supported repealing the ban on assault weapons, scored free face time on the evening news by threatening to establish a "code of conduct" (we had that in the fifties and sixties) to which entertainment companies would agree to adhere. (This would compliment the V-chip, which was designed to help parents monitor their childrens' viewing.)

Then the group Children Now issued a report that attempted to draw a parallel between television and violence. Boys from twelve to seventeen were studied to determine what TV shows they watched. Except for pro wrestling, most of the top picks contained no violence. In fact, most of the boys admitted that they also liked to watch *7th Heaven*.

Speaking of family dramas, in 1999 a group of major advertisers and their ad agencies struck a deal with the WB network to develop family-oriented scripts. Was this merely advertiser support? Or was it the beginning of a trend back toward advertiser control over content? Although many great dramas came out of the sponsor-controlled 1950s, the era was not without its drawbacks. In *The Days of Live*, producer George Roy Hill told author Ira Skutch about his experience producing a live TV version of *Judgment at Nuremberg*, which was being sponsored by the American Gas Association. "[A] few days before we went to go on air . . . the American Gas Association told us our contract said that 'gas' could never be used in a derogatory way. So their solution was to say that we couldn't mention gas in the show . . . you can't say that six million Jews died of apoplexy?"

On the positive side, there's no better role model for collaboration between advertiser and producer than *Hallmark Hall of Fame*, so perhaps the WB arrangement will portend well for the next generation of quality dramas.

Meanwhile, at the other extreme, some cable television networks, particularly MSNBC, CNBC, and CNN, were obsessed with President Bill Clinton's sex life, and by the end of 1999, his exploits had even slipped into the cultural lexicon. On an episode of *Law & Order: Special Victims' Unit*, a detective used the phrase, "getting a Lewinsky."

Racial Diversity

Congress's attention turned to another controversy before the close of the century—racial diversity on television. Early in 1999, the NAACP complained that the upcoming 1999–2000 season was devoid of black leading characters and that the industry had too few minorities in high-level executive positions. Congress went into high gear, and the big three scrambled as boycotts were threatened. Minority characters were added to some programs, but few people were willing to offer any long-term, substantive remediations. This was not a new phenomenon.

Glenn Altschuler and David Grossvogel, in their book *Changing Channels: America in TV Guide*, remind us that for most of the 1950s and 1960s, television avoided race. "Held hostage by local stations in the South, the networks dared not risk integrated casts or programs with racial themes." Altschuker and Grossvogel added that, in 1962, Sidney Poitier and Ossie Davis testified before Congress on discrimination in media employment practices—specifically "about the barriers black performers faced." None of the television networks covered or reported on the hearings.

George Hill and Sylvia Saverson Hill wrote in their book *Blacks on Television*, "From 1970 to 1979, blacks had starring or supporting roles in at least fifteen shows [but] there was one glaring error. The majority of these shows were comedies."

In 1977 and again in 1991, Congress appointed commissions to study racial disparities in the media, and, evidenced by the latest protest, neither of those previous efforts yielded appreciable results.

While Congress and the NAACP postured, Lifetime's *Any Day Now* continued to be television's lone beacon of weekly racial dialogue. In fact, after the 1999–2000 season premiere, the women-oriented channel teamed with vertically integrated partner ABC to offer a lively panel discussion as a follow-up to the preceding drama.

As a postscript to this ongoing saga, it can be said that this time around, the issue of racial diversity may be making some headway. By February 2000, all of the networks had agreed to some plan of action to assure racial balance both in front of the camera and behind the scenes. At the same time, *City of Angels*, with its predominately Black cast, landed midseason on CBS while Showtime ordered two minority dramas for summer, *Resurrection Blvd.* and *Soul Food*.

Ratings Games

Unfortunately, money, not social consciousness, still talks in Hollywood, and, at century's end, America was preoccupied, not with brown and black, but with the color green, in the form of ratings stunts such as ABC's *Who Wants to Be a Millionaire*, which spawned *Greed* on Fox and *Twenty One* on NBC.

Although game shows have always been part of the television landscape, they were never meant to air only in sweeps, or to run three or four nights per week. In the old days, game shows competed as weekly fare (*What's My Line, I've Got a Secret*), fifty-two weeks per year, and that's why "seasonal ratings boosters"—such as *Millionaire*—create nothing more than a false indicator of television's day-to-day program strength and normal viewing patterns. Speaking of gimmickry, as this book goes to press, reality programming has become the rage. Taking their lead from *The Truman Show, Ed TV*, and MTV's *Real World*, networks launched what critics call "Voyeur TV." CBS's *Survivor*, for example, followed the real life exploits of people stranded on an island, and viewers joined them in record numbers. Hour dramas suffered in the ratings because of these sorts of sweeps tricks, but, hopefully, the interruption will be short lived.

Course Correction

The year 1999, then, represented the best of times and the worst of times for America and for the television industry. It was a year fraught with horrible violence in our society, but one in which, thanks to TV shows such as *7th Heaven*, children learned to dialogue with parents on how to detect and deal with violent behavior by their peers.

As 1999 began, mindless sitcoms and trash talk shows dominated the landscape, and network television was still clueless as to what their role might be in addressing serious social issues. By year's end, however, an effort was being made to clean up the talk, and comedies and teen shows were being out-performed by thought-provoking dramas. Thanks to *Any Day Now,* race was talked about intelligently by actors and viewers.

Moreover, America's baby boomers, who had been abandoned by Madison Avenue and Hollywood, were suddenly being courted with programming designed to bring them back in front of the tube. Shows such as *Providence, Judging Amy, Family Law,* and *Once and Again* showed that adults, especially women in their late-thirties and forties, had much to offer, both in their art and as realistic role models.

Judging Amy's executive producer, Barbara Hall, told *Entertainment Weekly* (October 29, 1999), "The women's audience has been there, but for a long time they have not been addressed. . . . [T]he minute women see something even remotely like what their own lives are like, they will come out in force." And *Family Law's* cocreator, Anne Kenney, added, "At the start of this season it was 'kids, kids, kids!' Now everyone is talking about older women."

For a while it looked as if television had set itself adrift in a sea of mediocrity, but, by the time Y2K arrived, TV's ship had been righted and put on a course that made sense. It should be noted, though, that the real heroes of this course correction were the storytellers—men and women such as those profiled in this book. Because of their perseverance and vision, America (and the networks) came back around to a more intelligent and more entertaining use of the medium.

The FCC's Newton Minnow might have been wrong in the 1960s when he proclaimed television a "vast wasteland," but his assessment was pretty accurate for much of the 1990s—that is, until a select group of *TV Creators* stepped up to the plate and saved television from itself.

THE AGE OF DRAMA

Not that there was ever a conspiracy between China and A. C. Nielsen, but the Chinese New Year doesn't start until the middle of February sweeps. In 1999 the "year of the tiger" came and went, giving way to the "rabbit," who held honors until February 2000. It is fitting, then, that television reinvented and redistinguished itself with a genre that, like the tiger, quietly and stealthily slipped in and stalked its prey, then, rabbitlike, ran away with the prize—ratings and raves.

Americans too have names for months and days, even eras. The 1999–2000 television season could rightfully be called the "year of the drama." That moniker, however, doesn't do justice to the phenomenon. All indications are that it may have ushered in TV's seventh major era, the "age of drama."

For a historical perspective on the significance of this transition, it is helpful to review the previous eras. There are many ways in which we can delineate the stages of television history. One way is to categorize eras by quality. Author Bob Thompson, for example, describes the early 1980s and beyond as television's "Second Golden Age." TV's history can also be chronicled according to themes. The year 1964 was the "year of the rural comedy," the early 1970s, the "reign of detectives," and so forth. However, for this introduction, categorization is according to three factors. First, I ascertained what genre dominated an era in sheer number of entries, without primary consideration to the quality of the programs. Second, I factored in how those programs fared in Nielsen's top twenty-five. Third, I considered the impact and influence the genre had on the television industry and society. By these parameters, television has gone through six major eras before the start of the 1999–2000 season.

Era One (1948–1951): Vaudeville TV

Stage and radio performers made the transition to a new medium called television, and America was spellbound with laughter. Milton Berle's *Texaco Star Theater,* Sid Caesar's *Your Show of Shows, The Colgate Comedy Hour,* and other celebrity-driven "stage" shows dominated the era. In one year alone, Arthur Godfrey had two different shows in the top twenty-five. The emphasis was on slapstick comedy. The "stage" shows later turned to the variety format, which, led by a host of hosts, from Ed Sullivan to Carol Burnett, remained popular for most of the latter half of the twentieth century, though never as a dominant force.

Era Two (1952–1956): The Age of Lucy

Lucy and Desi were creators, not imitators. For that and for the influence *I Love Lucy* had on other programs in the genre, this era justifiably bears the star's name. During the period, Lucy begat a string of comedies with strong female leads, *I Married Joan, Private Secretary,* and *Our Miss Brooks* among them. Lucy never lost her appeal, and she would spin herself into a number of incarnations, such as *The Lucy-Desi Comedy Hour, Here's Lucy,* and *The Lucy Show.* Her contribution was most felt by her dominance of television in the 1950s.

Era Three (1957–1967): The Age of Westerns

In 1959 alone, no fewer than thirty-two westerns were on TV, and for eight of the ten seasons in this era, either *Gunsmoke, Wagon Train,* or *Bonanza* was the number one show. The genre began to lose its grip by 1962, giving way to the rural comedy surge (*The Beverly Hillbillies* was the only nonwestern to go to number one during this period), but even after the genre cycled out, *Gunsmoke, Bonanza, The Virginian, The Wild Wild West,* and others were still finishing well in the top twenty-five. All totaled, more than twenty westerns saw top twenty-five action during this period, and countless others missed the cut but filled the airwaves nonetheless.

Era Four (1968–1978): The Age of Classic Comedy

Ushered in by *Rowan & Martin's Laugh-In,* this era produced the most and the best comedies of any single period. In the ten-year period, forty different sitcoms dominated the top twenty-five, and there were no weak sisters among them. This was the time of *The Mary Tyler Moore Show, All in the Family, Bob Newhart, M*A*S*H, Happy Days, Barney Miller, Taxi,* and *Soap.* Not only did these classics garner high ratings—they have stood the test of time for their intelligent writing and brilliant ensemble performances.

Era Five (1979–1985): The Age of Soaps

Either *Dallas* or *Dynasty* finished first in the ratings for four of the six seasons in this era, and they were joined by top performers such as *Falcon Crest, Knots Landing,* and *Hotel* for top twenty-five honors. Other prime-time serials didn't fare as well (*The Colbys, Flamingo Road, Beacon Hill,* for example), but clearly participated in securing dominance for the genre. Many viewers had become enamored with opulence and greed, so this was, in a way, both a reflective and influencing television age. If you doubt their impact, evidence recent testimony by American-born Princess Lia of Romania, who credits *Dallas* with having inspired her countrymen to break from socialism in 1989.

Era Six (1986–1998): The Age of Cosby

As Lucy did in the 1950s, Bill Cosby ushered in, dominated, and shaped television in his era. *The Cosby Show* itself was number one for five years in a row, and many of the sitcoms it paved the way for carried the genre proudly for many years after "Cos" gave up his throne. In the 1990 season, out of ninety-three shows on air, fifty were comedies. And what comedies they were! This era gave us *Cheers, The Golden Girls, Roseanne, Designing Women, Evening Shade, Murphy Brown, Home Improvement, Seinfeld, Frasier,* and *Mad about You.* All of these modern classics graced Nielsen's top twenty-five, and all were among the two dozen or so shows that made up a second golden age of comedy. The only downside to this era is that, for much of the mid- to late-1990s, networks began to "green light" just about anything, and call it a comedy. These shows (and you know who you are) weren't funny when they premiered, and of those that remain, still aren't funny today. Unfortunately, these losers have to be categorized, and this is the only place to put them. Sorry, Dr. Cosby.

Era Seven (1999–): The Age of Drama

I believe this era will eventually become known as the Age of Drama. Since the early days of television, there have been outstanding dramas, beginning with shows such as *Naked City* and the early anthologies. There were *Perry Mason, Ben Casey, Dragnet, Marcus Welby, M.D., The Rockford Files, Columbo, The Waltons, Lou Grant, The White Shadow, St. Elsewhere, Hill Street Blues, thirtysomething*, and *L.A. Law*. The drama genre, however, has always been outflanked by more dominant program categories. In fact, from 1984 to 1998, the number of dramas on TV dropped from thirty-seven to twenty-three. A slough of sitcoms was still on the prime-time schedules, but quality dramas were slowly starting to return.

Law & Order, Homicide, NYPD Blue, Touched by an Angel, and *ER* all entered the scene in the early 1990s, and each was crafted by people who had learned the drama genre well, having earned their stripes by writing and producing top shows for other people. As dramas began their comeback, these beginning-of-the-decade pioneers seemed to beckon to other producers, saying, "Come on in, the water's not fine yet, but it won't be much longer till it is."

For networks, most of the 1990s was a trying time. Audience share was eroding, in part because cable channels such as HBO and Showtime were giving a voice to serious drama. *Any Day Now* became the signature show for the Lifetime network, and *The Sopranos* (HBO) in its first season won more Emmy nominations than any show, commercial or cable. This was the network's wake-up call.

In January of 1999, NBC took a chance on *Providence* as a mid season replacement, and, voila! Drama had turned the corner. By the time the 1999–2000 season rolled around, a whole new batch of hour programs appeared. Some were about women (*Judging Amy, Family Law*), others about relationships (*Once and Again*), others were political (*The West Wing*), and some were packed with drama and action (*Third Watch, Now and Again*). Together with veteran shows and the early 1990s pioneer dramas, these new offerings brought dominance to the genre.

At the start of the 1999–2000 season there were no fewer than sixty hour dramas on television (that includes network, cable, and syndication). Only four weeks into the season, eleven of Nielsen's top twenty-five were dramas, and, of those, five were new shows. All of a sudden, dramas (both established and new) were pulling in fourteen, fifteen, even sixteen million viewers each week. *Law & Order,* which had been hovering in Nielsen's high teens for the 1998–99 season, was now a steady top-ten show, finishing as high as sixth just a few weeks into the new fall schedule. At the same time, no fewer than eight sitcoms were under consideration for cancellation. Moreover, the drama genre became entrenched so quickly and completely that cable networks were scrambling to acquire groundbreaking rebroadcast rights.

Dick Wolf made a deal for *Law & Order: Special Victims Unit* to air on USA just thirteen days after its first-run broadcast, and *Once and Again* was snapped up by Lifetime for delay broadcast.

Is there a danger that these dominant shows will inspire five million drama clones? Yes. Could the Age of Drama be short-lived as a result? Absolutely. However, if the networks and cable channels nurture what they have, I believe that television's seventh era could run for another decade.

I hope that, as networks begin to clone successful dramas, they will take care to order only the highest quality imitators and innovators. The quickest way to destroy an era is by burning out the audience with "roadkill" (imitators that are DOA) and "overkill" (senseless piling on of one bad imitator after another). If we and they are vigilant, the Age of Drama could be our most literate era ever.

David Bianculli, in his book *Teleliteracy,* observed, "Sometimes life imitates art. Often times, TV instigates art. And at this point in time, TV deserves to be recognized as art." At least for now, Bianculli's argument rings particularly true, thanks to TV drama's "class of 2000." The question now is, Will that class graduate with honors, or fail the mark because of lack of creative or administrative support?

After all, according to the Chinese calendar, the "rabbit" is succeeded by the "dragon" who will escort us into 2001. And, as everyone knows, dragons are only an illusion. Fortunately, the reemergence of TV drama appears to be quite real.

Bill Croasdale of Western International Media, an ad-buying firm, told *TV Guide* (October 23, 1999), "The twenty-five to fifty-four year old viewer has fallen in love with the one hour drama . . . and this season, viewers are saying, 'Drama is where it's at'."

Let's hope drama is where it will stay.

Producer Profiles

The son of an accomplished violinist, **steven Bochco** is himself a talented musician (voice is his instrument), but writing was always his dream. Although the legitimate theater appealed to him, television claimed him. Bochco cut his teeth writing for several detective shows in the late-1960s and early-1970s. While at MTM (Mary Tyler Moore Enterprises), he created *Hill Street Blues* and redefined the TV cop show. He did the same for courtroom dramas with *L.A. Law*. His longest-running series, *NYPD Blue*, broke new ground for commercial television with its nudity and adult language. Bochco and his programs have won every major industry award.

A native of New Jersey, **David Chase** traveled west to attend film school, hoping to write for the big screen. Instead, some of his unsold screenplays and TV scripts landed him a spot on the writing staff of *The Rockford Files*. His street-smart prose gained him respect among industry insiders, but to the media and the public at large, Chase was still a relative unknown.

After having written for television across three decades, Chase's anonymity ended in 1999, when *The Sopranos* was nominated for an unprecedented sixteen Emmys (and won four). David was also named number two on *Entertainment Weekly*'s list of top entertainers for 1999, edged out only by Ricky Martin. So, at fifty-three, the creator, producer, writer, and director had become one of Hollywood's "newest" talents.

Tom Fontana is a product of a strict Jesuit education, but his teleplays have been anything but staid and traditional. After struggling as a playwright, Tom was discovered by MTM producer Bruce Paltrow, who hired the Buffalo native to write and produce *St. Elsewhere*. The groundbreaking medical drama earned Fontana two Emmys.

He later partnered with Barry Levinson to produce *Homicide: Life on the Street*, for which he won his third Emmy and three Peabodys. Levinson and Fontana also joined forces to create and produce *Oz*, an offbeat prison drama, and "The Beat," a police series for 2000.

In 1998 Fontana was number nine on *Entertainment Weekly*'s "Top Twelve Entertainers of the Year."

It should come as no surprise that, as a child, **Brenda Hampton**'s favorite TV shows were family comedies with a drama twist. After a stint as a writer for the military, and having made a nice living crafting jokes for stand-up comics, Brenda summoned those early influences as she launched a career in television writing about families. Skilled at comedy, Hampton wrote for shows such as *Mad about You*, but she found her niche in the hour format, creating *7th Heaven*.

Like his partner Ed Zwick, **Marshall Herskovitz** studied at the famed American Film Institute, then went on to write, direct, and produce episodic television for such programs as *Family* and *The White Shadow*. Together with Zwick, he coproduced *Special Bulletin* for NBC, which won four Emmys and the Humanitas Prize. The two friends also produced other highly acclaimed series, including *thirtysomething*, for which Marshall picked up two more Emmys, another Humanitas, and the Peabody. Their latest collaboration is *Once and Again*, a drama about two "fortysomethings" dealing with divorce and starting over.

Barry Levinson is best known for his films, among them *Rain Man*, *Diner, Avalon, The Natural*, and *Wag the Dog*. Along with Oscars, Levinson has collected his share of Emmys and Peabodys too. In fact, Baltimore's favorite son began his career in television, appearing in and writing for a number of comedy shows before breaking into films. Today, he continues work in both media, and with partner Tom Fontana, has created such memorable TV dramas as *Homicide: Life on the Street* and *Oz*.

John Masius, one of America's best storytellers, almost missed out on a career in television. On track to pursue business with his M.B.A. from UCLA, Masius was, instead, discovered by Bruce Paltrow, and given an opportunity to join the MTM family. From his first writing assignment on *The White Shadow* to his Emmy-winning work on *St. Elsewhere*, John has been associated with nearly a dozen TV series, including his latest creation, *Providence*.

David Milch has lived on the edge most of his life, and his television scripts reflect that influence. Exposed to gambling, drugs, and alcohol at an early age, Milch, nevertheless, rose to become one of Hollywood's most respected writers. He is a product of Yale and the prestigious Iowa Writers

Workshop, and his talent landed him a job on *Hill Street Blues*, where he won an Emmy and a Writers Guild Award for one of his first scripts. He has written, created, produced, and coproduced a number of programs, including *NYPD Blue*.

Nancy Miller grew up in the Old South, but was insulated from the scourge of racial discrimination. She discovered a love for writing while attending the University of Oklahoma, and dreamed of making that her career. Along the way, though, she worked as a bartender before finding her big break in Hollywood. While working steady as a writer and producer, Miller nurtured and pitched her pet project for eight years before *Any Day Now* was finally picked up. The Lifetime series deals with race relations, both today and back in the early 1960s.

As a child, **John Wells** was restricted on the amount of time he could spend with television. Thankfully, as an adult, that is not the case. As a production design major at Carnegie Mellon, and a graduate of the USC cinema department, Wells's writing skills were in demand almost immediately upon leaving college. One of his early efforts was as a staff writer on the TV series *China Beach*, but he gained notoriety as the writer/producer of *ER*, and, later, as cocreator of *Third Watch* and *The West Wing*. In 1999 Wells was included in *Entertainment Weekly*'s list of Hollywood's one hundred most powerful people.

Following in his father's footsteps, **Dick Wolf** began his career in advertising, first as a copywriter, then as a TV commercial producer. Later, he sought a different forum for his writing talents, first penning screenplays, then finding his niche as a writer, producer, and creator of television drama. Dick won an Emmy and a Writers Guild award for an episode of *Hill Street Blues*, and his hit series *Law & Order* has captured numerous honors, including a Peabody and an Emmy for Best Drama. In 1999 Wolf was inducted into the Broadcasting and Cable Hall of Fame, and named to *Entertainment Weekly*'s list of the one hundred most powerful people in show business.

Once a writer for *Rolling Stone* and *The New Republic*, **Ed Zwick** turned his powers of observation and his talent for storytelling to television and motion picture writing. A graduate of Harvard and the American Film Institute, Ed is singularly known for his award-winning direction of and involvement with such films as *Glory*, *Legends of the Fall*, and *Shakespeare in Love*. As a partner with Marshall Herskovitz, Ed has also left his mark on television, first writing for the ABC drama *Family*, and later cocreating *thirtysomething*. He has won Emmys for *Special Bulletin* and *thirtysomething*, and is cocreator of the forty-something TV drama "Once and Again."

TV creators

DICK WOLF | Law Man

Dick Wolf. COURTESY OF DICK WOLF.

TELEVISION CREDITS

1985	*Hill Street Blues* (NBC)
1986–88	*Miami Vice* (NBC)
1989	*Gideon Oliver* (ABC)
1989–90	*Christine Cromwell* (ABC)
1990–	*Law & Order* (NBC)
1990	*Nasty Boys* (NBC)

1991	H.E.L.P. (ABC)
1992	The Human Factor (CBS)
1992	Mann & Machine (NBC)
1993	Crime & Punishment (NBC)
1993	South Beach (NBC)
1994–98	New York Undercover (Fox)
1994	Swift Justice (UPN)
1995	The Wright Verdicts (CBS)
1996	Feds (CBS)
1997	Players (NBC)
1998	Exiled: A Law & Order Movie (NBC)
1999–	Law & Order: Special Victims Unit (NBC)
2000–	Arrest & Trial (syndicated)
2000–	Deadline (NBC)

ᨊᨊ ᨊᨊ ᨊᨊ

Dick Wolf was probably the town marshal in a previous life. He's tough but fair. He's a leader who can get the job done. More important, he and I both drank our milk from Hopalong Cassidy mugs and idolized western heroes.

"I went to the Roxy every Saturday with my parents," Dick recalls, "Either the Roxy or Lowe's on Fifty-second Street, which had the giant gold-fish pond in it. I also watched a lot of television, rode the arm of the easy chair in our library every day, and watched Hopalong Cassidy shoot bad guys. I still haven't shot anybody yet." (*Laughs.*)

Maybe not with bullets, but "buckaroo Dick" and his deputies certainly have "shot" a lot of bad guys on film over the years, many of whom bit the dust not far from Wolf's boyhood haunts.

Born in Manhattan, Dick, an only child, attended school on the Upper East Side before going to Andover at thirteen. He came by his love of and interest in show business honestly and genetically. "My grandmother wrote title cards for Paramount in the silent era. My father was a second-generation screen-writer. He did *Miami Story* and three or four other B movies in the early fifties. He also worked at NBC, so I spent a lot of my time sitting in the peanut gallery on the *Howdy Doody Show*. [Later] he was head of production for two major ad agencies, Ruthrauff & Ryan and Lennon & Newell that basically owned tele-vision shows. Ruthrauff & Ryan had a lot of Lorillard business and a lot of Colgate Palmolive business. My earliest memory is of being on the sets of live shows that were on Dumont and NBC. I think a couple of them were anthology series, not *Playhouse 90*, but "Dumont Theater" or something."

While still a student at the University of Pennsylvania, Dick would begin to follow in his father's footsteps. "I worked at ad agencies [Benton & Bowles and McCann Erickson] for two summers while I was in college. I've essentially never earned a dollar that wasn't somehow writing related."

After college, those writing skills landed him full-time employment with several ad agencies, where he created hundreds of national television commercials, including the famous "I'm Cheryl, Fly Me" campaign for National Airlines. His most prolific account, though, was Crest toothpaste, which, ironically, enabled him to brush off advertising and pursue a new career. "As I was approaching my thirtieth birthday, I realized that I really did not want to sell toothpaste for the rest of my life. That's when I was working on Crest with the actor Arthur O'Connell, who was playing Mr. Goodwin, if you remember that campaign. He owned sort of a general store and basically sold nothing but toothpaste. And I was spending a lot of time in California, almost three months a year shooting these commercials. It was 1975–76 and, nobody knew it because it really hadn't been diagnosed, but Arthur had Alzheimer's, so he could never remember any lines. We finally got up to eighty-six takes on one commercial. And he would screw up lines in ways that were really unique. There was one kid that he was pitching Crest to, and the kid wanted to be a lawyer, so the last line was: 'Bobby, you stick with Crest and you'll end up being a lawyer with the best teeth in town.' And on about take sixty-seven, he looks at the kid and says 'Bobby, you stick with Crest, and you'll end up being the best lawyer in town with teeth.' It was very sad, but the advantage to that is that everything took five times as long to shoot. So I was spending about three months a year in Los Angeles, happily ensconced at the Beverly Hills Hotel, and met a whole bunch of people, and bought a nonfiction book called *Trucker*, and turned that into a script that was bought by George Litto, who, I guess, was making *Obsession* at the time. *Trucker* became a 'go' project at Columbia. But by the time he got back to it, it had turned into an amber, then a red, light, because other studios were making *White Line Fever* and *Convoy*. So I was sitting here with this sold but unsold screenplay and was reading the *New York Times*, and read a Sunday magazine article about skateboarding, and quickly sat down and wrote a [film] script. *Bad News Bears* had been out the previous summer, and that's sort of how it took off. The picture was called *Skateboard*, which was like *Bad News Bears* on skateboards. That was in 1977."

Besides *Skateboard,* Wolf, in later years, would go on to write, produce, or coproduce other big screen works, including *No Man's Land* (1987), *Masquerade* (1988), and *School Ties* (1992). Dick would really make his mark however, in television, first as a writer on *Hill Street Blues* (after Steven Bochco's departure), for which he won an Emmy. He also began a long-term friendship with Tom Fontana, with whom he later teamed on several crossover episodes of *Law & Order* and *Homicide.* "We met at the MTM [Mary Tyler Moore Enterprises] graduate school of television," Dick laughingly recalls, "I was on *Hill Street Blues* and he worked for *St. Elsewhere,* in his youth and my middle age. There was always friendly competition, but remarkably similar attitudes towards getting shows done and keeping them at an A level. Everybody would occasionally have lunch together, because lunches were free, but it wasn't a question of going out and partying, because, as people don't seem to realize, on those shows you're a well-paid slave, and writing staffs were smaller in those days than they are today. It was kind of submersion for forty weeks a year."

After *Hill Street,* Dick moved from MTM to Universal, where, for two years, he ran *Miami Vice* (NBC), and created *Gideon Oliver* (ABC), starring Louis Gossett Jr., and *Christine Cromwell* (ABC) with Jaclyn Smith, all three of which were crime dramas. Then came Wolf's idea for a new kind of hour drama. With *Law & Order,* Wolf thought he had created a whole new type of show with a split-hour format. When he pitched it to Kerry McCuggage (then president of Universal, now chairman of Paramount Television Group), McCuggage responded that it had been done in the 1960s and was called *Arrest and Trial.* It starred Ben Gazzara as a tough detective who would catch criminals and Chuck Connors as a defense attorney who would often get them acquitted. The pilot for *Law & Order* was produced in 1988. Wolf first sold it to Fox, which subsequently backed out of the deal. (Ironically, Barry Diller, who headed Fox at the time, now helms USA Studios where Wolf is the star attraction.) Then he took it to CBS, who promptly rejected it because, according to Kim LeMasters (then head of CBS), the show had "no break-out stars." Finally, *Law & Order* found a home at NBC, where the late Brandon Tartikoff put it on the air. When Tartikoff left, Don Ohlmeyer came onboard as president of NBC West Coast, and he remembers an early meeting: "One of the first meetings I had when I got there was with Dick Wolf, and I said to Dick, 'You know, watching *Law & Order* is like watching Dr. Christian Barnard perform heart surgery. You know he's the best there is, you know it's pristine and pure, you know it's excellent. You know you're watching the best.' And Dick's sitting there, just beaming. And then I said, 'Now make me believe it's my fucking kid on the operating table, and you'll have a television show.' And three weeks into the season he called me and said, 'Do you believe your kid's on the table yet?' (*Laughs.*) It was so clinical, so I said, 'Put some heart in there.' And he would periodically ask me, 'Do you still think your kid's on the table?' And I'd say, 'Now that the kid is on the table, you can win an Emmy.' It's one of my favorite stories in the business. And I love Dick, he's a very talented guy."

Wolf was never content to corral that talent and rest on his laurels. *Law & Order* is stronger than ever, ten years after it debuted. Meanwhile, Dick has produced a variety of dramas during that tenure. They include *The Human Factor, Mann & Machine, Crime & Punishment, South Beach, New York Undercover, The Wright Verdicts, Swift Justice, Feds,* and *Players,* none of which made it to the new millennium. Dick's newest offerings include *Law & Order: Special Victims Unit,* a *Law & Order* spin-off that Wolf calls "a sibling, not a clone." *Special Victims Unit* follows New York City detectives who investigate sex crimes. The show features *Oz* veteran Chris Meloni, and allows Richard Belzer to reprise his role from *Homicide.* After only six episodes *Special Victims Unit* had broken into the top twenty-five, nearly doubling the viewers from its lead-in *Veronica's Closet.* In fact, it opened so strongly that NBC gave the show a full season pickup after only one airing. He also created *D.C.* (WB) and *Deadline,* starring Oliver Platt (NBC).

Today Dick Wolf is on top of the world, personally and professionally. On the home front, he and his second wife, Christine, have three children: Olivia, fifteen; Serena, twelve; and Elliot, six. Meanwhile, he was voted by *Entertainment Weekly* one of the "One Hundred Most Powerful People in Hollywood," and he continues to keep "law and order" in Dodge City.

Dick often admits that his goal in life is for *Law & Order* to make television history by beating (what else) *Gunsmoke*'s record on the air. I once pointed out to him that *Gunsmoke* lasted so long only because Matt Dillon never appeared naked on camera. I then asked Dick if he would promise never to show Jerry Orbach nude if it meant breaking *Gunsmoke*'s record. Wolf replied, "Absolutely! I'm willing to make that commitment. I can't guarantee the same about [Richard] Belzer." (*Laughs.*)

I caught up with Dick one Sunday afternoon as he took a brief respite from work. He spoke to me from the porch of his summer home in Maine.

Longworth: OK, so you've been inducted into the *Broadcasting and Cable* magazine Hall of Fame, you have an Emmy from *Law & Order* in your office, you have a long-term deal with USA for repeats. Since I'm fond of baseball analogies, let's say you're the player who's been hitting .400 every year, then gets all these honors and long-term deals, and suddenly, he starts hitting .210. How do you guard against something like that happening?

WOLF: (*Laughs.*) I guess I could credit my wife, which makes hitting .400 an economic necessity. (*Both laugh.*)

Longworth: You've been sounding a little exhausted lately—doing too many things. You're not destitute, so why do you push yourself to do three shows at one time?

WOLF: Let's put it this way. Two of the things that's strange about the television business is (a) you never know what's going to stick to the wall, (b) when you put stuff into development, you never expect that they're going to order everything. And I'm not being facetious about that. The WB show (*D.C.*) was just a straight development deal, there was no guarantee. And it was an area where, when I came up with it, it was the height of the Clinton scandal, and we got John August involved with the idea of doing something in Washington that was more hopeful than the current headlines. Something very appealing. And I thought there was an outside shot that the show was going to get ordered.

Longworth: Are you saying that being a successful production company is almost like running an airline, where you deliberately "overbook" with what you're pushing in development?

WOLF: I hate to say it's overbooking, but you never expect all the flights to be fully booked, and you don't expect everybody to show up. I don't think it is overbooking. We've had three shows on before. I mean, when *Law & Order* and *New York Undercover* were on, twice we had third shows, *The Wright Verdicts* and *Feds*. So as much as I suppose all of this would promulgate this ego-satisfying but untrue cult of personality around producers, the reality is that there are between 120 and 150 people working on each of these shows, without [whom] it literally is impossible to do the shows—none of us would be where we are. It's the people working on these shows, whether it's Ed Sherin, who's been directing episodes since the first season, or Rene Balcer, who started off as a staff writer in the first season of *Law & Order*, or Bill Fordes, who was originally the tech adviser in the first season and is an ex-New York City prosecutor, or Robert Palm, who has been working with me since *Miami Vice* on and off, and was a producer of the first two seasons of *Law & Order*, and now an executive producer on *Special Victims,* and Ted Kotcheff, who, to me, is one of the finest feature directors of his generation (I think *North Dallas Forty* is the best American movie about professional athletics ever made); he is the "Ed Sherin" of *Special Victims.* Or look at *D.C.,* where John Roman and Arthur Forney are running the show. Arthur's been with me, again, on and off for over a decade. John is an extraordinary producer who produced the *Law & Order* movie *Exile.* I mean, it's having this kind of bench strength that makes it even remotely possible to [have several programs on air at the same time].

Longworth: Speaking of doing several shows at once, the other day I was going over a complete list of all the shows that you had created.

WOLF: Oh, God!

Longworth: After all these years, don't you have some sort of internal gauge so that you know if an idea can make it as a series? Or is it still just a crapshoot?

WOLF: It's still a crapshoot. Ninety-five percent of stuff fails, but I hate to point out the obvious. If you went through the list, maybe I'm not the best judge of my own material.

Longworth: Nancy Miller [*Any Day Now*] told me that she doesn't consider a show to be a failure as long as it gets filmed and makes it to air. At least, then she would see her vision realized.

WOLF: I think that there are some shows that work and should have stayed on, and there are other shows that I miscalculated on. But for as long as they're there, they are all your children. Nobody sets out to make a bad show, but I can go through the list of some of the ones that I know where the big mistakes were, and they're still what I consider noble failures. For example, *Mann & Machine;* we never should have set it twenty years in the future. We should have taken that thesis and said, "It's right now." And I think the show would have worked much, much better.

Longworth: If you keep *Law & Order* on long enough into the new millennium, it will actually become *Mann & Machine.* (*Laughter.*)

WOLF: That's probably true. Those will be the beat cops. *Crime & Punishment* I'm still very proud of. I think if you look at some of those episodes, they're very good, but there was a fatal flaw in that one, which was breaking the fourth wall with the interrogator. I was completely dumbfounded. I thought the show was going to work like gangbusters, and I said, "Why didn't it work?" and someone said, "That goddamned interrogator." I said, "What was wrong with it, I thought it was really interesting." And he said, "Well, it just stopped the storytelling cold. As soon as you were getting into the story, bang! You went to this limbo cutaway of Rachel Ticotin and Jon Tenney, and that sort of took people out of the show." And believe me, that fooled everybody at NBC, too. They really liked it, but the audience didn't accept what they couldn't see.

Longworth: Well, you know Marshall Herskovitz and Ed Zwick are gambling on that same technique working for their show *Once and Again.*

WOLF: I know, and a lot of critics loved *Crime & Punishment.* (*Laughs.*)

Longworth: Since we're talking about what shows get on and which ones stay on, let's focus for a moment on the pilot system, of which you have been very critical. You've even suggested that pilots be replaced by short videos, and that the system should be revamped.

WOLF: It doesn't work. I mean the amount of money that is wasted every spring on shows—the pilot system—all you have to do is look back after they're bought, how much they're retooled, and how much they're recast. A much better expenditure of money to me would be (and at NBC I think you're going to see them doing it more) the way the WB does, even though I think that they're making too much film in the presentation. I think these presentations should be ten minutes long just to kind of know how the actors look on film, and make sure they don't bump into the furniture. But the real development money should be spent on scripts. And I've been saying this for years. I'm getting a little bit ahead of myself, but the two shows that have come out the most fully developed that I've done have been *Law & Order,* which was, luckily, a failed pilot, and then we went back and wrote six scripts before Brandon (Tartikoff) ordered it, and we knew what the show was. And the same thing has happened on *Special Victims Unit.* When we started production, there were eight teleplays in. And I think the level of finish on this show is higher because everybody had an idea of what the show was. Normally, the ludicrousness of the whole system is that you make a pilot in February or March, you wait around until the end of May when it's ordered, and then you're supposed to be in production seven weeks later doing twelve or thirteen more of these things. You haven't been able to hire a writing staff, you're starting from ground zero, and it's not really a surprise that most new shows suck.

Longworth: Since you mentioned the WB, what do you think about their new deal with advertisers who have agreed to put up eight million dollars to develop "family friendly" scripts? After all, you just said that money being spent on pilots should go toward script development. So let me put you in the middle of this issue. You're a former ad man, and you also have a contract with WB. Is this deal good for young writers and consistent with your philosophy on script development, or is there a danger that it could start shifting content control back to the advertisers and their agencies?

WOLF: It's a wonderful diversionary tactic, because there's not enough money involved to really make—I mean, you're talking about essentially a little more than high-end, pilot script money for this whole thing to develop family programming, and I think the extra money will probably be eaten up by WB executive salaries listening to these endless pitches.

Longworth: So you think it was more PR than—

WOLF: Yeah, but I think the idea is absolutely right. I'm not worried about content control. When they say "family-oriented" programming, the mandate is pretty clear. I don't think there are many content concerns on *7th Heaven* or on *Touched by an Angel*. When you say "family friendly" or "family-oriented" program, by its very nature it's not going to be controversial. I think that the idea of getting advertisers in early is a wonderful idea. I've been pitching this for years. But don't forget this is literally new wine in very, very old bottles. At the beginning of television, the ad agencies owned the shows, so this is hardly new. This is going back fifty years in terms of how programming was developed. The difference is that, in the old days, the advertisers essentially rented the delivery system from the networks.

Longworth: I knew you liked westerns as a kid, but as I looked over your credits, every show you've produced has had something to do with crime, cops, and sleuths.

WOLF: Well, we did a medical show that was on Thursdays at ten with Eriq LaSalle. (*Laughs.*)

Longworth: Just like *ER?*

WOLF: Well, it was actually medical students, which was the fatal flaw in that show. As I said, it was a very good show. John Mahoney [*Frasier*] was the head of this program in a med school that was associated with a hospital where he taught a course on human values and medicine; [it was] called *The Human Factor* [1992]. It had Eriq LaSalle in it. There is a basic problem about doing a show about medical students. They can't make life or death decisions, and are sort of observers. But it was on Thursday at ten on CBS, so we were about three years early with a little bit of the wrong franchise. But, you're right, the rest have been sort of legal or police oriented, and there's a reason for that. For the last fifty years, the most successful shows have been either crime or medically oriented, and that's because drama is conflict, and the ultimate conflict is life and death. And those are the shows that deal with it on a weekly basis without being a huge reach.

Longworth: Have you ever wanted to produce a western series?

WOLF: Oh, are you kidding? I'd love to do a western. Waylon Green and I developed a western for ABC that I'm still in shock didn't get on air, called *The Regulator*, which was a ten o'clock western that was really a kick-ass show. I can't believe it didn't make it.

Longworth: The guys with the long rifles who—

WOLF: Well, the regulators were essentially guns for hire. They would get people in Arizona and Texas literally out of prison to go take care of these range wars and towns that were overrun by bad guys. They were sort of sheriffs with an attitude.

Longworth: You could make them modern-day regulators in New York.

WOLF: Well, we're doing something like that. (*Laughs.*) That's in development, too. (*Laughs.*) It's called *Mafia Cop*, which is based on a book by a guy named Lou Epileto, who was the ninth most decorated cop in the history of the New York City Police Department, but whose family [his father and his cousin] was mobbed up.

Longworth: True story?

WOLF: True story. And basically, Lou believed in mob justice on the streets. If he caught you, he wasn't big on Miranda warnings.

Longworth: (*Laughs.*) Well, the mafia's hot right now with *The Sopranos*. But going back to westerns, those were great dramas.

WOLF: Yeah, [but] I still think that everybody conveniently forgets that up until about 1955, there were nothing but half-hour dramas. And you can sure get story acceleration [in a half hour].

Longworth: Exactly, and one of my favorite half hour dramas was *The Rifleman,* but it was classified as a "western."

WOLF: Well, it was a western but it wasn't a western. It was like *Have Gun Will Travel,* which became *The Equalizer* when it moved to New York.

Longworth: Now, whether it was Crest toothpaste commercials or motion pictures or television shows, are the writing skills the same? Did commercial writing help you become a better TV writer? Or, once you had the talent, did it matter what you were writing?

WOLF: I think it's all additive and cumulative. It's one reason I'm not a big believer in the unsullied power of youthful writers in Hollywood, that especially in drama you need some miles on the odometer before you understand the depth and breadth of the human condition. But it's [also] one of the old clichés that "writers write." And the best advice you can give to anyone trying to break in is to just keep writing, because unless you are blessed by

God in a way that very few people are, your initial efforts are not going to be Emmy-quality scripts. There is a lot of skill to the craft in terms of knowing how to structure stories, knowing how to tell stories. And I think that [in the constant search for new writers], I can teach structure to the proverbial fifteen monkeys in a room with typewriters, but you can't teach people how to write dialogue. They can either do it or they can't. And there are certain rules even in dialogue that you can teach, but it's one of those things like having a tin ear or having perfect pitch, it's a skill that you can't really teach.

Longworth: I've written a lot of commercials and news-style documentary features, but I don't think I could ever write dramatic dialogue.

WOLF: Well, it's a very funny thing. There are some people who can write excellent prose and you'll read something that they put in dialogue form and go, "Wow!, this doesn't cut it," because the tricky thing about dialogue is that it is not speech. It's decidedly different. It's kind of an enhanced reality, a false reality. People don't speak that way. It's a false positive in a sense. It's not real. And yet, when it's flowing and it sings, it sure sounds right.

Longworth: You once commented that the "thing that keeps *Law & Order* going is the very thing critics said would kill it." Explain.

WOLF: The conventional wisdom on television is that people watch television for the characters and that episodic and series television is successful when people clue onto a character and that's who they want to see every week. And ours is the most story-driven show on television since *Dragnet*.

Longworth: Yes, but unlike *Dragnet*, *Law & Order* fans have become invested in the characters as well as the stories. How do you create three-dimensional characters in a story-driven genre?

WOLF: The one thing we do on *Law & Order* is the character information is doled out much more realistically than it is in most shows. The term I've used is that it's dispensed in an eyedropper as opposed to a soup ladle. And you look at a lot of pilots and you know when the main characters were toilet trained, people sort of regurgitating their inner secrets and their souls on camera, which makes my teeth itch. But if you think back to the way you get to know most people, they don't stand up in the first three hours of a business or a social relationship and tell you everything about their parents, their siblings, where they went to high school, and when they lost their virginity. There's constant character revelations in human relationships, and I think that in *Law & Order* it actually is parceled out much closer to the reality of day-to-day life.

Longworth: And where did you lose your virginity?

WOLF: I can give you the state. (*Laughs.*)

Longworth: What state?

WOLF: New York. (*Laughs.*) Surprise!

Longworth: Some shows try to create fast pacing by using a jerky camera, which is kind of stupid I think, but—

WOLF: Did you tell Fontana that?

Longworth: Yes. We're no longer speaking.

WOLF: (*Laughs.*)

Longworth: But you quickened the pace by simply eliminating wasteful action.

WOLF: Well, the reality is that *Law & Order* is a show that if you put in establishing shots and drive-ups and people talking more about their personal lives, *either* half of it could be a perfectly acceptable hour show. Therefore, one way is looking at it as massive story acceleration, the other way would be trying to put five pounds of shit in a four-pound bag every week . . .

Longworth: (*Laughs.*)

WOLF: . . . which doesn't give you the freedom to indulge in extraneous action, or else you wouldn't be able to finish the episodes, and you wouldn't be able to air them because you'd run out of time about the end of the third act.

Longworth: That was really your second big innovation, the first being the split format. But before *Law & Order*, everybody else had wasted a lot of minutes of screen time.

WOLF: Not only wasted, but it's cheaper. That's why after nine years there have been more than seven thousand speaking roles on *Law & Order*. We've got thirty speaking parts or more almost every week. The story keeps moving and the one thing I've said when the writers ask me, "How can it move that fast?" I say, "When was the last time you saw a movie that moved too quickly?" You get bored when it's slow. It's amazing what people absorb if you feed them meat instead of filo.

Longworth: Speaking of moving the story along, where did you come up with that masterful percussive two-note bridge?

WOLF: The "ching, ching"? That's to Mike Post's credit and chagrin. Mike says he's done something like thirty-seven TV series now, and what he's going to be most famous for is two-notes.

Longworth: It's a great device because if I think a scene is ending and I head for the bathroom, then I hear the two-note bridge, I know I have to rush back in the room.

WOLF: (*Laughs.*) Yep, you know there's going to be a shift.

Longworth: It seems appropriate that you produce a split format show using split operations. What are the advantages and disadvantages of a bicoastal arrangement?

WOLF: The biggest advantage, and I'm very serious about this, is that I think it keeps everybody more on their toes when the writing and postproduction is done in L.A. And whether it's New York or some other location, it's almost like the home team and the away team. There is a good, combative edge that is not lost. Both coasts want their point of view to prevail on a weekly basis, which leads to everybody sort of "maxing out." That may sound simplistic, but I think there is a tendency when shows are all done in the same place that you don't get that creative cauldron going on a weekly basis, or it's hard to keep it going, and everybody gets sort of too comfortable with each other. Drama is conflict, and I think in hour television to keep the drama at a certain level, there has to be a certain amount of conflict.

Longworth: Did you choose to shoot *Law & Order* in New York because that's where you're from, or could you just as well have shot in Chicago or L.A.?

WOLF: Well, there are a lot of reasons that I like New York, and the bulk of my shows have been set in New York. The ones that have moved out or didn't get done there, I think really suffered from it, the two most notable examples being *Crime & Punishment* and *Players.* And I think *Players* would still be on if it had been in New York. The reality is anything that happens anywhere on the planet, you can set in New York and it's totally believable. There is a different energy in the city that is translated onto film. The vertical upthrust of the buildings, the mass of people, the mass of conflicts, everything, the pace of the city, all seeps into the film. The acting pool is better trained because they're basically stage actors. You don't have the same day players, you know the usual suspects. You don't run into the situation that I ran into with one show when the villain of my show at ten o'clock had been the hero of the drama that had been on at nine o'clock.

Longworth: (*Laughs.*)

WOLF: There are thirty-eight reasons why I like being in New York, or certainly being out of Hollywood.

Longworth: Another comment you made at the Museum of Television seminar was that you've yet to produce the perfect episode of *Law & Order.* Well, I think I know what it should be. Recently, I came across an old *Mad* magazine satire of your show and—

WOLF: Oh, wasn't that great? The original artwork for that is in the waiting room right outside my office where Lydia is.

Longworth: Mort Drucker is a great caricaturist.

WOLF: Oh, yeah, the drawings are amazing. He captured everybody dead on.

Longworth: But anyway, *Mad* magazine suggested an episode where Logan kills off everyone. Would that be the perfect episode? (*Laughs.*)

WOLF: No, the closest we came to a paradigm episode was "Life Choice," which was the first season, the abortion clinic bombing episode. The "perfect" episode is one where all six characters have different points of view on the same moral conundrum or idea and they're all right. The points of view they present are all logical and compelling in their own right, and you can see how well intentioned people can disagree. I don't know what subject you'd get all six of them on different sides, but "Life Choice" had certainly three really dispirit points of view.

Longworth: Speaking of the abortion clinic bombing episode, you, as a former ad man, had to know that as soon as the script came out of the hopper, there was going to be a shit storm coming down all around you.

WOLF: Oh, yeah. Look, I think you've probably heard me say this, if *Law & Order* came out now, I don't know if it would survive the first six episodes. And believe me, *Special Victims* I think is going to be very contentious too, because the subject matter is not initially advertiser friendly. But *Law & Order* has no advertiser pullouts now, no matter what we do, because advertisers are incredibly self-serving, and the reality is that *Law & Order* delivers not just a gold-plated, but a platinum-plated audience.

Longworth: How much money did NBC lose on the abortion clinic show in terms of ad revenues?

WOLF: Eight hundred thousand dollars. And that was ten years ago. They lost 80 percent of the advertising in it.

Longworth: But if the network lost that much money, it looks like they would have come to you the next day and threatened to kick your ass if you ever did that again.

WOLF: Oh, yeah, but Brandon was running the network and he didn't care. He thought it was an Emmy-level show, and they were willing to lose money on it, but "could we please not do abortion or child killings more than once a season," basically.

Longworth: Is it your job to entertain me for an hour, or to send me a message that I can talk about with my family?

WOLF: No, I think my job is to entertain you. To quote Sam Goldwyn, "If you want to send a message, use Western Union." We don't have a message.

I'm very serious about this. You'll see it in "Gun Show," the first *Law & Order* episode of this year [1999], which my kids just watched last night, which is about a mass killing that will be reminiscent of what happened in Atlanta. And McCoy takes the gun manufacturer to court. And without giving away the ending (which I think would take away some of the enjoyment of the show), my two oldest kids saw it and were arguing at the end of the show.

Longworth: That's good.

WOLF: That's great, but you can't look at this and say it's either pro- or anti-gun manufacturers.

Longworth: Well, perhaps you don't take sides on the show, but you personally have taken public swipes at, for example, Senator Sam Brownback for his position on guns.

WOLF: Not even picking on him, but he is one of the more egregious examples along with John McCain who are political opportunists trying to take Hollywood to task. This guy is saying we should not have violent images on television, and it's rank political opportunism. I feel like it's the Army/McCarthy hearings, you know, "Senator, have you no shame?" This guy [Brownback] wants to have hearings about Hollywood's irresponsibility, and yet he voted to repeal the ban against assault weapons. Liddy Dole, whose husband he replaced in the Senate, came out and said (and she's running for president), "I don't think it's necessary for Americans to have AK47s to defend their families." Assault weapons are different to me than handguns or shotguns. Look, I have nothing against gun ownership, I own guns. But if you want to own a deadly weapon, you should have a license to own it and be fingerprinted. I would want on the books that every gun sold in this country should have to go through a ballistics computer, which is readily available, so that if it's used in a crime, within five minutes they can punch it into a computer and know who the last legal owner of the gun was. I mean, this is a shameful situation. And to have these senators sitting up there saying that the fault lies with Hollywood, when they're voting to put previously banned guns back on the street, I mean, I think they should just be ashamed of themselves.

Longworth: You're a man of deep convictions, and clearly you're not known as someone who backs down, so I'm curious. Why did you give in and change the name of *Sex Crimes* to *Special Victims Unit?* Was it because of outside pressure from politicians and others?

WOLF: No, it was because of the network—and both networks [USA and NBC] feared that the show would be boycotted by advertisers just because it had "sex" in the title, which I still think was a mistake. I mean, if you test that title—I'm very familiar with concept testing and politically correct testing—and if you ask people, "Are you going to watch a show called *Sex Crimes?* they'd say, "Absolutely not, you think I'm crazy?" But they'd watch. It's just like when *I'll Fly Away* was the second highest testing pilot in five years because, if you call up a bunch of people on a cable test and ask, "Would you watch a show every week about the civil rights movement in the sixties?" what do you think people are going to say? "No, I'm a racist, I have no interest in watching that"? Of course they're going to say "yes" but nobody watched. This is sort of the same situation in reverse.

Longworth: And while we're on the topic of nobody watching. Why on earth would NBC put *Special Victims* up against *Monday Night Football?* That makes no sense.

WOLF: Well, wait a minute. It's opposite *Monday Night Football, Everybody Loves Raymond,* and *Ally McBeal.* I mean, it's the most stupid programming decision of the past ten years, and it has nothing to do with the show. It has everything to do with NBC News. And this is not speaking out of school, I'm rip shit about it! The show is a very good show and . . . there has been great conflict inside NBC about this. But this is the News Division wagging the entire network.

Longworth: Well, that's happened before, though.

WOLF: Yeah, but I mean, let's face it. *Dateline* is on five times a week and it's a very good show. I watch *Dateline.* That's not the point. The point is that at nine o'clock it's a very logical programming alternative against what was the number one show on television last week, *Everybody Loves Raymond,* which is a comedy. *Ally McBeal,* which is a comedy/drama, "dramedy," whatever you want to call it, and *Monday Night Football.* Give people an alternative. Don't put a ten o'clock drama on at nine o'clock, or eight o'clock central time zone, and expect not to take a lot of heat about it. [Subsequent to this interview, NBC complied with Wolf's wishes, and in January 2000 moved *Special Victims Unit* to Fridays at 10:00 P.M.]

Longworth: There used to be a strategy of counterprogramming and nobody seems to do that much anymore.

WOLF: Well, this is the reverse of counterprogramming.

Longworth: Well, you know how years ago, CBS put *Chicago Hope* against you guys.

WOLF: Oh, I know. These are the myths of programming. Everybody forgets that nobody liked *ER* when they saw the pilot at NBC. And any executive who tells you different is lying, because I remember that spring, and the reason that they ordered *ER* was to dent *Chicago Hope.* So, as William Goldman once said, "Nobody knows nothing." He said that a long time ago and he was right.

Longworth: Same question for you that I put to John Wells: One week this past summer, *Law & Order* tied *ER* in the ratings. *ER* costs nearly 13 million per episode, *Law & Order* costs nearly 3 million per episode.

WOLF: Something like that.

Longworth: Then is *ER* 10 million dollars better than *Law & Order?*

WOLF: Don't be ridiculous. The *ER* deal is the worst deal in the history of show business. And if they had made it a year earlier, it would have been about 3 million an episode. NBC lost football, they lost *Seinfeld,* and this was a perceived emergency. There's nothing on television worth 13 million an hour.

Longworth: Speaking of revenues, your deal with USA was considered groundbreaking.

WOLF: It is groundbreaking.

Longworth: But it also caused some concern among network traditionalists. Why was it both?

WOLF: Well, it is groundbreaking because with the cost of programming, it's the wave of the future, and especially if this show works you're going to see a lot more of it. And your definition of network traditionalists are affiliates who are a nice bunch of guys who are still living in 1956. And that's the bottom line. Exclusivity is going to go the way of advertisers owning their own programming.

Longworth: What are the specifics of the deal—when will *Special Victims Unit* replay on USA?

WOLF: Thirteen days later.

Longworth: Will they also be able to replay *Law & Order?*

WOLF: No. A&E's got *Law & Order* until 2002. It goes to TNT in 2001, so in 2001, you'll be able to see *Law & Order* on NBC, A&E, and TNT. And *Special Victims Unit* on NBC and USA.

Longworth: Of course, *Law & Order* has a new cast member for season ten. And you hired Jesse Martin [a black actor formerly of *Ally McBeal*] long before the NAACP raised questions about racial diversity with the networks. Nevertheless, did you feel as a producer you had a responsibility to effect racial balance in casting?

WOLF: The simple answer is "no." The reason I put Jesse in it is because he was really hot last year, and within a week of me offering him a job on *Law & Order,* he got, I believe, offers from Bochco and David [Kelley] and two other networks for a blind holding deal. I was just a little bit ahead of the pack, and I think I also had another advantage in that *Law & Order* is shot in New York and Jesse loves New York. He loves the show. But this show is a workplace show. I think the only responsibility I have—and this is both self-serving and vaguely altruistic—but I think dramas work better when they accurately reflect the full palette of American society. In an ensemble about the police department in New York, and the legal system, the reality is there are a huge number of minorities in both places, and that's why they're in the show.

Longworth: Does *D.C.* have a diverse cast?

WOLF: Yep.

Longworth: And it's an hour?

WOLF: That's an hour ensemble. There are five regulars.

Longworth: Is it fair when people say, "Oh, Dick Wolf's doing a *West Wing* show?"

WOLF: No. It's not a *West Wing* show. It's about twenty-three- and twenty-four-year-olds in their first jobs in Washington. It's really the best and the brightest. It's much more—if I had to call it anything, I'd say it's an anthem to why people still go to Washington. It's not about inside politics.

Longworth: I suppose you have no free time these days, but if you do, are there any dramas that you like to watch other than your own?

WOLF: Oh, yeah. I love *Homicide.* It never should have been canceled.

Longworth: What do you think of your friend Tom Fontana's work?

WOLF: In all seriousness, Tom is undoubtedly one of the best writers ever to work in this medium, and though he is selling himself on a weekly basis, the stuff that comes out of that head is incredibly unique, and in very much a way that is immediately recognizable. I mean, you look at episodes of *Homicide,* and that's all Tom. That's not to take anything away from the other writers who do a terrific job, but the head of that show, or what the head is wrapped around, is really Fontanavision.

Longworth: What other shows do you like?

WOLF: I really like *The Sopranos.*

Longworth: I found David Chase to be fascinating.

WOLF: Not only that, he's a great guy. My favorite hour show of all time is *The Rockford Files.* And David wrote probably 30 percent of those episodes. He's got a unique voice, and he's one of the only people who can tell really, really good, self-contained stories that have good drama in them, but can also be hysterically funny.

Longworth: And nobody had heard of him until now all of a sudden—

WOLF: Oh, sure. Nobody had heard of him maybe in the current crop of television writers, but I've known him for fifteen, sixteen years. He was at Universal for a long time when I was there. He did *A Year in the Life*. He's been around. He did *Northern Exposure*. He's an enormously talented writer.

Longworth: So you do get a chance to watch *The Sopranos?*

WOLF: Oh, yeah, on the weekend.

Longworth: Does that in any way put you at cross purposes? In other words, your rooting for a drama on HBO that essentially takes viewers away from NBC?

WOLF: I don't care where it is. Good programming is good programming. And there's not very much of it.

Longworth: Final question. You've innovated so many things—the split-format drama, the streamlined pace. What's going to be your last innovation?

WOLF: My last innovation will be coming up with a show that can't be canceled. (*Both laugh.*)

Longworth: What will it be called?

WOLF: I guess, probably "Stay Tuned." (*Laughter.*)

ᯤ 2 ᯤ

DAVID CHASE | "Hit" Man

David Chase. PHOTOGRAPHER, ANTHONY NESTE. COURTESY OF HBO.

TELEVISION CREDITS

1976–80	*The Rockford Files* (NBC)
1981	*Off the Minnesota Strip* (ABC TV movie)
1982	*Palms Precinct* (NBC pilot)
1982	*Moonlight* (CBS pilot)
1986	*Alfred Hitchcock Presents* ("Enough Rope for Two")

1987–89	*Almost Grown* (CBS)
1991–92	*I'll Fly Away* (NBC)
1993–95	*Northern Exposure* (CBS)
1995	*The Rockford Files* (CBS Movie of the Week)
1996	*Not Fade Away* (CBS pilot)
1997	*The Sopranos* (pilot)
1998–	*The Sopranos* (HBO)

MW   MW   MW

Even the most casual reader knows who the author of the book that he just read is. But spend an hour watching a great television drama, and hardly any of us can recall the name of the writer just moments after end credits roll.

It should come as no surprise, then, that in 1999, when the name David Chase first began to seep into the public psyche, we assumed that the creative genius behind *The Sopranos* was an overnight success. But if Chase is an overnight success, his is the longest night on record. For nearly thirty years he has toiled in television and told us countless tales about private detectives (*The Rockford Files*), divorce (*Almost Grown*), the civil rights movement (*I'll Fly Away*), quirky Alaskans (*Northern Exposure*), and now, the mafia (*The Sopranos*).

In a sense, David Chase has been a utility player in the big leagues for decades, reporting to work every day, and manufacturing hits when called upon to do so. But this is the era of Mark McGuire and Sammy Sosa, and just as the new millennium approached, Chase became a TV power hitter. *The Sopranos* struck a nerve with more than 7 million fans, and made the all-star team by piling up an unprecedented sixteen Emmy nominations after its first season on HBO (winning four, including one for Chase's writing). The show, about a mafia boss and his insecurities, is (considering all the media hype and critical acclaim) the TV equivalent of seventy home runs, and Chase is driving them out of the park and into our living rooms. A "tape measure" success to be sure, and all this from a shy, unassuming man, who, as a boy, didn't even like baseball.

What he *did* like was writing, and that's fortunate for those of us who enjoy his work, especially *The Sopranos* and its tales of the mafia—a topic that has been a lifelong fascination for Chase and for generations of Americans.

Catapulted by newsreel accounts of Al Capone, the gangster movie genre made stars out of Edward G. Robinson, George Raft, and Jimmy Cagney, and set the stage for a continuous string of crime flicks, culminating with *The Godfather* trilogy, which spanned several decades.

Despite the popularity of hoods on the big screen, television seldom dipped its toe into mob waters. Certainly, there were mafia-related story lines running through episodes of myriad police and detective dramas, but only a few programs focused their attention exclusively on organized crime. *The Untouchables* (1959–63) took us back to the Capone days and was the most successful small-screen drama of the genre. Later attempts were short-lived, including *The Gangster Chronicles* (1981), *Crime Story* (1986–1988), and *Wiseguy* (1987–90).

Today, almost forty years after Robert Stack waged war on mobsters, we finally get to see the flip side through Chase's *The Sopranos*, about a mafia boss waging war on himself as he battles inner conflict. Of course, *The Sopranos* wasn't a guaranteed hit. After all, it premiered at the end of a decade in which TV gangsters were limited to an occasional movie special (*Gotti*) or miniseries (*The Last Don*), none of which generated widespread interest.

Will *The Sopranos* spawn or otherwise inspire other serious crime sagas on television? Not long after David Chase's New Jersey–based drama bowed, Showtime came forth with *Bonanno: A Godfather's Story* and CBS with *Falcone*, but it is too early to predict either the longevity of *The Sopranos* or its potential for shaping prime-time programming.

The Sopranos may do for the mob drama what *Lonesome Dove* did for the western, but remember, *The Young Riders* and *Dr. Quinn* were much easier to program than a show about ruthless, modern-day murderers, especially in this age of parental and congressional concerns about the correlation between television and its effect on societal violence. Speculations aside, what we do know is that David Chase, like any good Mafia don, is taking us for a ride, and we're all too happy to go with him.

David is a third-generation Italian-American, whose grandparents settled in New Jersey and subsequently changed their name from De Cesare (pronounced DeChezeray) to Chase. He comments on that name change: "I have occasionally thought of changing my name back because people always told me, 'God, what a beautiful name.' And it has this ring to it. When I was in high school I thought it would be a cooler name than the one I had, and when you're that age, any name is cooler than the one you've got. And then again, when we had a child I thought, 'You know what? Her name's not really Chase, we should go back to De Cesare, but it's just such an aggravation.'"

Though an only child, Chase was surrounded and supported by a large (make that huge) extended family. "I think I had ten aunts and uncles on the one side, and twelve aunts and uncles on the other. A lot of cousins."

David's wife, Denise, has been part of that family for more than thirty years. They met in high school, were married the summer after he graduated from NYU, and have been together ever since.

Over the years, coworkers have been amazed at Chase's proclivity for being able to depict the mob mentality so authentically in his writings, though no one in his immediate family was ever "connected." Now in his fifties, David is (to return to the baseball analogy) much like Barry Levinson's film character Roy Hobbs (*The Natural*), who, when finally making it to the major leagues, was greeted with a sarcastic salutation from his new manager: "Mister, you don't start playing ball at your age—you retire!" Roy Hobbs sure showed 'em, and so has David Chase. "He's a natural, a natural."

I spoke with David as he was preparing for the second season of *The Sopranos*.

Longworth: There's an industry phrase for someone who both writes and produces, but what do you call a guy like you who creates, produces, writes, *and* directs?

CHASE: I call it filmmaking.

Longworth: Chris Albrecht at HBO is a big fan of yours, but admitted that he was a bit nervous initially about you directing the first episode, because of putting so much control in one person's hands.

CHASE: It's news to me that that was the reason. (*Laughs.*) I just assumed they thought that maybe my directing chops weren't up to speed, or that they might have had visions in their head of doing it. I don't know, maybe they wanted a feature director or something. In fact, it's always in one, or maybe two, person's control, but I can see his point.

Longworth: How many episodes do you write and direct, and how do you delegate the work?

CHASE: That's very difficult on this show because I have great people working with me, Robin Green and Mitch Burgess, with whom I've worked before. Frank Renzulli and a few other writers were hired, but the show is very idiosyncratic, and it's very much what some people like to call a "personal vision," and delegating really doesn't work that well. Now, this will go in complete contrast to what I'm about to tell you, which is that I don't really originally write all that many of them. But I do have a lot to do with the final script on each one.

Longworth: So you're the master story editor?

CHASE: Well, I'm the final story editor.

Longworth: Let's talk about your family background. I read that your father ran a hardware store, and that he was big on your going to college.

CHASE: Extremely.

Longworth: My parents were too. You're not much older than I am—wasn't that a generational thing? Do you see young parents today putting the same emphasis on college?

CHASE: I have a daughter who was a senior in high school last year, and was on her way to college . . . I mean, I saw a lot of yuppie parents who were totally into it, utterly obsessed by it. Now, that may just be *her* school, but I think it may be like that across the country.

Longworth: It's like in Little League when parents would push their kids. You could always spot the kid whose parents made him play, and he didn't want to be there.

CHASE: That was me by the way. (*Laughs.*)

Longworth: Where did you want to be?

CHASE: (*Laughs.*) I really wasn't that comfortable out there on the baseball field. Actually, I was a pitcher. I was a lousy athlete.

Longworth: So you walked a lot of batters?

CHASE: I played Little League two seasons, and I think I was in one game. We were winning like 20-4, and they put me in. (*Laughs.*)

Longworth: And you didn't blow the lead?

CHASE: No, I held for all of six pitches that I actually made.

Longworth: (*Laughs.*) Well, then, that's why you got the deal at HBO, they obviously knew you could hold a lead. (*Both laugh.*)

CHASE: That's right. You don't have to pitch that many times.

Longworth: What about grade school, high school, did you display any talent for writing?

CHASE: I liked the idea of writing in high school and I liked the idea of writing stories, but everything I wrote was total shit, and I had no discipline whatsoever. Or maybe I had discipline, but I didn't understand about rewriting at all. And I don't think the teachers there would really do enough—you know, you gotta really write and rewrite and rewrite, and I never did that. And the stories I wrote were sort of mindblowers, like somebody spies the Apostles sneaking Jesus' body out of the tomb, right before they go, "Oh, my God, he's resurrected!" (*Laughs.*) Real mind-blowing stuff like that.

Longworth: Did you do a rewrite on that? That sounds pretty good as is.

CHASE: (*Laughs.*) Well maybe I could have fixed the dialogue. (*Laughs.*)

Longworth: So what college did you go to?

CHASE: Well, I started at Wake Forest down where you are.

Longworth: Well, I'm in Virginia, but my family is still in North Carolina.

CHASE: Then I transferred to NYU, and then I went to Stanford Graduate School.

Longworth: What attracted you to Wake Forest?

CHASE: My best buddy in high school was going to go there, and we thought we would continue—that our fun would be unabated by this geographical move.

Longworth: You said you went from Wake Forest to NYU to Stanford. Those are some big leaps. What was the logic behind that? Did you just want to go to different places to get laid?

CHASE: No. This was the early- to mid-sixties in the South—not a happy time there.

Longworth: Yeah, tell me about it.

CHASE: And, frankly, at that time I thought it very prejudiced.

Longworth: Still is.

CHASE: Well, I found it very prejudiced then. There were a lot of Klan rallies. I didn't leave because of the Klan rallies, but I never felt really welcome on that campus as a Yankee. Now, some people did. Some people didn't have any problem with it. But what was going on with me was I'd seen the Rolling Stones and that's kind of who I wanted to be like. And that wouldn't go down at Wake Forest.

Longworth: So you actually saw Klan activities on campus?

CHASE: No, no, no, absolutely not. But nearby, where they had the hugest rallies when the grand dragon was there—I forget his name. And it wasn't an atmosphere I liked. It's not that I'm some freedom fighter, I just found the South to be at that time stodgy, strange and bigoted, and kind of unsophisticated. I mean, I was from New Jersey, I grew up twenty-five miles from New York City and I missed that.

Longworth: It amazes me when I talk to young kids about racial prejudice in the South; they think I'm talking about the Civil War. And I say, "Well, tell me when the last major cross burning was in Virginia," and they think it was 1865. But it was 1977 on the lawn of the ABC affiliate TV station the night *Roots* aired. So this still goes on.

CHASE: I guess it does. I was back in the South off and on for two years doing *I'll Fly Away* and I still saw it, but I also saw a lot of changes, but what do I know? I'm an outsider looking in.

Longworth: Speaking of *I'll Fly Away*, were you disappointed about it's cancellation by NBC?

CHASE: Very much so.

Longworth: Not just because you thought, Well, there goes a paycheck?

CHASE: Well, it wasn't the paycheck so much, because that show was always a loss leader for everyone who worked on it. The Business Affairs Department would always throw it in our face that it wasn't doing that well, that it was a noble effort, and that Warner Brothers . . . we were all sort of being good guys just by doing the show, in view of the fact that the ratings were so low. I did not create it. All the credit for that goes to Josh Brand and John Falsey, and I worked with them, and I was glad to be a part of it. By the way, it was because of my experience in Winston-Salem in the early-sixties that I was drawn to that show. Because I remembered it, I remembered a lot of details about it, and I remembered how unhappy I felt about the situation for black people then. It was quite a time.

Longworth: Yeah, I remember going to church one Sunday in Winston-Salem right after Martin Luther King was killed, and right as we turned off Broad Street downtown, I looked up, and on the upper parking deck of the Sears Roebuck store were armed National Guardsmen.

CHASE: It was a strange thing.

Longworth: Since we're back in time now, let me ask if *Rockford* was your first big break?

CHASE: Yeah, I'd say it was my first big break.

Longworth: Help me out here, you get out of college and—

CHASE: I got out of graduate school—I was knocking around, I could not break into the business at all, and I did not come down to Hollywood to work in television, I wanted to work in features. This was a very exciting time in movies. This was in the early-seventies and movies were starting to be called "film," and there was a lot of influence from European, Japanese, and all kinds of foreign films. And that stuff just blew me away, and I had always loved movies, and that's what I wanted to do. That's what I went to film school for.

Longworth: But how did you just walk in and get a job on *Rockford?*

CHASE: What happened is I wrote a feature script which got the attention of a TV producer, who, in fact, hired me to do a teleplay, and I didn't get hired again for two years. But having done that teleplay got me into the Writer's Guild—I had to join the Writers Guild and, because of that, when the Guild went on strike, I had to go out on picket duty. I was very naïve at that time, and I pissed and moaned about why should I have to go out on picket duty for the union when they haven't gotten me a job? And that's not the way it works, but that's what I felt. But I went out there and I had the best time of my life. (*Laughs.*) I was actually in the business, you know? I was standing there with writers that were working—names I had heard. One day I was on picket duty with Steve Allen, and that was the best experience of my life.

Longworth: What a great guy he is.

CHASE: Well, a great guy to be out on the street with. You remember his "Man on the Street"? You're standing there for four hours on your picket duty shift with Steve Allen, and he's going, "Look at this guy's car. What's he putting in there? Let's go ask him." (*Laughs.*)

Longworth: In my twenty-eight years of interviewing people for television and feature articles, I was most in awe of Steve Allen. When I was on the phone with him and Jayne for the first time, she sensed my angst and said, "I understand, he's Steve Allen. He's different."

CHASE: Well, he *is* different. He's very cool. When I was in high school and he had done that show, it was like, man, he's great.

Longworth: Do you ever have the feeling that if Thomas Jefferson had hosted *Meeting of the Minds,* that he would have wanted to interview Steve Allen?

CHASE: Probably.

Longworth: But back to *Rockford,* post–picket duty. Who actually hired you for that show?

CHASE: Meta Rosenberg and Steven Cannell.

[Cannell told *Emmy* magazine that the credit goes to Rosenberg, who had read some of Chase's scripts and then brought him onto *Rockford* for the second season.]

Longworth: Did you cross paths with Steven Bochco during that time?

CHASE: I did. When I was doing *The Rockford Files,* Bochco and Cannell had a show called *Richie Brockelman,* and we did a couple of episodes in which Richie and Rockford got together and solved a case. I think part of it was an attempt to bolster the *Richie Brockelman* prospects—sort of have Rockford walk through there and do his magic. So, yeah, we did brush up against each other and were in story meetings together.

Longworth: Speaking of story meetings, let's skip forward. There's a funny story Jeff Melvoin tells about you during *Northern Exposure.* He says you used to get on top of the conference room table during meetings and stretch out as if it were a psychiatrist's couch.

CHASE: That's true, I used to lie on the table.

Longworth: Was that the beginnings of your fixation with psychiatry?

CHASE: No, it had nothing to do with psychiatry. It had to do with the fact that those meetings go on for a long time, and I had kind of a bad back, and I love to lie down. I'm very lazy and phlegmatic. And after two or three hours in there, I'd just get on the table and lie down in the middle of it. It had nothing to do with psychiatry.

Longworth: Still, I want to ask you where the idea for having a shrink on *The Sopranos* came from. Was that an idea floating around in your head for many years?

CHASE: Well, I was in a lot of psychotherapy myself beginning in the early 1970s. Actually, it was when I started working in the business. As soon as I had money to spend on it, I was in therapy. I was always interested in it. I took a lot of psychology in college, and it's always disappointing there. You think it's going to be really mysterious and it isn't. I think I had sort of a half-assed minor in it, but I had read Freud as a kid—even in high school I was interested in Freud—but when I got into therapy I was very taken with it. And in a sort of foreshadowing, I created this character for *The Rockford Files* [played by Katherine Harrold] who was a psychologist. At that time I was going to private therapy and group therapy and, for a writer, it was amazing to watch how that all works.

Longworth: But were you doing it for you, or doing it for the "writer's experience"?

CHASE: Therapy?

Longworth: Yeah.

CHASE: Oh, for me—yeah, I was miserable.

Longworth: Why? From what I've read about you, you had a big, supportive family.

CHASE: Yeah, my extended family was very supportive and very nice. Did you ever read the Alice Miller book *The Drama of the Gifted Child*?

Longworth: No.

CHASE: It's actually about narcissistic people, and neurotic people. And that fit me to a tee. Without getting into a lot of detail, my mother was a very frightened person. She passed a lot of that on to me. I was messed up as a teenager. It was just the three of us, and the dynamic of it, being very much involved in each other's lives, wasn't always healthy. For whatever reason, whether it was genetic or not, I had psychological problems, and I had to go to therapy.

Longworth: So we know now that the role of the psychiatrist in *The Sopranos* had its roots in your childhood, the character in *Rockford,* and your therapy sessions. Let's talk about *The Sopranos* specifically. Was there a defining moment where you came up with the idea for the show? When did the idea first take shape?

CHASE: In 1988 I had a very short-lived show I created and executive produced, *Almost Grown.* It starred Timothy Daly and Eve Gordon, and was on CBS Mondays at ten o'clock. We were only on for six episodes. It was quite an ambitious undertaking, and slowly it was working its way into getting a lot of critical approval, but the numbers were not there, and the network canceled it. Anyway, somehow I made the acquaintance of Robin Green. She was a writer on the show, and had worked before that on *A Year in the Life.* So I was telling her stories about my mother and myself that she found hilarious. She said, "You should write a story about a TV producer and his mother." And my wife had also told me this, going back twenty years, saying, "You've got to write about your mother. Your stories about her have people on the floor laughing at her outrageous behavior." The way her reactions were, they were just not your typical reactions to anything. So I thought to myself, Yeah, that would be kind of funny, and not only funny, but interesting. Of course, everyone wants to write about himself to a certain extent, but what kind of thing can you do about a TV producer and his mother? And the idea just kind of popped into my head about making him a gangster.

Longworth: That's a big leap from TV producer to gangster, or maybe it's not.

CHASE: Yeah, maybe it's not. I think it was the Italian thing. I suddenly saw how it would be very interesting to have a gangster in therapy. And at the time, I pictured Robert DeNiro and Anne Bancroft (this is like 1988). I'd have a gangster in therapy—a middle-aged guy going through a midlife crisis. His mother is driving him crazy. His mother feels cut out of the loop, not given her due, abused by a lack of attention. And somehow or another, they get into a gang warfare situation over who's running the mob, and he would be in therapy and the therapist would be trying to help him through all this stuff, but it would actually play out on the streets, and I didn't know then if it would be serious or comic. So that's basically what *The Sopranos* is.

Longworth: [citing an episode of *The Sopranos*] Now, your dad never wanted to move the hardware store to Las Vegas, and your mom never said, "I'd rather smother the kids with a pillow [than move]."

CHASE: My mother never said that. But my father did want to go to California. At that time, he was an engineer and he was designing printing presses, and the company he was working for broke up, and one of the guys who was one of the mainstays wanted him to come to join him in business out there, which in the fifties was the land of opportunity. My father told me that he really wanted to go, but my mother couldn't make it. She said, "My sisters are here, everything's here, I won't go out there." And so, naturally according to him, these guys became multimillionaires. My mother came from New Jersey, and she thought it difficult just to move to Westchester, just across the Hudson River. Anyway, that story always struck me—well, it speaks for itself.

Longworth: Well, if you had made *The Sopranos* about a TV producer, it would have played out as Rob Petrie and his mom. Instead it's about a mafia family. But in the wake of so much violence in America, do you feel as a producer that you have some sort of responsibility not to glorify violence? There's the episode where Tony Soprano took his daughter off to visit colleges, and then he ends up killing a guy. It's a weird juxtaposition.

CHASE: Well, it's interesting that you would use the term "glorifying violence." Many people found that to be repellent. Which is what the object was. Especially if you were to talk to a lot of women who had seen that show, they'd tell you that it was really hard to take. But I've also heard that from some men. This is a violent man. He makes his living this way.

Longworth: But indictments notwithstanding, it seems that the violence isn't punished—the Sopranos can off a guy, but they don't get killed themselves.

CHASE: That's an interesting thing because certainly there were no consequences for it. In my reading and research, and lifelong obsession with the mafia, I've seen very few times when those guys get sent to jail for murder. Gangland killings are notoriously unsolved. Maybe in the end it's because the cops don't really care, because the less of them around the better, but notoriously unsolved. So it was not my intention. I did not want to do a cop show. I didn't want to do a show about crime and punishment. I want to do a show about the crimes that people wreak on each other, psychic punishment, and psychic self-punishment. I didn't want to do a show about the legal system. Now, to answer your question about the wake of all this violence, do I feel it's my responsibility? I can't answer that directly. Here's what I'd like to know. What's the problem with the white male that he just can't hack it? That he's just so miserable, so weak, so puny, so self-centered, so self-glorifying, so self-mythologizing that he's compelled to grab guns and shoot people indiscriminately. And I mean it. It's the white male. So, I'd like to know what the fuck the story is there? And in some sense, I think *The*

Sopranos in certain ways at least begins to touch on some of those themes—repressed rage, on a link between depression and violence, and also the role of the media in violence. Now, every TV producer will say something self-serving about his own show, and how it relates to the violence argument, and I guess that's what I've just said, but this is a mob show. It's hermetically sealed. It's about a group of men who have elected to live a life in which violence solves issues.

Longworth: It's organized.

CHASE: No, it isn't. It's allegedly organized. It's supposed to be organized. It's not as organized as they would like to believe. It's really about a bunch of sociopathic, very cutthroat, tough guys. And they have paid lip service to a certain amount of organization, but as we've seen now, it's falling more by the wayside. However there *is* some kind of a code. And in fact they don't shoot women, and in fact they don't shoot children. And in fact, they don't go bullshit in fast-food restaurants and spray the place with gunfire, killing people they don't even know. They kill their enemies. And maybe you could say, "Well, that's not much of a step up." (*Laughs.*)

Longworth: But it goes back to the glorification issue. These people do what they do, and there's some honor to it. Whereas with the random acts of violence today, the rage, there's no organization, there's no honor. What's the difference?

CHASE: Well, I think if you watch *The Sopranos*, you're not seeing happy people there, the ones that are committing this violence. I think you're seeing largely tormented people.

Longworth: There's a book called *Culture of Honor* that talks about the Southern white male, the rage, the violence; it goes into some things you've seen and referred to.

CHASE: When I was working on *I'll Fly Away*, there was this great book called *The Encyclopedia of the South*, really quite well researched, and I was surprised looking through it, when it comes to "Violence," and there was like eight pages about the reasons for violence in the South, or the suspected reasons. You know, we talk about westerns. But those guys all have Southern accents. (*Laughs.*) The western is, to a certain extent, a Southern art form. So it just goes to show you how influential, possibly, the Southern white male has been in our culture.

Longworth: Let me go back to the mafia for a moment. James Garner once commented that your scripts for *Rockford* were "some of our most literate," while Charles Johnson, one of the *Rockford* producers, observed that you always had a penchant for how gangsters would talk and act. So that begs the question (which I know you've heard a thousand times) if there are no "mobbed up" folks in your family, how did you have such a feel for this lifestyle so early on?

CHASE: Well, there were some connected people in my extended family. We're not close relatives, but a cousin of mine married some guy who I found out was a loan shark. And when I was in eighth grade, my best friend was adopted—he was a blond, blue-eyed kid and he lived with a very dark-haired Italian family. They had a boat and a Cadillac and all that stuff.

Longworth: So Tom Hagen was living with them, huh?

CHASE: (Laughs.) Yeah, and as it turned out, my aunt had dated the father in high school and she told me he was one of the bigger loan sharks in New Jersey. Now, I never said two words to that man, so I have no idea how he spoke. In fact, actually I did. I was with him a lot, and he said very little. But I went to high school with people who you could tell were certainly going to end up there. What I really think it is, is just growing up in New Jersey that taught me that. I don't mean that everybody was going there, but there were guys who probably were going to wind up in the mob maybe had aspirations to wind up there. But there's a certain cadence in the way of doing business with these guys.

Longworth: *Sopranos* star James Gandolfini, in praising your writing, said the show would be interesting even if it were not about a Mafia family, but do you really think if *The Sopranos* wasn't about the mob, that you would have picked up sixteen Emmy nominations, and that everybody would be watching? Would Tony Soprano be as interesting as an insurance salesman as he is a Mafia boss?

CHASE: No, of course not. All of that's a contradiction. I don't think people would have been watching a working-class Italian guy in New Jersey selling insurance, no. It would not be interesting. But that gets into a whole other question. Why do Americans and also the rest of the world love Mafia stories?

Longworth: Exactly, and that goes back to the issue of glorification. If there wasn't some kind of prurient interest in this stuff, you wouldn't be on the air. There wouldn't be the sixteen Emmy nominations, and everybody in the world wouldn't be calling you for interviews.

CHASE: What's prurient about it, though? I don't even know what prurient means. People love gangsters. Prurient to me always sounds like curiosity, and I don't think there's much left unknown about the mob. We've had these people on the screen now for a hundred years. I just think people love the Mafia.

Longworth: Another issue that keeps coming up with television is race. As you know, the NAACP has been threatening to boycott the networks. Now, I noticed on *The Sopranos* the Jewish character Hesh uses the N-word several times. He was telling a black guy . . .

CHASE: Yeah, he said, "My people were the white man's nigger when your people were still painting their faces."

Longworth: Well, there used to be a line that white writers didn't cross, where even on cable, you had to be a man of color to say the N-word. So are *The Sopranos* sort of the equal opportunity offenders here? And do you have any problem getting away with crossing that line?

CHASE: No, we don't have a problem. No one has yet complained to us about it. But it just occurs to all of us that it would be absurd to portray these killers as politically correct. I mean, it's the truth. I'm a white person, you're a white person, I don't know what you hear, but when white people are together and white Christians are together, and they're by themselves, you hear a lot of stuff. You hear a lot of derogations about Jews, about blacks, about anybody. And I'm sure when black people are together there's a lot of derogation about white people.

Longworth: As with the race issue itself, there are lessons to be learned I believe from just reading the comments you and the other producers are making for this book, so let's talk about your learning curve. What is it you've been able to learn or take away from each TV show as you go on to the next, that makes the next one better than the one before? Is there baggage that you take with you along the way that makes you better at what you're doing?

CHASE: That's a tough one. In my case I didn't spring full blown from the head of Zeus, I'm just kind of a writer. I told you, I started writing and I wrote a story about the Apostles trying to spirit Jesus' body away in the night, so that people would think he was resurrected (*Laughs.*), so maybe I haven't changed at all. I have no idea. I guess you just learn more what works and what doesn't work. It's trial and error. And it becomes harder and harder to do things you haven't done before, and you get bored with yourself, and so it makes you push to try something different.

Longworth: But you've come to great success later in life, whereas a lot of the writer/producers today are being recognized in their twenties and early thirties. Even some of the network executives are extremely young. I'm thinking of a couple of issues here, one being the college issue, the other being career. It's often said that older folks who go back to college usually do better because they appreciate it more, and they'll say, "College is wasted on the young." Now, having achieved superstar status at age fifty-three, do you think you have a better perspective on success and more of an accurate appreciation for what got you there?

CHASE: No, not at all.

Longworth: Have things changed at all?

CHASE: Well, I spend a lot more of my time talking on the phone.

Longworth: To people like me. (*Laughs.*)

CHASE: (*Laughs.*) But more important to people—just getting positive response. Now the enemy is self- consciousness.

Longworth: This has to be a great validation for you, no matter the reason. You've paid your dues, and you've hung in there, and now all of the sudden—

CHASE: Yeah, it was about my last go-round. I really had had it. I've been very lucky. I've only worked on good shows. But my own stuff never really found a home on network television, or in movies either. A lot of the guys you're talking to—Bochco, Fontana, all middle-aged guys—they found more acceptance than I did.

Longworth: It's interesting because John Masius told me almost the same thing, that if *Providence* hadn't made it, that was going to be it for him. Is there a point you guys get to where you just say "screw it?"

CHASE: You get bored, and I don't know if you can tell it from looking at *The Sopranos,* but I had just had it up to here with all the niceties of network television. I couldn't take it anymore. And I don't mean language and I don't mean violence. I just mean storytelling, inventiveness, something that really could entertain and surprise people. I just couldn't take it anymore.

Longworth: Do you wish you had broken out of your boredom earlier if you had known that's all it took?

CHASE: I was trying, I was trying. I mean I wrote pilots, pilots, pilots, pilots. And they never got shot.

Longworth: What other current dramas do you like other than *The Sopranos?* Are there any series on the air that you wish you had created?

CHASE: I don't.

Longworth: Do you watch any TV?

CHASE: No.

Longworth: Do you even *have* a TV? (*Laughs.*)

CHASE: Yes. Oh, I mean, do I watch any serious television? No, I do not. I watch *Larry Sanders*—that was the last one.

Longworth: What a great show.

CHASE: Yeah, it was fantastic. And the last one I liked before that was

Twin Peaks. Then I had a long dry spell. I liked *I'll Fly Away,* I was proud of that and I enjoyed watching it.

Longworth: Why don't they put *I'll Fly Away* on home video?

CHASE: Probably the same reason it was canceled. They say (*In a mocking voice.*), "We spend all this money, who's gonna buy it after we sell it, and package it." (*Laughs.*) There are also projections that say *The Sopranos* won't sell in boxed sets.

Longworth: Speaking of packaging, I guess you also have to make a decision about future syndication. Would the show play OK in reruns if people see episodes out of sequence, or is it compartmentalized enough to where you get a good story each hour?

CHASE: Yes, I think so. Our goal last year (and I hope we're keeping it this year) was to make every show a little movie. See, I love movies, I don't like television. And what I've always wanted to do is movies.

Longworth: Didn't I read somewhere that you had a deal pending on a movie?

CHASE: Oh, there are big deals all over the place. I've had deals pending to make movies since 1980 (*Laughs.*) and not a one of them got made.

Longworth: But I read something in a trade magazine that—

CHASE: Yeah, sure, I've got scripts out there, I'm trying to find a home for these things. But no, as yet I've never had a movie made. But I mean, I've written for the studios probably nine screenplays and a couple of specs for myself.

Longworth: Do you want to do what Levinson and Zwick do, which is to say, "Well, I'm going to write and direct a movie while I'm on hiatus from the TV series then I'll go back—"?

CHASE: No. I would rather just do one thing at a time. But that's a financial decision. And you have to say to yourself, "OK, I'm not going to make as much money."

Longworth: Is there a point where you know *The Sopranos* will end, because you have an ending in mind already?

CHASE: I don't have that. But here's what I do know. I know it's always been about "the rise and fall of . . ." so, that's all I know. That's what's been done in the past. But there's never been a series about it either.

Longworth: So say there's a Movie of the Week about David Chase. How are they going to wrap it up? Will you go back with the Apostles? (*Laughs.*)

CHASE: No, there'll be something like a really good paté or fish, and I'll be about to put it in my mouth, and then I'll fall gently to sleep.

Longworth: You're kind of a sick man, aren't you?

CHASE: (*Laughs.*) No. I'd just like to live in Europe—watch the sun sparkling on the water.

Longworth: You would like to spend your last days in Europe?

CHASE: Oh, yeah.

Longworth: You and Jerry Lewis?

CHASE: Yeah, me and Jerry Lewis, but he's not there either. (*Laughs.*)

TOM FONTANA | The wizard of *Oz*

Tom Fontana. COURTESY OF TOM FONTANA.

TELEVISION CREDITS

1982–88	*St. Elsewhere* (NBC)
1987	*The Fourth Wiseman* (ABC)
1988	*Nick Tattinger* (NBC)
1992	*Home Fires* (NBC)

1993–99	*Homicide: Life on the Street* (NBC)
1997–	*Oz* (Showtime)
2000–	*The Beat* (UPN)

ᗱ ᗱ ᗱ

John Tinker (*St. Elsewhere, Chicago Hope, Judging Amy*) once described his longtime friend Tom Fontana as "ever evolving," and yet, within that evolution is a predictable pattern of the unpredictable. From his early childhood years producing neighborhood plays, to managing a college theater group, to writing and producing *St. Elsewhere, Homicide,* and *Oz,* Tom Fontana has always pushed the envelope of traditional drama, and challenged audiences to follow him into new territory. Ironically, Fontana claims to be a total dinosaur. "I still write longhand on a yellow pad with a Flair pen." Yet, no one in television today is any more cutting edge than Fontana, a talent that has elevated him to among the top ranks of producers, in both critical acclaim and financial success.

In December of 1998, *Entertainment Weekly* ranked Tom ninth on their list of the top one hundred "Entertainers of the Year," placing him in the company of DiCaprio, Spielberg, and Cameron. Although Fontana is only now receiving the widespread recognition he deserves, his place in the annals of television history has been secure for nearly two decades, again, a result of an ongoing evolution.

Tom Fontana first "evolved" in 1951 to parents Charles (a wine salesman) and Marie (coordinator for the ob/gyn department at Millard Fillmore Hospital, where Tom was born). Early on, young Tom displayed a work ethic far beyond his years, something that family and friends partly attribute to the Catholic influences on his education, first by the Sisters of St. Joseph at Cathedral School, then by the Jesuits at Canisius High School. His disciplined manner even transferred to his boyhood hobby and future career of writing. Tom comments on that early Jesuit influence: "I would say that the Jesuits, in general, had a profound influence on my life in the sense that I learned about discipline. I mean, I can get up at 5:30 in the morning to write, having had no sleep the night before, write for five hours, then come to work and produce, because the Jesuits taught me that you have to set up a schedule every day. For a writer there is no bigger lesson to learn as far as I'm concerned. You can start writing at five in the morning or ten at night. The point is you have to do it every day, and you have to do it at the same time every day, because what happens is that something kicks in, and you suddenly go, 'Oh, it's time for me to write.'"

Besides adopting a strict, Catholic work ethic, Tom (and his writing style) was also influenced by some rather offbeat, off-the-wall television programs. "The truth is, my favorite show as a kid was *Green Acres*, because I found it so incredibly, wonderfully absurd. The world they created was very specific, very funny to me. It was existential."

After graduating from Canisius High School, Fontana attended Buffalo State College, where he was involved in numerous theater productions. During that time he also worked with the Buffalo-based Studio Arena Theatre. "Studio Arena Theatre was, for me, like a graduate school because my intention was to become a playwright. At the same time, the very best actors, directors, and designers were coming through Buffalo working at that theater, so all I had to do was just keep my ears open and my mouth shut. I had a lot of different jobs. I was originally the house manager, then I worked in the publicity office, and then I was a stage manager."

After college, Fontana sought his fortune in New York City. "I came to New York to be a playwright in 1975. . . . I'd have a play done here or there, I'd get a commission to write a play, but it was a very hand-to-mouth existence that was mostly subsidized by my parents. I basically starved from 1975 until I was hired for *St. Elsewhere*."

On the way to his big break with *St. Elsewhere*, Tom began making a seasonal mecca up the road to Williams College, to become a jack-of-all-trades for the prestigious Williamstown Theater Festival. One season he penned a play that would change his life forever. "I had this play being done in what was the second company, an adaptation of *The Specter Bridegroom*. Blythe [Danner] and Jake and Gwyneth Paltrow came to see it opening night and seemed to really like it. Then Blythe said to her husband, Bruce, 'You should go and see Tom's play.' Now, Bruce and I had gotten friendly at Williamstown because I was probably the only guy who wasn't asking him for a job [Paltrow was then producing *The White Shadow* for CBS]. At that point I still had an attitude about television. I was a playwright and very self-righteous about my art, so Bruce and I would hang out together, but we never talked business, and it was great. So Blythe is after Bruce to come see the play (but he never does). Now, the distance between the front door of the theater and the front door of the house Bruce had rented for the summer was about from home plate to first base, and all through the summer, he had to drive or walk by the theater. He didn't go see the play, and he didn't go see it, and every time he'd see me, he'd say, 'I'm going to see your play,' and I'd say, 'Bruce, it doesn't matter.' Summer ends, and he never sees the play. He now comes to me out of Jewish guilt or some motivation, and says, 'Look, I didn't see the play, but I heard it's very good, and I have this new TV show that I'm doing (a medical show), and I would like you to come out to L.A. and write an episode.' So, I'm convinced to this day that if Bruce had seen this play, he never would have hired me (*Laughs.*), and I would still be in Williamstown earning $1.50 an hour. So it's some kind of lesson. I've yet to sort out what the true meaning of that story is, but it is the true story."

The first season of *St. Elsewhere* was marked by low ratings and the defection of two of the show's original producers, John Falsey and Josh Brand. As shooting wrapped, cancellation was a foregone conclusion, so cast and crew dispersed to find other opportunities. For Fontana, that meant returning to New York. "I had been a starving playwright. After the first season of *St. Elsewhere,* I had already made more money in one year than I thought that I was ever going to make in my lifetime. So I came back to New York the happiest little boy because I had money in the bank, and I was married to a woman I loved [*St. Elsewhere*'s Sagan Lewis], and I thought, 'Wasn't that a great experience?' and I was out of television. I had said good-bye to everybody and I was gone. Well, I'm sitting there at the Writers Theater, and the phone rings, and it's John Masius and he goes, 'Guess what? We're doing it again. You've got to come back to California.' And that was scary because Falsey and Brand were gone, and NBC waited until the last minute, so we virtually had no lead time. This was late May, and we always start shooting in July, so we had no time to write anything. We had no staff. It was Paltrow (who wasn't writing at that point), Mark Tinker (who was occasionally writing) and Masius, and me. I got to L.A. and Masius and I started writing. I think we wrote every day, weekends included, for six months. I mean, we never saw the light of day, because once we started, the race was on and you couldn't stop. The wonderful thing about Bruce is he says, 'You're a writer—I'm paying you to write. So write!' So you'd be in this kind of forced march behind Caesar, going, 'Well, Caesar's going to the Rubicon, I guess we're going too,' you know? (*Laughs.*) That's the kind of leader he is, I mean, you don't think about the consequences, you just jump."

As it turned out, *St. Elsewhere* and Fontana returned for five more seasons, winning two Emmys for Tom, including one for "The Women," guest starring Blythe Danner. Consistent with his flair for the unpredictable, Fontana's final episode of the series turned the tables on cast, crew, and audience alike. It even suspended the characters themselves, as he revealed that the entire series had been the fantasy of an autistic child. Fontana continued, "I loved the fact that the entire show had existed in the mind of a little boy named Tommy. What I thought that said to the audience and to the writers on the show was that this was only a fantasy. As much as it was a part of my life, I needed to let it go and put it in its proper perspective, which was, after all, that it was only a television series. . . . It was a very hard thing for me to do."

St. Elsewhere went off the air in 1988, but Fontana and the Tinkers stayed with Paltrow to produce a few short-lived series (including *Tattingers* and *Home Fires*) and myriad unsold television pilots. Then, for Fontana, it was time to change direction. "I was going to go to Italy for a month, rent a villa outside of Florence [and] write epic poetry."

Before he could pack his bags, Tom's old buddies were inadvertently setting him up to return to television in a big way. John Tinker and John Masius were originally offered jobs as writers on a new cop show being developed by big-screen director Barry Levinson (*Rain Man, The Natural, Wag the Dog*) but declined. The two Johns departed, but suggested that Levinson contact Fontana. "I went out and met with Barry, and when the whole idea of a cop show was presented to me, I was like, 'Well, there's never going to be a better cop show than *Hill Street Blues*, there's no other way to do it better.' And Barry said, 'I want to do a cop show without car chases and without gun battles. I want to do *Homicide* as a thinking man's unit.' And so, the minute he said that, I said, "That's impossible. I have to be part of this!"

Tom's evolution moved from offering audiences an irreverent view of health care to producing an offbeat, yet cerebral world of police detectives. While producing *Homicide,* he picked up a third Emmy and three more Peabodys. His next challenge was to take us all to prison, with the groundbreaking HBO series *Oz.*

In 1999 I spoke with Tom on several occasions about the business of television in general and his thoughts on *Homicide* and *Oz* in particular. At the time of the last interview, Fontana and Levinson were still awaiting news from NBC about the renewal of *Homicide*. Don Ohlmeyer, a champion of the show, had just changed jobs at NBC and would no longer cast the deciding vote on programs like *Homicide* as he had for most of the nineties. "As NBC went from third to first", Ohlmeyer commented, "the thing I was happiest about was . . . it meant that I could renew *Homicide*. It was like we were doing twenty-one hours for the rest of America and for NBC and the 213 affiliates, and were doing one hour for me (*Laughs.*), and *that* [*Homicide*] was my hour.

Ohlmeyer could no longer protect that hour, however, and in late 1999, after seven seasons, *Homicide* was canceled. *Oz,* on the other hand, was renewed for the 2000 season, UPN picked up *The Beat,* and a *Homicide* movie arrived in February. Our interviews with Tom pre-dated these developments.

Longworth: Mark Tinker said of you, "Tom never likes to let the viewer get comfortable." From *St. Elsewhere* to *Homicide* to *Oz,* is this a recurring theme of not letting viewers get comfortable?

FONTANA: I think so. I think that because I watched so much television growing up, I got to figure out the rhythm of it. I've always thought, and part of it comes from the "great book of Paltrow," who, when I first got into television, said, "If anybody else can do it, you don't want to do it." Well, we've all seen every kind of idea and every kind of character and every kind of plot. We've been watching television forty-five, fifty years, right? So it's very hard to fool the audience. You know as well as me the number of times you've sat watching a good show, going, "Oh, I know what's going to happen." Well, my goal is to have people watch my shows and—not that they're never going to say, "I know what's going to happen"—but at least occasionally go, "Holy shit! I never thought that was going to happen."

Longworth: I actually *do* know what's going to happen when I'm watching *Oz.* About ten minutes into it, I throw up.

FONTANA: (*Laughs.*)

Longworth: So it is pretty predictable.

FONTANA: (*Laughs.*) Well, you see, you shouldn't eat beforehand. That's the mistake you're making.

Longworth: If you hadn't been doing these other shows, and it had fallen to you to be the writer/producer of a family show like *Dr. Quinn,* and knowing what we know about your offbeat style, what would she have been like?

FONTANA: Well, first of all, it would have only run for a season because she would have been raped by the second episode. (*Laughs.*) I think probably it would have been a lot rawer. Actually, it's funny, because I had talked to Pat Hingle years ago when we were doing *St. Elsewhere.* He had given me a book about a country doctor in roughly about the same period of time that Dr. Quinn lived. And he and I talked for a while about developing this book into a TV series, you know with the buggy and the going the long distances to get to people. And I always thought it would be fascinating to do a show about medicine when there was no medicine. When there were no machines. And especially in counterpoint to *St. Elsewhere,* it would have been interesting to do a show where the doctor had to trust his or her instincts, and cure people. And also the kinds of things a doctor back then would have had to deal with as opposed to somebody today.

Longworth: Are you incapable of writing and producing what critics would call a "traditional" drama?

FONTANA: I don't know. Every once in a while I'll develop something for one of the networks that I think is like a commercial show, a mainstream show. I did a thing for ABC a couple of seasons ago called *murder.com*, a script about a middle-class couple in their early thirties, living in New York with a kid. And he's a retired cop—she's a teacher at the John Jay Criminal College. But basically, it was my version of *Murder She Wrote*, my version of *Hart to Hart*, because it was about a married couple. My problem with *Hart to Hart* was they were too rich and they were too infertile for my taste (*Laughs.*), in a sense that it was this very elegant couple that didn't have any children and kind of ran around solving murders. My thought was to do a show about a couple who had to pay a mortgage, they had to get the car fixed, they had to get the kid to school. And in the midst of a life, a real life, solving murder mysteries.

Longworth: And why didn't that fly?

FONTANA: Well, I don't know. I mean, it's still out there somewhere, God knows someone may eventually want to make it. But there was nothing in it that was provocative. There was nothing in it that was controversial. The darkness level of it was equal to a *Murder She Wrote.* ABC passed after reading the script. They just didn't seem to think it worked. And maybe it didn't, I don't know. For me, the challenge was, OK, I've never done this kind of thing so I should try it. I only want to do something that I've never done before. When *St. Elsewhere* went off the air, and I think I said this to you once before, we had done 137 episodes; I never wanted to see a gurney again for the rest of my life. And all the offers I got after that until *ER* started were "just do a medical show." I'd go in and pitch a show about a pizza parlor, and they'd say, "Yeah, but can they be doctors?"

Longworth: (*Laughs.*) At what point does an established producer have the clout to say to the network, "Hey, I've got an idea, let's do a show about a clockmaker," and they say, "OK, can you start tomorrow," or does he or she ever get there?

FONTANA: I think it's very rare, given the economics today, especially. I think that might have happened twenty years ago. It doesn't happen today. I mean, David Kelley makes pilots, Bochco makes pilots, everybody makes pilots. It's a hideous system. You don't want to get me started on pilots, because that's a forty-five-minute tirade right there. In the old days of television they ordered thirty-nine episodes of a show for a season. Then they got to the point where they only ordered twenty-two. Then they started ordering thirteen, and on the back nine, you waited to get the pickup. Then it was, "OK, we'll order six." Now we're at a point where the rift for the networks in terms of money is so large that they don't want to make that kind of commitment.

Longworth: What effect did *ER*'s 13 million per episode deal have on other NBC programs, like *Homicide*, for example?

FONTANA: Well, I'll tell you, it's had an effect on NBC. In the sense that with the loss of *Seinfeld* and with paying *ER* this much money, NBC's capacity for profit has been basically eliminated. That's not to say they're losing money, but they're not making money. I'm told GE has a policy that, if one of the companies which it owns doesn't earn 10 percent profit a year of its budget, then they sell that company. Right now, NBC is not going to do that, so they're in the process of downsizing in order to make itself attractive for a buyer. Now, all of that is very corporate, and has to do with stuff that I have no control over and almost no interest in, except that NBC the network airs *Homicide*, and NBC the studio produces *Homicide*, so I have been asked to try to reduce the budget in the eighth year, if we go to an eighth year.

Longworth: You were being asked to reduce your budget, but *ER* was not?

FONTANA: I guess not. But see, my approach to the business has never been "oh, what is John Wells getting, what is Steven Bochco getting, what is David Kelley getting?"

Longworth: I understand, but isn't there a point where the whole team, that is, all of the network shows, suffer because of the *ER* deal?

FONTANA: We're at that point, we're at that point, we're at that point. Helen Hunt and Paul Reiser are making a million dollars each [per episode]; what that does is put an enormous amount of pressure on the producers of other shows, because their actors are now saying, "Well, how come I'm only making $45,000 per episode?"

Longworth: And no show is worth 13 million an episode?

FONTANA: Personally? No. I don't think so.

Longworth: You made a statement one time that your shows don't have real, clear-cut heroes and villains. In his book *Morality and Social Order in Television Crime Drama*, John Sumser references an episode of *Homicide* where a friend of one of the police officers shoots his father as an act of euthanasia.

Sumser writes, "[E]veryone involved is both innocent and guilty," and he goes on to analyze how we've moved from the age of Reagan to Clinton. And I'm wondering, Is TV now in the "age of Clinton," where "nothing is my fault," where there are no heroes or villains, everything is allowed, therefore the story lines for *Homicide, NYPD Blue, Law & Order,* and other shows are not going to have clear-cut rights and wrongs?

FONTANA: Part of my job is to chronicle the time in which I live and reflect society as I perceive it in these waning days of the millennium. Having said that, I've always believed that the great thing about television is that it has room for everybody. It has time for *Touched by an Angel* and *Dr. Quinn.* And it has time for *Oz* and *NYPD Blue.* I think that part of my goal in writing is to say, "The world is not as simple as we would like to believe," and to fool yourself into thinking that it *is* that simple only leaves you open to an enormous danger and an enormous amount of pain, eventually. But that isn't to say that a good simple morality play isn't as effective as an hour of *Homicide.* So, I would hope that we're not getting homogenized, I don't think we are, and that's the God's honest truth. Every conversation that I have with everybody at any network is not about "oh, let's blur the line of morality, let's blur the line of good and bad." In fact, it's the opposite, it's "we need more *Walker, Texas Ranger,* we need less of Tim Bayliss's quandary about the meaning of his life."

Longworth: You told me you would never move back to L.A., but is there one actor who *could* entice you to move to L.A. and produce a new TV series?

FONTANA: If they said to me Jack Nicholson wanted to do a TV series, I might go back to L.A. (*Laughs.*) But the truth of the matter is that television *is* a young man's game, and the recent statistics from the Writers Guild about who gets hired to write and who doesn't only further prove that. I would like to believe that I'm going to stay in television a long time. My gut feeling is that I won't. So I hope that by the time I'm at the point where they don't want me anymore, that I won't want to do it anymore. (*Laughs.*) You know what I'm saying? I have this joke now that I'm going to stop writing episodic television when I get beyond the prime demographic, which is forty-nine. Of course, they just upped it to fifty-four, which could fuck up my plans.

Longworth: (*Laughs.*) Speaking of age, why didn't you just change the name of your show to *Homicide 90210,* and stay young forever?

FONTANA: (*Laughs.*) *Homicide* was going on in Baltimore, which got a lot of press for being the number one town for sex diseases. Someone once said I should change the title to *Gonorrhea: Life on the Street,* which I'm tempted to do—it would probably do better numbers.

Longworth: At what point does a producer reach a level of financial security? At what point can you mark off on the calendar that you are financially secure after a particular number of episodes?

FONTANA: The studios are still notorious for creative bookkeeping. Homicide is in profit, and Barry and I are owed a nice chunk of change from NBC Studios, which we are having trouble getting. So, the truth be told, I don't know. I don't know if I'm ever going to see the money that NBC studios owes me for the profit part of *Homicide*.

Longworth: So I guess you and Fess Parker and James Garner can just stand in line trying to get your money from the network.

FONTANA: Having martinis together in the Will Rogers home.

Longworth: And waiting on a class action against the networks?

FONTANA: Well, this is actually the studios and not the network. It gets crazy because it's the same three letters, but NBC studios owes us this money, and it's fascinating to me, because the thing is, we're good producers. We're very cost conscious, not like a lot of people who just don't give a shit. I give a shit. I take the responsibility of somebody else's money very seriously, probably more seriously than I take my own money. And so, we've produced this show for a real amount of money, and we are in profit, and when people say to you, "Well, we're not sure we're in profit," you say, "Wait, I know what the numbers are the same as you do."

Longworth: Let's shift gears a bit and talk about casting. One of your friends speculated that you gave Andre Braugher a prominent role in your *Homicide* ensemble because it was a way for you to make up for not having given Denzel Washington enough to do on *St. Elsewhere* years earlier.

FONTANA: No, I don't think so. Writing an ensemble show is a very tricky thing. Different writers respond to different actors, and that had nothing to do with color, but more how I could write with greater ease for Ed Flanders and Billy Daniels than I could write for anybody else on the show. That isn't to say I didn't like writing for the others. I liked writing for everybody on the show, but in terms of the guys who kind of inspired me to write deeper stuff, those were the two guys, and it literally had nothing to do with color. I think Denzel's a fine actor. I think that when we got him, he was young, and I think he has grown into being an extraordinary actor.

Longworth: So it wasn't a makeup call, it just sort of "evolved."

FONTANA: It was me responding to the individual actors at that particular moment in their growth.

Longworth: Now to the subject of the written word. Is it difficult to be a writer/producer who relies on other writers? Is it difficult for you to let go and not interfere?

FONTANA: Well, I'll tell you, if they're on my staff, then they're on the staff because I believe in them as writers, and I believe in their individual voice. It's much harder for me with a freelance writer because if a script comes in, and it's "not there," I get frustrated because it's very hard to teach people how to write a television show. But once they get it, then they fall into another category: help them, see their vision through, not to tell them how to write.

Longworth: But can you really teach that, though?

FONTANA: No, that's my point. My point is that we use x-number of freelancers a year on *Homicide.* Out of that, maybe we find one or two people where maybe we say, "Let's put this person on staff." So once we put them on staff, I don't have to teach them to write, that's how they got on staff. All I need to do is guide them. My opinion is that David Milch and Jimmy Yoshimura are probably the two most talented people writing television today, or, at least, episodic television. My whole attitude toward Yosh is when he comes to me with an idea that he is excited about, I would be an idiot to stand in his way.

Longworth: But isn't the talent of writing for television, and writing creatively, something that you're pretty much born with?

FONTANA: Let me put it this way. I know that everyone who is breathing has a story that they want to tell. And I think that it takes a certain amount of courage to start writing that story. And then it takes even more courage to finish the story. Now the question then becomes, what kind of avenue do you use to tell that story? You could write a diary, you could write an essay, you could write a poem, you could write a novel, a short story, a play, a movie, or a television show. You could write a comedy show, or a drama show—a two-hour movie. In my mind, not every writer can write everything. There are a lot of incredible writers who could not write an episode of *Homicide,* and that doesn't mean they're not good writers. That just means that they're not right for this particular show. I don't like to make judgments about writers and say, "Well, this writer sucks." My feeling is always to go, "Well, this writer works in the context of *Homicide,*" and therefore is somebody that we need to bring onboard. When I was starting out a thousand years ago, a lot of people told me I couldn't write. They literally told me not to even think about being a writer. I mean, professionals, not just my cousin.

Longworth: You want to mention a name.

FONTANA: No, I'm not going to, mostly because it was when I was writing plays, and what they may have meant was "don't write plays," which I've stopped doing.

Longworth: Speaking of stopping, did you ever have to pull a story because of network standards and practices?

FONTANA: The only time I can think of where I pulled a script that we were going to shoot was we had done a story about a SIDS death; it was based on a true story about a woman who had had a number of her children die, and they were supposedly SIDS deaths, but the truth was she had murdered them. Roz Weinman, who is the head of broadcast standards, called me and she said, "Listen, I'm asking you not to do this story, not because I think you've done it badly, but because, for parents whose children have actually died of SIDS, it's such a painful thing to have gone through, that to then have a show with the kind of clout that *Homicide* has, implying that they might have killed their child." She said, "I don't think you really want to do that to these parents." And when she said that, I said, "You're absolutely right." And I pulled the story. But that was the only reason I did it. What was great about it was that Roz and I fight all the time about everything, and I mean everything! And it was the only time she called me not out of a concern for the advertisers or the lobbyists or anything like that. She was coming at it from the same place that I like to think that I come at my writing from, which is the human heart. And I couldn't *not* do it.

Longworth: *Homicide* was nearly canceled after the third season, then, in order to placate the network, you introduced more blood and guts into the stories. David Kalat implies in his book on *Homicide* that what you learned from nearly being canceled, and then from inserting more blood into the next season's stories, was that violence drives ratings, that viewers like blood. I can't help but recall our earlier interview where you told me that Barry said *Homicide* was going to be the "thinking man's" cop show.

FONTANA: Yeah, no gun battles, no car chases. Well, what happened is we thought we were going to be canceled after the thirteenth episode. Yosh and Julie Martin and Jorge Zamacona, who were the producers at the time, developed this story about three of our cops getting shot. I was against it, because up to that point, I don't think a gun had been fired, I think maybe a gun had been pulled out once or maybe twice, and I was very proud of that. And Barry said to me, "Well, you know if they're going to cancel us, let's go out with a bang, literally and figuratively, in the sense of let's shoot three regulars, and just leave it like that. Let's end it, after thirteen episodes these guys got shot and you never know if they lived or died, or whatever happened." So I said, "OK, let's do it, let's try it." So we did it. In the interim, the show got picked up, so we were able to complete the story which we'd already started. Well, lo and behold, those three episodes were probably the highest-rated episodes of that season, probably of the past couple of seasons, to which the network said, "Oh, well, see, this is what people really want." And my attitude is yeah, that's probably true, and I will do it on occasion, but I don't want that to become the show, because it's not the reality of the way things are.

Longworth: But is Kalat's assessment correct about what you learned vis à vis the audience's thirst for violent stories?

FONTANA: Yeah, I was stunned that the numbers spiked as high as they did. I learned that, but it didn't necessarily mean I repeated it. My attitude was OK, we can't kill a member of the cast every week, as much as I would sometimes like to. (*Laughs.*) Well, if we were actually killing the actor, I probably would have gone along with it a lot quicker anyway. (*Laughs.*) But I said, "We can't do this every week." We can do it occasionally if it makes sense.

Longworth: Finally, let's talk about *Oz*. *TV Guide*'s Jeff Jarvis once said that *Oz* is "aggressively profane and mocks God . . . it is insulting to God and to us." How do you respond to that? And no profanity please.

FONTANA: The day that I truly believe that a *TV Guide* critic knows the mind of God, I will get out of the business. I mean, I found that line to be so incredibly pretentious and self-righteous, and I was stunned by it. Because here's a guy who not only pretends to know the mind of God, but then pretends to assign human emotions to him, like being offended, as if God would be offended by a television show. Just the preposterousness of it made me dismiss the entire review.

Longworth: Well, maybe Jerry Falwell should start writing for *TV Guide* as well.

FONTANA: Exactly. It's one thing to say that it offended Jarvis and *his* religious beliefs, that's fine with me. I would imagine that there would be a lot of people that would be offended, but to think that God is represented by *TV Guide!* It's fucking *TV Guide* . . . they have a crossword puzzle at the end of the book, you know what I'm saying?

Longworth: (*Laughs.*) Did you say anything profane as you read that review?

FONTANA: (*Laughs.*) I probably did, but I didn't say anything profound when I read it.

Longworth: Profane but not profound.

FONTANA: Oh, by the way, about a week or so after that review came out, the publisher of *TV Guide* called me up and asked me out to have lunch with him, and I said sure. And we had a lovely lunch and he just basically said to me, "I just want you to know *Oz* is my favorite show on television." (*Laughs.*) So it's to his credit that he didn't censor Jarvis. He did tell me Jarvis was pissed off that he had to do the review because he was on vacation.

Longworth: How did the idea for Harold Perrineau's soliloquies on *Oz* come about? Is it like some ancient Greek tragedy? What's the deal?

FONTANA: Well, obviously my theater roots are showing, but what I thought was, in *Homicide,* when our guys are going to or from a murder, they get in the car or they go to the coffee room and they do these little debates. Now, in prison, guys aren't that forthcoming about what they think and what they feel 'cause that leaves them open and vulnerable to attack, and to potentially become dead. So I thought to myself, Well, how do I accomplish on *Oz* what we accomplish in those car scenes on *Homicide?* In other words, how do I initiate discussion about the point of the hour if I don't have those car scenes? So my thought was to just let someone articulate some thoughts about what all this craziness meant. I also thought, given the honesty with which we were trying to approach the storytelling, that it would be good every once in a while to take the audience out of the prison, give them a chance to breathe if you will, so that it's not fifty-eight minutes of nonstop brutality. It's fifty-five minutes of brutality. (*Laughs.*)

Longworth: How did the idea come about to do Oz in the first place? And don't tell me that you've been to prison.

FONTANA: No, no. I was in jail briefly for civil disobedience, but that was a long time ago.

Longworth: For civil disobedience?

FONTANA: Back in the sixties, we don't want to go into that. Anyway, here's the point. First of all, having done *Homicide,* a show about murder, we were often sending the murderer away. And I started to think, Well, OK, now we know what effect all this has on the homicide detectives and on the victims' families, but what really is the long-term effect on the guys who commit the crime? So in a way, it's a rumination on what happens after *Homicide.* Obviously, my next series should be about the afterlife, where we follow the victims themselves to see what they're up to in hell and heaven.

Longworth: So what's your frame of reference?

FONTANA: Every character that I create, I create three parts to him or her. One is the mind, one is the heart, and one is, for lack of a better word, the balls. In other words, what do they think about? What makes them weep and laugh? And makes them want to fuck? Now, that is universal whether they're doctors, cops, criminals, or my Aunt Tilly. So, once I have those characters defined in such a way, the environment then becomes the thing we try to capture. My knowledge of hospitals (even though my mother worked in a hospital all those years) was minimal until I started doing *St. Elsewhere*. My knowledge of a homicide investigation was even less before I started doing *Homicide*, and my knowledge of prisons was infinitesimal before I started researching *Oz*, but what I did was I went to a number of prisons . . . all levels, medium security, maximum security. I went to experimental prisons. And what I went there looking for was not stories. I wasn't looking to steal anybody's life, and put it on TV. What I was looking for was more of a sense of what it felt like for them to live in this life day after day, and to a man, the common answer was: loneliness, fear, never being able to relax. Those elements, the idea of survival, how does one survive in an impossible environment. So once I plugged into that as the common experience of all these guys, writing it became relatively easy.

Longworth: But doesn't every show have to have some kind of sympathetic character? Most viewers of *Oz* would say, "Gee, I just can't sympathize with any of these guys, it's just so foreign to me."

FONTANA: Chris Albrecht [head of programming at HBO] said to me when I went in to talk about this show, he said, "I don't care if any of the characters are likeable as long as they're interesting." Now, I have taken that to heart, and what my feeling has been is that I think people watch *Oz* not because the characters are likeable, but because they're interesting, and because the actors playing these parts are interesting. So here is a prime example that goes against the conventional wisdom of television, which is you must have likeable characters in order for people to watch them week after week. But I've always thought that was the great lie of television. Because if you look at a show like *Seinfeld* or *Cheers*, they were mean to each other. They were incredibly selfish, they were incredibly narrow, they were incredibly self-absorbed, and mean to each other on both shows. This idea that for an hour drama you have to have a hero is, I think, something coming out of a lack of vision by network executives, as opposed to an expectation on the part of the American public. Another example would be probably the most popular hour drama character of the last twenty years was J. R. Ewing. Not a pleasant bone in the man's body, OK? People were fascinated by him. Part of that was the outrageousness of what he did, but part of it was the fact that Larry Hagman was immensely popular, from *I Dream of Jeannie*. But that isn't to say, having learned this lesson from *Oz*, that I'm now out there trying to sell the networks on doing shows with incredibly unlikable characters (*Laughs.*). I'm not.

Longworth: As the networks' audience share keeps shrinking, will that bode better for niche shows like *Homicide?*

FONTANA: I think so, I do, I do. I have no desperate need to be on NBC, unless I'm doing a show that I want to do. You know what I mean? If they called and said to me, "Oh, we'd like you to take over *Profiler,* and we're going to offer you all of the money in the planet," I would still say no. That's why I've gone to HBO, I've gone to Showtime, I've gone to Lifetime, to develop things. I have this deal with UPN. In my mind, I'd rather go to a place that needs me than be on a network that doesn't. I'm not picking on NBC per se, because the bulk of my career has been there, and I feel very affectionate toward the place, but if you have a conversation with any of the network presidents and you're having a conversation about "we need this at this hour," you are basically a tailor making a suit. You talk to Chris Albrecht and the people at HBO, they don't have a season, they don't have a schedule. They put shows on or they don't. If they don't like a show, they don't put it on. If they like it, they put it on, and they support it. They develop less things and, as a result, make better things, I think.

Longworth: Why don't we see more half-hour dramas?

FONTANA: I think that what happened was there was that period of time when the "dramedy" was in vogue. You know, like *Molly Dodd?*

Longworth: And *Frank's Place.*

FONTANA: *Frank's Place,* and *Wonder Years* to a lesser extent, because it was always a little softer. But the networks said, "Well, people don't want that." I think that also simultaneously what occurred at the time was "you get me a stand-up comic and build a show around him or her," and that's how you do a half hour. We went through that period after *Roseanne*. So, again, I think it's the narrowness of the network executives. The other thing that I would worry about if I was going to do a half-hour drama is that I don't know if it really *is* enough time to take on a big issue. Every time I watch a half-hour comedy try to deal with racism or alcoholism or something, I always feel like I'm getting the *Reader's Digest* version of a problem, you know what I mean?

Longworth: Tom, what's going to be the last unpredictable thing you'll ever do?

FONTANA: (*Laughs.*) You mean in TV or on my deathbed?

Longworth: Both, or they can be the same.

FONTANA: (*Laughs.*) Yeah, they may be. God knows if I keep this up I'm going to kill my career. I have no idea what the last unpredictable thing I will do on TV is. Because part of the reason that I think I'm unpredictable is I have no clue myself. It's not like I have a grand plan of the universe here.

Longworth: Well, you know how to offend God, so . . .

FONTANA: I guess I've gotta offend the Devil next. Make a series out of that. Well, I guess Martha Williamson has done that. (*Laughs.*) But in any case, the last unpredictable thing I'll do on my deathbed I hope will be fucking a sixteen-year-old girl. (*Laughs.*)

Longworth: Thanks, you've just ruined my whole chapter. But really, do you feel unpredictable?

FONTANA: No, I don't actually. It's not like I wake up every morning and say "Now, OK, what can I do to be unpredictable?" What I do is, I think, and this is going to sound incredibly pretentious, but I think for myself to keep growing in an industry that does not want you to grow (it wants you to follow the formula), I just want to keep reaching, because the minute that I feel like I'm done reaching, I will get out of television. I love television too much to end up being one of those guys who makes the same show over and over again.

NANCY | Poster Girl for
MILLER | Perserverance

Nancy Miller. COURTESY OF NANCY MILLER.

TELEVISION CREDITS

1987–88	*Houston Knights* (CBS)
1992	*The Roundtable* (NBC)
1993–94	*Against The Grain* (NBC)
1995	*The Monroes* (ABC)

MW   MW   MW

In *Star Trek VI The Undiscovered Country,* Spock volunteers Kirk as a peace envoy to the captain's archenemies, the Klingons. "Why me?" asks Kirk. Spock replies, "There's an old saying from the late-twentieth century, that only Nixon can go to China."

Perhaps it is only appropriate that a white girl who grew up in the Deep South during its most shameful era has "gone where no man has gone before," creating a television program not only about civil rights, but also civil life in America, then and now.

That person is Nancy Miller, a tough Southern belle who has spent most of her adult life first tending, then "raising" the bar.

Born in Donaldson, Louisiana, Nancy is one of three daughters brought up in a Catholic household that was run by her stay-at-home mother. Her father was a veterinarian. Both parents were originally from Birmingham, Alabama, where each summer they and the girls journeyed to spend their vacation and revisit family roots. Nancy's family began to move from place to place, including a brief stint in Baltimore, but by the time she was in fourth grade, they settled in Oklahoma City. She attended Bishop McGuiness High School, and later enrolled in the University of Oklahoma, where her writing skills began to emerge. "My father died when I was a freshman in college, and that's when I really started writing 'cause I didn't know what to do with that pain. So I put it on paper. I wrote this skit for my sorority a couple of years later, and that was the first time I heard people laughing and being moved by something I'd written. I thought, 'God, I liked that. That's kind of cool.' I was a physical education major, but screwed up my knee, so I had to transfer my credits into recreation. I knew I didn't want to do that, so it was like 'what the hell am I going to do with my life?' I was a Vista volunteer for a year right out of college. It was in Beaumont, Texas, and that was the worst year of my life. So then I thought, 'I guess I'll move to Los Angeles and try to write.'"

While she struggled to make it as a writer, Nancy supported herself by working as a bartender, learning about the human condition, and making contacts along the way. Both paid off, and finally, in the mid-1980s she began to get work in television. Soon, her name was appearing steadily on prime-time credits. She served as story editor for the CBS drama *Houston Knights,* described by Brooks and Marsh (*The Complete Directory to Prime Time Network and Cable TV Shows*) as "a youth-oriented police-action series, in the *Starsky & Hutch* mold." She then created and produced *The Round Table* for NBC, which Brooks and Marsh describe as a "cross between *thirtysomething* and a violent TV cop show." Miller served as supervising producer for NBC's short-lived family drama *Against the Grain* (starring a young Ben Affleck) and for *The Monroes,* about a powerful political family. In 1996 she was coexecutive producer on *Profiler,* then created and produced another short-lived series, *Leaving L.A.,* for ABC.

Having amassed these considerable credits, Miller was now a proven quantity, so much so that in 1990 CBS agreed to buy six episodes of *Any Day Now.* The show, about two girls (one white, one black) growing up in the South in the early 1960s, was originally slated as a half hour. Nancy's life was coming full circle, and she would finally have an opportunity to face the injustices of racial discrimination that she was too young to understand or do anything about three decades before. "Our family trips to Birmingham in the summers, the genesis of *Any Day Now,* was experiences that I remember down there. Spending all those summers in Birmingham, we were in the middle of all this, the middle of the sixties, and I'm embarrassed to say I didn't even know it was going on. I was catching fireflies and worrying about boys, and a half a mile away, children my own age were being hosed by policemen."

Nancy's good intentions aside, not everyone was ready to revisit the civil rights struggle. According to an article in *Entertainment Weekly,* CBS canceled their order because Orion "couldn't market the series internationally." Miller told *Entertainment Weekly,* on September 3, 1999, "Every pitch session I went to for eight years, I'd say 'I want to do this half hour show about two little girls and the Civil Rights movement.' Invariably, they'd say, 'What about dropping the Civil Rights aspect'."

Miller persevered, holding steadfast to her vision of producing a drama that could make a difference. During those eight years, she might have been inspired by the words of two famous writers. A century before, Harriet Beecher Stowe said, "Never give up, for that is just the place and time that the tide will turn," and Henry Wadsworth Longfellow once noted, "If you only knock long enough and loud enough at the gate, you are sure to wake up somebody." Miller kept knocking, and she "woke up" the Lifetime network who shared her original vision. Some changes were indicated, however, to insure a better fit with the cable network's audience and mission. The architect was Lifetime president Dawn Tarnofsky-Ostroff.

"If you had read the half hour of these two little girls", Tarnovsky-Ostroff commented, "you would see that the characters are so well drawn that the dimensions, the level of depth in these two girls, was really astounding, especially for half-hour television. And I think anybody who read the script would have said the same thing I said, which is 'what happens to these girls when they grow up?' Did they miss anything? Did they spend a good part of their life focusing on one area, and wake up one day and say, 'Oops I forgot this part over here'? And all of this just started to gel and come together, and it was almost as if Nancy had drawn a straight line that stopped, and then she just picked up a pen and drew the rest of the lines. What Nancy really did was flush out these people as adult characters—just a level of the things that they deal with in their feelings, that everything is not black or white, but that there's a lot of gray in our emotions, in the way we deal with things, and we're not always perfect people, we're always struggling for the right answers. I think that that is so in tune with what women feel today. And as hard as we try, it's really damn hard to get it right. (*Laughs.*) She understands that. She really does. And I have just an incredible amount of respect for the way in which she's gone about producing this kind of show, which could have been extremely controversial. It could have been a show that didn't receive the kind of acclaim that it did from all different organizations as well as the press. But I think that Nancy's sensitivity to what is actually happening in our country right now, and her sensitivity to what she faced when she was growing up, has all just come together under one big television show. You don't walk away feeling angry, you don't walk away feeling frustrated. You walk away feeling as if there's sort of a new beginning, and there's hope. And it's a very encouraging sign for us to be able to present a show like that."

Any Day Now soon became Lifetime's most watched series. In the first season, the program attracted about one million viewers, but by the opening episode of the second season, that number had nearly doubled. "Although ratings are important to a certain degree", Tarnovsky-Ostroff continued, "it is sort of the signature show for our network, and it's a show that we stand behind emotionally and creatively. And I think one of the luxuries of being in cable is that every show is not ratings driven. You know, there are different reasons to do different shows. Some shows really *are* ratings driven, and they've got to really look at the numbers. And other shows are there because it reflects the tone of what we want the network to be about. It really has characters that we believe in, it really shows issues that are very hard to find on television, and it's a critically acclaimed show really beyond our wildest dreams. And I think for those and other reasons there are a lot of other factors that go into being what makes *Any Day Now* a success. Now, it just so happens that the ratings are really going up this year, that the demos are pretty fantastic, and I don't foresee that changing. If anything, I think that in the second season it's really going to catch on even more. So I don't think the ratings issue will ultimately be a big thing for us. It's a show that will be around for a long time."

TV Guide critic Matt Roush noted in an August 21, 1999, review that *Any Day Now* "harks back to a nearly vanished form of well-crafted family drama." He ended his article by asking a rhetorical question, "Do the networks know what they're missing?" Sadly, they probably don't. But two million of us do, and that's quite a tribute to the former bartender who always knew *our* limits, but refused to be held back by her own. I interviewed Nancy just before the networks had announced their 1999–2000 season, which included a number of dramas featuring women leads.

Longworth: Nancy, the other day my wife told me to be more like a man of the nineties, and I replied, "I am. I'm a man of the 1890s.

MILLER: (*Laughs.*)

Longworth: Well, I began to think about her charge that I was a sexist, and, as I started to research this book, I realized that I was only writing about male producers. What's wrong with the industry today when it seems to be such a white boys club in terms of producers? And what does it say about Aaron Spelling, who has several outstanding women producers in his TV family?

MILLER: I think there's nothing more wrong with the industry than what's wrong with the world. It's a white man's world, you know? That's the truth. I've been very fortunate in my career to meet men—it's always been the men that have had the power. I've been doing this for years. I sold my first script in 1980. I was the only woman in the room for years and years and years and years. I was grateful to be there, and I learned my craft. I made a lot of great contacts, and I've never personally experienced any overt sexism beyond the regular tale. I think every woman in this business (and probably a lot of the men) have experienced some stuff.

Longworth: I'm hoping that you will harass me, as a matter of fact.

MILLER: (*Laughs.*) Right. I don't know what goes on behind closed doors, but I never felt like I wasn't being heard, that I couldn't do what I wanted to do. Now, saying that, there's still not enough women and there's not enough people of color in our business. But I think it's just a reflection of things in our society. I don't think there's anything deliberate. I haven't felt a territorial thing where the guys are closing in and don't want any women. I haven't found that at all.

Longworth: But back to the second part of my original question. What's so special about Aaron Spelling? I'm thinking Connie Burge (*Charmed*), Nancy Miller, Brenda Hampton (*7th Heaven*)—most of the women creator/producers of TV drama today work for Spelling. Why is he so progressive? This obviously is not a coincidence.

MILLER: I don't know if it goes back to his background as a little Jewish boy growing up in Texas and feeling not a part of the club. Aaron has always been—he's just always been fair, and he's always been open. Aaron gave me a huge boost in my career when I did *The Round Table*. I came in as a coproducer. And through a sequence of events the guy they hired as my boss left the show, and Aaron bumped me up to supervising producer, which was like three bumps in one day.

Longworth: Like a battlefield command promotion?

MILLER: Yes, but he had faith in me. And I'll never forget that. And he's just a very fair person from all of my experiences with him. He's got this unbelievable talent for recognizing stars. His casting ability is unparalleled, and his knowledge about the business. And he's really kind of like this figurehead— he comes in when you need him, but he isn't intrusive. And it's just been wonderful working there. And everyone that works with him has the same experience, Duke Vincent, Jim Conway, Jonathan Levine. I've never felt any sexism, and I have my radar up for that. Unless it goes on behind—who the hell knows what happens when I leave the room, you know? And as far as the progression in my career, in my mind, nothing was going to stop me, and I think you almost have to have that kind of mind-set in this town.

Longworth: How did you hook up with Aaron in the first place?

MILLER: Eight years ago I met Gary Randall, who is now my partner. He was president at Orion Television [slated to distribute *Any Day Now* for CBS]. We sold *Any Day Now* to CBS, Deborah Joy Levine and I did. They ended up pulling the plug and we didn't make the series, but Gary then went to Spelling as president, so that's how I ended up at Spelling. Gary brought me in, and we did *The Round Table*. So the man who pulled the plug on *Any Day Now* is now my partner. (*Laughs.*) It's so ironic.

Longworth: Let's use one of those *Any Day Now* flashbacks and go back in time. How was it you could just pick up and move to L.A.? I wouldn't have had the courage to do that.

MILLER: You know, ignorance really is bliss. If I knew then what I know now, I never would have stayed [in L.A.]. The odds against me doing what I've done, you know? And this is what I tell people, and I don't know if it's good advice or bad advice. If you have a second choice of something you love to do, you'll never make it in this business. Because if I had had a second choice, if I had wanted to teach, if there was something else that I loved, I would have given up and gone home. But I had no second choice, so I was either going to be a bartender all my life or a writer. So I *had* to make the writing work. And like I said, I've been fortunate. I've met good people.

Longworth: Who gave you your first break?

MILLER: Sally Robinson. She read a *Family* script that I wrote, in fact, this is a pretty interesting story. I knew no one in this town. The guy I was working for—I quit my job and moved to the beach and said, "I want to be a writer," and he goes, "You idiot, don't you know this whole town is based on relationships? Why didn't you tell me that? Let me introduce you to a friend of mine who is a writer." Sally was a writer for a show called *Family,* and she read one of the spec scripts I had written (I had bought books, and for a year all I did was read books on screenwriting, and then I wrote three spec scripts, with *Family* being one of them), and if she had said, "Nancy, I don't think you have it," I would have left and gone home to Oklahoma. But she was very encouraging, and she said, "You're very raw, but you have talent." So I rewrote the script and I asked her for an envelope from her agent, 'cause I knew you couldn't send scripts in unless they're from an agent. So I steamed off the return address and put it on my envelope and I found out that they had just changed story editors. I wrote a letter to the old story editor, Carol McKeon, who had just left. Sally Robinson was the new story editor, but I had written this to Carol. I said, "Dear Carol, here is the script we talked about, I hope you like it, blah, blah, blah, blah, blah." About three weeks later, I get a call from Sally Robinson, saying, "Carol's not here now, but I'm the new story editor—I read your script and I love it." (*Laughs.*) And I'm wetting my pants I'm so excited. I'm just out of my mind. And she said, "I don't know if we're going to get picked up, but I either want to use this script or have you write another one for us." So they didn't get picked up, but I stalked Sally Robinson for like two years. I would call her about once every six months, and I saw where she was at some seminar, so I went to the seminar and I introduced myself. And about two years later I'm making my twice-a-year phone call, and she says, "I've been trying to get ahold of you; I just got a new show and I want you to do a script for it." So that's how I wrote my first script.

Longworth: And what was the show?

MILLER: It was called *Secrets of Midland Heights*. And she was great. I wrote the draft and she gave me notes and said, "I'm going to be sending you the rewrite but I don't want you to be upset—the first script that I had on the air, I only recognized two words." She had done a *Lou Grant* and only recognized "Hello Lou." (*Laughs.*) So she goes, "Don't be upset that we had to rewrite this." She was amazing. She was great.

Longworth: Now, help me with the chronology. When did you get hooked up with MTM where you did *Profiler?*

MILLER: That was two years ago.

Longworth: Were you in the MTM system prior to that?

MILLER: No, I was under a development deal at that time with Warner Brothers, but I was free to go on a show. And *Profiler*—I did that show for eight episodes and got the hell out, basically.

Longworth: You wrote for a strong woman character in *Profiler* and you write for two strong women characters on *Any Day Now.* Can only women really write for women?

MILLER: *Ally McBeal* is a show written by a man about women. But he [David Kelley] has every right in the world to tell that story the way he wants to tell it. If you look at my show, which is about two women, men scream all the time, "Oh, it's a woman's point of view," like you're dammed right it is! And it's about time. (*Laughs.*)

Longworth: But what's wrong with me, then? I like *Any Day Now,* and I watch it with my wife.

MILLER: Well, thank you very much. I think men hear Lifetime and they think "The Chick Channel," and they don't tune in. The ones that do, I've only met one man out of countless men, who said he didn't like it. I wish Lifetime would promote it more to men, as well as women because I think they're all universal things that men can relate to as well as women.

Longworth: Exactly.

MILLER: Now, what *does* upset me is the lack of interesting female characters on television. It's not only color, it's also if you look at the women, except on *Touched by an Angel* and *Ally McBeal,* there's really no other leads with women.

Longworth: *Providence.*

MILLER: *Providence,* and Melina [Kanakarades] is a dear friend of mine. I'm thrilled about that show, and hopefully because of *Providence,* next year there'll be more. I know that because *Providence* went well, they were looking for more female leads. But one reason I developed *Any Day Now,* and every-thing I do, I'm sick to death of writing women as victims, rape victims, breast cancer victims, homicide victims. If I had to write another dead woman, I was going to scream. So that part of this drives me crazy. Television is from a man's point of view, and it's how they think women talk and think women act.

Longworth: Well, since you mentioned that. I was researching your career, and wondering what you were going to be like, and I'm thinking I'll find a bunch of credits like "Loving Women" or something. And I'm reading this credit sheet, and there's *Houston Knights,* and *Round Table,* you know, cop shows! One critic described *Round Table* as a cross between *thirtysomething* and a violent cop show. And I'm thinking, Is this the right Nancy Miller? That's 180 degrees from *Any Day Now.* Were you just cutting your teeth then because it was the white man's industry, and you just kept *Any Day Now* inside your head all along? Or are you just an industry whore?

MILLER: (*Laughs.*) I was learning my craft and I was a bartender for years. I'm from Oklahoma, I moved here in '78, not knowing a damn thing about this business or anyone in it. Didn't even know what a script looked like. And I took any show I could get. Any assignment I could get, I took. Now within that assignment, if you read those scripts, you would find that the women are strong, the women are smart. So within my abilities, I did what I wanted to do. I was hired to write a show for *Houston Knights* that is about two cops. That's what I was hired to do and I had to do that, but within that I would always try to portray women as positively as I could. I don't think it's fair to take a job from someone and then go, "I'm not going to do this," you know? It's like, well, don't take the job. (*Laughs.*) So, and I love cop stuff. Some of the shows I'm going to pitch this year are about cops. So I love that world, and the men and women in that world are so fascinating to me.

Longworth: But you've never been a cop.

MILLER: No.

Longworth: But a few minutes ago you critized men who write shows for women. So why did you think you had the right to write about cops?

MILLER: That's a good question. Because what I write about is the char-acter. I write about these people. Now these people are working on a case, and I've done extensive research. I hung out with cops, I've gone to I don't know how many crime scenes. I completely immersed myself in their world.

Longworth: Ever been arrested by a cop?

MILLER: Yep, one of the most horrible nights of my life. But we won't go into that.

Longworth: That's exactly what Tom Fontana told me about his background. I was just kidding with him when I asked the question, and he said, "Yeah, but I don't want to talk about it." What's with you producer types? When were *you* arrested?

MILLER: That was like fifteen years ago. But anyway. You're right. I probably shouldn't have said that a man shouldn't write about a woman, because otherwise the only thing I could write about is a writer, because that's the only thing that I'm doing. But we are so much more than that. And *Ally McBeal* is a lawyer, so that part of it comes from David's world. And like I said, he has every right to do that. I have every right to have it drive me crazy.

Longworth: (*Laughs.*)

MILLER: So you write about what you know.

Longworth: So then you were paying your dues, doing what you had to do, but you always sort of had these ideas in you that you wanted to explore?

MILLER: Yes. The name of my company is Paid My Dues Productions. And I bar tended and wrote anything I could for years and years and years.

Longworth: How did being a bartender help you become a better writer?

MILLER: It was like, if I'm not a success as a writer, I've got to do this [tend bar] all my life. (*Laughs.*) So it was great motivation. And working with people and talking to people, you know, when you create characters, what's really amazing is that we're all so much alike. When you get beneath all the crap, we all want the same thing, and that's love. And we all have different ways of going about it. So any time spent with the masses of people like my customers at the bar, the waitresses, the janitor, it was all an education, just studying—and I love to do that. People fascinate me.

Longworth: We talked earlier about your summers in Alabama. Did you have black friends?

MILLER: No, and that part of it—I originally started—I wanted to do a show about little girls coming of age. We know about little boys coming of age, we've seen that a hundred times.

Longworth: Yeah, I'm still doing it.

MILLER: (*Laughs.*) And I wanted to do stories about the civil rights movement, so I married those two ideas and came up with the idea of a secret friendship between a little white girl and a little black girl. That was eight years ago; when we sold it to CBS it was only a half hour. Lifetime had the idea to put it in the present as well as the past, which I just loved.

Longworth: A successful producer of network shows once warned me that if you go to cable, you give up a lot of creative control. Is that true? And what would have happened if you had said to Lifetime, "No, I don't like your idea about putting the show in the present?" What's the relationship there?

MILLER: OK, a couple of things. If I hadn't liked that idea I would have said no, and I would have kept the project and not written it for Lifetime. Over the eight years that I tried to sell it, I had people say, "I love this, but make it about boys," and I said, "No, I'm not doing it." If you have—it's either the guts or the stupidity to say that word no—you can keep [going] . . . this is a very collaborative business. You shouldn't be in this business, I don't think, if you're not going to collaborate. Now, saying that, there has to be one person with a vision of the show. If that person allows all of this other input to come in and water down the vision of the show, that's that person's fault. Now, you have to be willing to accept the outcome, which may be "then you're not doing your show." I've always been fine with that. I've saved my money, I've enough "fuck you money" that I can hold on to my projects. I have like five projects that I am determined to get made. Two of them have already been made. *Leaving L.A.* two years ago on ABC was a script that circulated around town for a couple of years, and everyone loved it, but it scared the hell out of them. ABC, Jamie Tarses, and Stu Bloomberg had the guts to put that on the air. Now, it didn't work, OK. And they took it off after six episodes, but at least they tried and at least, to me, that was a success. Now, to my agent or to other people, it might be a failure because the show was canceled, but I got to see that thing come to life the way I wanted to. I mean, it was exactly what I wanted. I fought like hell for the director I wanted. I knew I had one shot. If I had gotten the wrong director, this thing would have been a disaster. And if you have the courage of your convictions, you just have to hold them off, and you have to fight for what you believe in. That's not to say I don't believe—I am not a control freak. In fact, I'm exactly opposite than a control freak, I like to have a life. So I don't write every script, I'm not there every moment of the day, I have an amazing staff that is great and I depend on a lot. I have a partner, Gary, so that I don't have to deal with the crap I don't want to deal with, so I love collaborating. And if someone has a good idea about something, great! It's all about making it the best you can be.

Longworth: When you first pitched the idea for *Any Day Now*, did anyone ever say to you, "Well, that's been done with *I'll Fly Away?*"

MILLER: Oh, all the time. Every damn time. I'd say, "God, it's not the same show at all." *I'll Fly Away*, I thought, was a great show. It was well produced, but it didn't have a lot of humor. And I think that was its downfall. *Any Day Now* has a surprising amount of humor in it. Also, *I'll Fly Away* was kind of about the racial part of the show right on the head. We usually come about it in a backdoor way. We've done some episodes that are only about race. But usually, it's about a little girl who wants her first bra. And she can't try it on because there's no colored dressing rooms. So we take a step back, and it's through the eyes of the little girl. So what I just said to you I've said to them year after year after year, this is not the same show at all. I'd say, "Here's how it's different" and they'd go, "Well, oh yeah, but."

Longworth: Speaking of the bra scene, the transitions in *Any Day Now* are outstanding, such as the one where in flashback Lorraine is trying to get her first bra, and you cut forward to present day when she, as an adult, is packing her bra for a trip. Do you work hard at those transitions?

MILLER: Every single transition from past to present and present to past has to be scripted. I even sent a huge memo to all the writers. So that was always a part of the show that I loved, and some of the shows, if you watch them, we were kind of lazy, and we didn't do it. Then we clicked into it towards the end of last year. And, from now on, every single transition, unless something happened on the set that day that screwed it up, they're all scripted, so they're thought out very carefully.

Longworth: Since *Any Day Now* is on cable and since cable never has the same ratings as network, is it fair to say that the show would never be killed because of low ratings—or would it?

MILLER: If it goes down to like a .2, we'll get canceled, I think. They tell us they don't care about the ratings. It's not that, they say, "Don't worry about the ratings," you know, we're their first drama, so we're really breaking new ground here and we're all learning as we go. That is the most frustrating thing about being on cable is the number of eyeballs that don't see it. However, I could never do this show on network television, I could never do the episodes that we're doing, so—

Longworth: Because it wouldn't pull the numbers?

MILLER: Well, no, because it's about women, it's about civil rights—the reasons the networks never bought it for eight years.

Longworth: Well, in order to pull bigger numbers and get more exposure, why not cross-promote the show and get ABC to run repeats of *Any Day Now* during filler times or in the summer?

MILLER: That's exactly what we tried to do.

Longworth: See, we Southerners aren't so stupid.

MILLER: I know, but exactly what you just said is what we proposed to them. The problem is—say they put it on during the summer at nine o'clock on Tuesday night. People aren't going to be able to see *Spin City,* and if they fall in love with our show, then when the new fall season comes up, instead of watching their show that's on in our time slot, they'll watch our show.

Longworth: Yeah, but they could put it in a place where they have a real dog show, that they knew wasn't going to be renewed, and put *Any Day Now* in there. What do they have to lose?

MILLER: That's what I say. And with all this synergy crap that's supposed to be going on within the corporation, you would think that ABC would want it to do well because Lifetime is owned by ABC and Disney.

Longworth: Right, but if you had gotten it on network—

MILLER: I think this would have been a huge hit on network, I do. But I think every show I do will be a huge hit. (*Laughs.*) But people—when they find this show, they love it. Now, my mom has friends, and the older generation—and you probably experience this too—some of my mom's friends won't watch the show because it has blacks in it. So I know that that would have been out there, but if this was on network, it would have created a controversy I think. It's the only show on the air that's dealing with this stuff that has two female leads, one of which is black—well except for *Touched by an Angel.* I think the time would have been right for this. But yes, if we were on and got terrible numbers, we would have been canceled. Definitely.

Longworth: You mentioned civil rights again. Let's talk about racial diversity on television. Most other industries, as well as the government, seem to have programs in place to nurture diversity, except the entertainment industry. Do you think it will ever get better?

MILLER: Just my experience over the years, I have seen doors open more and more. I think there are some minority-planning things, but I don't think it's a priority, though. Every year, and I'm sure you've read about, this fall it's a white landscape—no leads for blacks. I know the people, a lot of the people who make these decisions, and I know they're not racist so I think it was a matter of they just got caught with great surprise. You know, a creator comes in and pitches an idea, and we come in and we go, "OK, here are our characters." Now, every show I've ever done, I've always included black characters and other people of color because they're interesting people, and it only contributes to the dramatic elements of the show. I don't know if this year [1999–2000] the creators came in and they didn't have black characters. I can't imagine that they said, "You know what? Make that black character white."

I can't imagine that that happened. Now, on the other hand, I'm going in this year with an idea for a TV show based on a white female and a black male lead. You all have said that you want this, so here's a great idea, it's time that it's done. If they don't want to, then they're going to have to say no.

Longworth: They're going to tell you that Eriq LaSalle would not approve your project.

MILLER: Right, right. (*Laughs.*) I've got the actor I want.

Longworth: (*Laughs.*) [In 1999, according to widespread media reports, *ER*'s LaSalle opposed the continuation of a story line in which his character was involved in an interracial romance.]

MILLER: So I can't imagine it was done maliciously. Now, on the other hand, there wasn't a great concern to make sure that there was inclusion. So that's a problem—they're not thinking about the landscape. And everyone gets caught up in this business, it's so crazy. Then one day all the schedules are laid out and they go, "Oh, my God, they're all white." I don't know what happens, but I do know the people I dealt with are not racist or sexist.

Longworth: Are you going to pitch your new idea to Lifetime out of loyalty, or will you go to the networks?

MILLER: I'd love to develop it with Lifetime, but I'm pitching these ideas to the network.

Longworth: And you're prepared for what they might say?

MILLER: Well, if they don't want to do it, I want them to have to say no. I don't know if all the ideas that came to them were void of all this stuff, and they just went with those ideas, or if they were presented with ideas, multiracial, all these other things, and then they said no. Now that there's been this publicity, I would think they were going to be open to discussions like this.

Longworth: You have a very diverse cast. How did you decide on them?

MILLER: Oh, God, we were just blessed. The two little girls we cast first, Mae and Shari Dyon Perry. And we looked here in L.A., in New York, in New Orleans, and we found them finally in Atlanta. And they walked through the door together, and we about fell off our chair. I saw Mae Middleton, and I went, "Who did she grow up to be?" She grew up to be Annie Potts, because we were talking about Annie. Lorraine I knew from *Leaving L.A.* She was in that show, and I had actually written another pilot with her in mind, but ABC didn't pick it up. But she wanted to read this, and once she read it, she said, "I don't care about the other pilot, this is what I want to do."

Longworth: She was great in some *Law & Order* episodes.

MILLER: Yeah, she's great. And those are usually the roles Lorraine got to play, the tough D.A., the tough coroner. Now we get to see this other side, there's this playful side, this giggly girl side to her, so it's really fun to write this stuff for her.

Longworth: I was really moved by Courtney Vance's performance in the pilot, so why didn't he continue with the series?

MILLER: Because Courtney is a movie star, and the reason he did the pilot was he loved the show and he was very good friends with our casting director. And he wanted to do the series, but we would have to do it according to his schedule. In other words, if he got a movie, he couldn't shoot. And there's no way to write scripts like that, because we may need James in episode five, he has a huge episode. So Courtney would have said "great," but then two weeks before we start shooting, if he got a movie, he would have gone to the movie. So with great heartache we decided we just couldn't take that chance.

Longworth: What a tough decision.

MILLER: It was a very tough decision. But I love John, who got the part, and I think it's worked out well. But I know that Courtney was an important part of that pilot.

Longworth: You also have a very diverse staff of writers. Are you all working to effect change in our society?

MILLER: *Any Day Now*—I know it's not going to solve racism. But what it can do is lead to a dialogue, and that's the beginning of understanding. The writers—we have seven writers, five women and two men. Two of the women are black, two of the people on my staff are gay. It's a very diverse staff, and the story meetings we have—when we break an episode—[well,] we did one about if you tell a racist joke, does that make you a racist? We did a whole episode about that, and it nearly killed us. We got into some of the most heated, emotional discussions, and I remember coming home one day just completely drained and mad. I was so mad at these people I love. We all have such different opinions and it hit me. We're doing the work that the nation should be doing, in this little room, doing this little TV show, we are having the most incredible conversations on race and gender and these other issues.

Longworth: That's one of the things I want to try and communicate to college kids about what television can do and what it can teach us to do.

MILLER: Yes. Well, I mean, and that's what's frustrating to me that more people aren't seeing the show, because so many of our episodes, if you've watched them, you can't help but talk about it at the end of it. Whether you are pissed off at a stance someone took that you don't agree with, but it makes you talk and what that leads to is maybe a glimmer of understanding. *I* think that you can tell racist jokes without being a racist. I've told jokes about disabled people—doesn't mean I hate disabled people. Some of my other writers—categorically, if you tell a racist joke, you are a racist. Now, I still think the way I think, and they still think the way they think, but now I understand a little bit more why they think the way they do, and they understand me. You know, I'm the only one on the staff that's from the South, and there was a real attitude about the South. And I was determined to make the people in this show—Mary Elizabeth and her family—they were not going to be rednecks. They were not going to be Southern idiots, because I know these people. I know Collier Simms, I grew up with them, and I know their hearts. And all of the writing staff—and I don't think you'll find this with any other TV show—all of us plus about ten of the actors went on a pilgrimage to Birmingham, and for four days we had roundtable discussions with women that were in the movement in the Civil Rights Institute, black women and white women. We went to the Sixteenth Street Baptist Church. They cooked us this incredible meal—I'm getting emotional just talking about it—we went upstairs to the church and we had a fellowship. And we talked and we asked them questions. We asked them, "What about our show have we gotten wrong? What can we do better?" And what we got back was how important our show is to them, and how important this story is to be told.

Longworth: That's great.

MILLER: We came back from those four days changed people with this incredible mission to keep this show on the air, and keep telling these stories. So it was amazing. They had a screening of our show at the Alabama theater, this great beautiful old theater. I had about twenty family members all around Alabama come, so I had this whole other layer going on of family. And it was really remarkable. And I'm hoping—we want to go back and shoot our season opener next year—if Rene gets married, have her married in the Sixteenth Street Baptist Church. And they've already told us we can shoot there.

Longworth: That would be neat.

MILLER: It would be great.

Longworth: Well, how many episodes are you contracted for?

MILLER: We have just these twenty-two. We had our first season, and we got picked up for the second season for a full twenty-two.

Longworth: So you're going year to year?

MILLER: Yeah, and I see a long life for this show.

Longworth: What is it you want to do now?

MILLER: I have about five shows I want to get on the air. Now, I always say I want to get two more on the air and then retire, because it's just hell, this business—it just takes your life. But my agent tells me everything that I do is a little bit off—there's something about it that makes people nervous. Now, there's also something about what I do that people like. What I think is the greatest problem at the networks is fear. They're afraid to trust their guts, and I don't even know how many screening meetings I've had about research. Research shows this, research shows that. And I go, "I don't give a shit, I don't care about research. Two days ago you loved this character, and because some twelve idiots in the Valley said they don't like him, now you want to get him out of the show?" That drives me crazy. Now, ranting and raving about all this, let me just say I don't know anything about programming or that side of the job. I really am about my passion and my vision. I've watched TV since I was a little girl. I grew up on *Bonanza* and *Patty Duke,* all that shit, and I never wanted to write for movies. I've always just wanted to do television. It's the most powerful medium we have, and I know these shows are good, and it's a matter of pride. It took me eight years to get *Any Day Now* on the air, but that's OK. It's now on the air. I'm having a blast. I'm getting to do my show. I would so much rather wait eight years and do what I want to do then sell some stupid show that can get on the air and last five years and I hate it and I'm embarrassed by it. So I'm constantly getting advice to be more commercial. Be more mainstream. So I tried to, with my quirky ideas—I tried to put something mainstream in there, and I listen to what they say, and I know they have a point. But I can only go so far. So it's going to take me longer, but I've said for twenty years I want to be the female Bochco.

Longworth: Well, actually the two of you *have* never been seen together, so everyone thinks you could be the same person.

MILLER: (*Laughs.*) Actually, in New York a couple of years ago I got to have a drink with him and it was a thrill. I only know of him through people who work for him, and they all respect him a great deal. His shows are very— you know a Bochco show, like *Cop Rock?* I will forever applaud that man for trying to do that, and for having the guts to try it. So what that it didn't work. At least he tried something new and different, and that's what I think the problem is with the network. They're just afraid, they're afraid unless it's by a Bochco or a Kelley. You know those of us who are under the radar a little bit—if Bochco came in with my ideas they'd be bought in half a second.

Longworth: But it wouldn't insure that it would work once it got on the air.

MILLER: True. Just because it's a Bochco doesn't mean it's going to work, but you know it's going to get attention and the audience will make a choice. But I believe in the stuff that I want to do. I've been lucky enough to find those people who also believe in it and support it, and I'm just going to keep ticking away.

5

MARSHALL HERSKOVITZ | TV craftsman

Marshall Herskovitz. PHOTOGRAPHER, DANA TYNAN.
COURTESY OF THE PHOTOGRAPHER.

TELEVISION CREDITS

1977–79	*Family* (ABC)
1979–80	*The White Shadow* (CBS)
1982	*CHiPS* (NBC)

1982–83	*Seven Brides for Seven Brothers* (CBS)
1983	*Special Bulletin* (NBC movie)
1987–91	*thirtysomething* (ABC)
1988–89	*Dream Street* (NBC)
1994–95	*My So-Called Life* (ABC)
1996	*Relativity* (ABC)
1999–	*Once and Again* (ABC)

〰〰 〰〰 〰〰

Marshall Herskovitz cares deeply about his work and he cares deeply about the human condition. Not surprisingly, both passions have effectively complemented each other over the past twenty years.

Herskovitz's work (much of it while partnering with longtime pal Ed Zwick) has been loved, lauded, lampooned, and once even launched a fashion trend. Much like his contemporaries Zwick, David Milch, and other scholars-turned-television producers, Herskovitz is a brilliant conversationalist, whose ability to transform discourse into dialogue has helped millions of Americans better understand themselves.

Herskovitz is an accomplished screenwriter, but he is best known for his teleplays. With television as his chosen arena, he has dramatized a variety of emotions and moral dilemmas: from tapping into our fear of nuclear weapons (*Special Bulletin*) to portraying the fears of marriage (*thirtysomething*) to examining the fears of being a teenager (*The White Shadow, My So-Called Life*) to confronting the fear of starting over (*Once and Again*), Herskovitz's writings, by exploring relationships between people and ideas, reflect who we are and what we seek to learn about ourselves.

Marshall Herskovitz is a wordsmith who in 1952 was born into a family of artisans. Growing up in Philadelphia (the youngest of three brothers), he learned about quality workmanship from his father. "My father owned an architectural woodworking business, which was a sort of formative influence on me because he did a kind of woodwork that doesn't really exist anymore—a very fine, high-level of craftsmanship—moldings and panelings, installations, and wood rooms. It was very, very fine craftsmanship, and I was raised with an uncompromising attitude about craftsmanship and doing the job well. And that has certainly influenced me in my approach to directing and writing, and it's something that I'm always very aware of—getting it right, [and] how important it is that it be well crafted. You can't fake that. You have to do the work to make it good."

Besides his father, Marshall's other great influences were television and movies. Although he watched a lot of TV (he loved *Have Gun Will Travel*), his favorite film, Frank Capra's *It's a Wonderful Life*, most reflects his own writing style. In the film, Jimmy Stewart's character, George Bailey, is a sympathetic savings and loan officer in the town of Bedford Falls. His uncle misplaces their cash reserves, and George is on the verge of suicide when he is saved by an angel. "Angst with hopefulness"—it's a Herskovitz trademark. Not surprisingly, he and Zwick would later name their joint venture the Bedford Falls Company.

Marshall graduated from Brandeis University in 1973 with a degree in English; then, based on a short film that he wrote, produced, and directed (*In Footsteps*), he was accepted at the prestigious American Film Institute where he met Zwick. The two would-be filmmakers became fast friends, and even collaborated on Marshall's second-year graduate video, in which Marshall directed and Ed acted. Tom Stempel, in his book *Storytellers to the Nation*, references an article in *Playboy* (December 1989) in which Richard Kramer, a longtime friend and associate of Herskovitz and Zwick, commented, "What happened [at AFI] was that recognizing each other as the other smartest person around, they had declared a pact of mutual disarmament."

One of Marshall's first jobs after leaving AFI was as a writer on *The White Shadow* (CBS, 1979–81) at MTM Studios. "I worked for Bruce Paltrow, and it was Bruce's little kingdom there. There was no sense that Bruce Paltrow owed fealty to anybody, I mean, it was his show. It was a very lively, masculine, occasionally difficult atmosphere on that show as I remember. . . . Bruce was a very charming but also a very difficult guy, often cutting, often sarcastic, very funny. It was a very jock kind of show. You had to be very well defended when you walked in there."

Longworth asked, "So you had to wear "a cup" to work?" and Herskovitz replies with a laugh, "Exactly. Now, the thing is Grant Tinker, as a studio executive, let his executive producers [such as Paltrow] set the tone for their shows, which I think is the most important thing in television.

Still a freelance writer, Herskovitz went on to write for *CHiPS* (NBC) and *Seven Brides for Seven Brothers* (ABC) before teaming with AFI buddy Zwick to write and produce *Special Bulletin* (1983), an NBC movie about antinuke terrorists who threaten to detonate a nuclear bomb in Charleston harbor. NBC felt that the two rookie producers needed a guiding hand, so Don Ohlmeyer (who had just left the network to form his own production company) was brought in as executive producer. *Special Bulletin* was really about the way the news media cover a breaking story, and that didn't sit well in some corners at NBC.

"Tom Pettit was executive vice president of the News Division then", Ohlmeyer commented "and he screened the [movie] about ten days before it went on the air, and he went bat shit. (*Laughs.*) He went crazy. He said, 'This is about us! It's not about nuclear stuff, this is about news!'"

Despite numerous on-screen disclaimers from NBC, (who wanted to avoid another *War of the Worlds* panic), *Special Bulletin* still had a significant impact on viewers, especially with its jolting surprise ending. It also helped us understand for the first time the dangers of nuclear weapons that reside within our own borders, much less the ongoing threat of world conflict. (The Cuban missile crisis had been dramatized eight years earlier in *The Missles of October*, but did not focus on the graphic horrors that could result from imminent and localized detonation.) The movie went on to win four Emmys (including two for Marshall), and the veteran Ohlmeyer became a fan of his young partners.

"The success they had afterward never surprised me," continued Ohlmeyer. "These were some diamonds that were just polishing themselves, and were going to be major forces. And not only have they done things that are successful, but they've done things that are really important."

However, the success of and critical acclaim for *Special Bulletin* was bittersweet for Marshall. Just as he was honing *his* craft, Herskovitz's father, the artisan, passed away. It was a momentous year for Marshall and for Ed. Marshall reflects, "That was the crucible of our partnership and our friendship. In that year [1983] I had my first child, had my first success in this business, and my father was diagnosed with brain cancer and died. In the same year, Ed got married, had the same first major success, and his mother was killed in a car accident. It was just this astonishing year of highs and lows, and sort of life intervening that we were both experiencing together. And we were both changed by it for sure, just by the intensity of it, and the fact that we were going through it together."

So, besides the very personal emotional effects of that year, Marshall emerged from 1983 empowered with two important career boosts—the legacy of his father's work ethic and the strength of an unshakable partnership.

Soon, Marshall and Ed were collaborating on *thirtysomething*, which lasted four seasons on ABC. The Bedford Falls boys picked up thirteen Emmys plus shelves full of other awards (including the Peabody and Humanitas) for their Reagan-era saga of introspective yuppies. The show was widely praised and panned. Bob Thompson, in his book *The Second Golden Age of Television,* references Clifford Terry's review in the *Chicago Tribune:* "The only thing worse than living in the middle of yuppies is having to watch a program about them."

Mad magazine, meanwhile, satirized the show, dubbing it "thirtysuffering," where the Michael character comments, "The network has discovered there are millions of Americans who get off on misery—next season they're laying in a sob track."

In Thompson's book, Herskovitz himself defended the realism of *thirtysomething's* presentation: "If you go into any home . . . in America and get close enough to those people, you will find that they are incredibly upset about incredibly minor issues . . . the so-called petty issues become the major issues in people's lives."

Petty or not, millions of Americans identified with *thirtysomething's* characters, and many became caught up in spin-off marketing, even purchasing a line of clothing inspired by the TV series. Like it or not, Marshall and Ed had changed the face (and the course) of television by helping define, mirror, and amplify the feelings of an entire generation of Americans.

Throughout the run of *thirtysomething,* Marshall and Ed managed to maintain their individual lives and interests while working closely together (both of their wives were also on the writing staff). Ed would take time off to direct a film (*Glory*), then it was Marshall's turn (*Jack the Bear*). In later years, they would occasionally collaborate on films (*Legends of the Fall*). Three years after *thirtysomething* left the air, the boys were back on ABC with *My So-Called Life,* starring a young and unknown Claire Danes. The show was ahead of its time, and became the prototype for today's teen dramas. *My So Called Life* was short-lived as was their next effort, *Relativity,* which also lasted only a season.

In 1999 Herskovitz and Zwick decided to tackle relationships from a new angle with the series *Once and Again,* starring young fortysomethings Sela Ward (*Sisters*) and Bill Campbell (*The Rocketeer*). The hour drama is about adults and kids starting over after divorce. *People* magazine hailed it as "a mature look at the course of love between single parents . . . a good, grown up romance." Matt Roush of *TV Guide* raved, "Easily the best show of the new season." Marshall himself told *TV Guide* that *Once and Again* is a show "about the baggage you acquire in life, and how difficult it is for two people to construct a new life together." That's something with which Herskovitz can identify. He has experienced divorce firsthand upon the breakup of his marriage to former writing partner Susan Shilliday. Despite the critical acclaim, though,

Once and Again faced an uphill battle because of ABC's jam-packed schedule. The show started in *NYPD Blue*'s time slot, then, after a squabble between Steven Bochco and ABC, had to switch nights in midseason. However, with a little luck, *Once and Again* will be on the air long after this book is in its second printing, and we can look to Marshall's craftsmanship to sustain us as we grow old in the new millennium.

At the time of our interview, the 1999–2000 season was about to launch, and *Once and Again* was slated to hold down the Tuesday night ten o'clock time slot until *NYPD Blue* returned for November sweeps.

Longworth: I had a good talk with Ed the other day. You're going to have to defend yourself now.

HERSKOVITZ: I'm used to that. (*Laughs.*)

Longworth: Actually, I'm sitting here with a photo of you in front of the telephone, because I thought I'd do what CNN does when they have a foreign correspondent on the line.

HERSKOVITZ: (*Laughs.*) You're supposed to hear bombs dropping.

Longworth: (*Laughs.*) Well, maybe that'll happen. Now, at the risk of alienating you right off the bat, my guess is that most people think of you and Ed not as individuals, but, as a team, like Woodward and Bernstein, or Laurel and Hardy. Does that offend you in any way, or your sense of individualism?

HERSKOVITZ: No, actually, it doesn't. The interesting thing is that I don't get the impression that people do think of us in that way. I think that Ed and I are safely anonymous to 98 percent of American culture anyway. There's probably some group of people that knows us as filmmakers, especially Ed. And some groups that know us as television producers. But I don't think we're well known enough to be seen as one thing.

Longworth: But let me continue exploring the relationship theme here. As I listened to Ed recount your history together it seemed that both of you would trade positions from time to time. You'd write, he'd direct. You'd direct, he'd write. Put that into historical context for us, and bring it forward to *Once and Again.* How do you determine, as the "blue collar" guy would say, who takes what shift?

HERSKOVITZ: You know, I'm hearing a weird echo on my line, let me call you back.

[Hangs up; calls right back]

Longworth: Hello, is that better?

HERSKOVITZ: Yeah.

Longworth: Actually, I had a fear that you would never call me back.

HERSKOVITZ: (*Laughs.*) Yeah, I *so* wanted to avoid that question. (*Laughs.*)

Longworth: So how do you determine who takes what shift?

HERSKOVITZ: It's really been very organic. I mean, we have occasionally argued over who's going to direct something. That's the only kind of conflict we've ever gotten into. And even that was easily resolved based on passion. You know, it just would emerge when we started to develop something, who felt more passionately about that particular project. And he who felt more won.

Longworth: But, in other words, you never codirect anything?

HERSKOVITZ: No, we don't codirect. Of all the things we handle well, we don't handle being on the other person's set very well. When I visit him, I can't keep my mouth shut, and when he visits me, he can't keep his mouth shut and we get into arguments. And it's sort of amusing to the people who know us, but we find that it's best to sort of leave the other person alone when they're directing. By the way, we produce for each other while the other's directing. This has to do with literally what happens on the set. It's not a problem any other time.

Longworth: But what happens if you're directing and he kibitzes and makes a suggestion that might actually make the product better, or vice versa?

HERSKOVITZ: No, no, they always *are* better. I mean, we always have good advice for the other. I think our relationship is very complicated, which is to say that it's easy for us to acknowledge that the other person has good advice while we're saying it, and then you say, "You know what? Get out of my fucking face, I don't want to talk to you anymore," (*Laughs.*) and we both understand that. It's not whether you're right or not. It's about how it feels to have someone undermine your authority in front of a hundred people, and the shame of not always having the right answer, and a million things. And we both understand that, and we give a lot of room for that. So we really understand that it's problematic to go on someone else's set and tell them what to do, even if you're right. I can think of very particular instances in our working relationship where each of us had something very important to offer the other when the other was directing, and may even have been crucial to what the other needed at that moment directorially, and they were *still* very upsetting, painful experiences.

Longworth: Back in the days when you and Ed were together at the American Film Institute, he said everyone there worked collaboratively, yet were also very competitive. Is that still true of your relationship today?

HERSKOVITZ: You know, what's interesting is that I think Ed and I are both deeply competitive people, but we learned very early on that competition between us was potentially toxic to our relationship, and so, I think without saying it out loud, over the years, we have kept a very tight rein on our competitive instincts toward each other. We tend to stay away from areas that the other excels in, and we just give that to the other person. You know, like Ed never took up golf because I play golf. I didn't take up tennis because he plays tennis. (*Longworth laughs.*) No, honestly, I think those are things that were consciously decided—it's just we stayed out of the other's way in that sense because we knew those things can get out of control. And, by the way, we acknowledge them, we joke about them. Occasionally, we do compete, but we know that that's potentially dangerous. You know, by the way, I think it's important to say that the main glue of our relationship has been our friendship, not our professional partnership. It's the fact that we're best friends, and we've been best friends for twenty-four years, and that we have enormous affection and respect for each other. I mean, that's the honest truth. It's very funny because people who know us see a particular kind of bantering, bickering, funny relationship we have where we yell at the other, and insult the other, and make fun of the other, and we do that when we're around other people. And when we're alone, just the two of us, we're very, very sweet and quiet and sensitive generally. It's a very sort of easy, loving relationship, actually.

Longworth: A good marriage?

HERSKOVITZ: Yeah, it's a good marriage. And that's really at the heart of it.

Longworth: Ed said he acted in a play for you in film school.

HERSKOVITZ: Yeah, in a tape project.

Longworth: He said there were two main characters. One wanted to be a protestor and one just wanted to get laid. Which character did he play?

HERSKOVITZ: Oh, he played the guy who wanted to get laid. (*Laughs.*)

Longworth: What was the name of that project?

HERSKOVITZ: *Cambridge Nights.*

Longworth: How do you rate Ed's acting skills?

HERSKOVITZ: They've improved greatly over the years. (*Laughs.*) He was in a pilot a couple of years ago. The pilot of *The Player,* the Altman movie they wanted to make into a television series. And he was in the pilot playing a director named Edward Zwick. (*Laughs.*) It wasn't him. The personality was different. He did quite a good job, I thought.

Longworth: So you would hire him as an actor?

HERSKOVITZ: Yeah, I would hire him.

Longworth: Let's talk about *Special Bulletin*. Did you do that for some kind of shock value? Thinking, Hey, this is going to be the *War of the Worlds* of our generation? Did you do it to warn people about the possible threats that could occur? Or was it purely for entertainment?

HERSKOVITZ: It started out from a notion of Ed's. Ed has a sort of an endless curiosity about form, in terms of storytelling—about the sort of different modes of storytelling. He's very analytical about it, and is quite creative in an amazing way. And he just started talking one day about how television news had become a language of storytelling, and that you could tell a story through the language of television news. And I was quite amazed and fascinated by that. You know, he was saying you would never have to go behind the scenes. You'd never have to have a narrator. You'd just see what you would see if you were watching television. And you could tell a whole story that way.

We didn't want to fool people.

Longworth: Yeah, but the networks still put those disclaimers on screen.

HERSKOVITZ: But we always planned to have some disclaimers. In other words, what we always said was in the beginning and end of each act, we'd have a disclaimer saying "this isn't really happening."

Longworth: That's what I think when I watch *Suddenly Susan*.

HERSKOVITZ: (*Laughs.*) What NBC said at the time was, "No, you need more disclaimers than that." And that's what we objected to. When we came up with this idea—it was 1981, early 1982, and we were in the middle of Ronald Reagan's new arms race where very frightening things were being said by the United States. They were saying we would use first strike nuclear weapons, they were declaring that the doctrine of mutual destruction was dead, and there was a very frightening thing going on at that time. And I said, "You know what? This would be a good opportunity to illustrate just what we're talking about here, because the only way these conversations happen about nuclear weapons is if people don't really think about what nuclear weapons do. Because you can't have that conversation if you really think about what they do, it becomes insane." So that was my contribution—was, OK, let's tell a story this way, but let's tell it about this issue that's so important in the culture right now. A cautionary tale.

Longworth: So Ed's playing with the form and you're coming up with the cautionary tale?

HERSKOVITZ: That's right. And we married them together in a way that was very fruitful. We first wrote it for NBC without any production company involved. And they put us together with Don Ohlmeyer. And Ohlmeyer was a very tough character. I really respect him, very tough, though. He read the script and said, "This is a good idea but you guys don't know what you're doing. You don't know anything about television news. This bears no relation to how television news really works." He said, "I'm gonna make this be ahead of its time. We're going to use stuff in here that you're going to see happen on the networks five years from now."

Longworth: And he did.

HERSKOVITZ: By damn if we didn't do that. And you know, I look back on it now, and it's sort of quaint, but in the movie by the twelfth hour of the coverage the network had come up with a computerized graphic and a theme song for the crisis. That was just beginning in those days. And now, of course, they have the most elaborate things for that immediately, you know. It was very interesting how we did sort of get ahead of the curve on what was happening in TV news.

Longworth: With *Special Bulletin* you were doing a drama about TV news. In New York, at the Museum of Television and Radio, I seem to remember that you said something about TV dramas not being protected by the first amendment the same as news. Was there, then, a weird, fine line you had to cross with that movie?

HERSKOVITZ: By the way, what I said there (because it pertains) is that broadcast television is not covered by the first amendment.

Longworth: OK.

HERSKOVITZ: That includes TV news. TV news is not protected by the first amendment either, because the FCC has the right to censor anything on broadcast television. So that changes your question, but here's what I believe. I believe that if you're telling a fictional story and you're not pretending that it's true (and we were not pretending that it was true, clearly), then there is no line. You can say whatever you want. That's what fiction has always done. So with *The Blair Witch Project* they say, "Oh, this was done by these filmmakers that disappeared three years ago," so you can do that because that's a device of fiction, a narrator. This manuscript was discovered in a desk somewhere, blah, blah, blah. That's a time-honored technique in some way, and I don't think there's ever anything wrong with that. What's wrong is when people whose job it is to tell objective truth, which is news people, start fictionalizing. That's when it's wrong. So I think certain codes of behavior apply to them that will never apply to fiction writers. They're of a different nature.

Longworth: Though *Special Bulletin* had some suspense and action, it seems that over the years, you've stayed away from writing those kinds of shows. Your writing is usually about relationships.

HERSKOVITZ: Well, oddly enough, my aspirations as a filmmaker have been much closer to what I loved as a kid. All I ever wanted to do as a filmmaker was *The Vikings,* you know—or a story of 1066 ("The Battle of Hastings") or a western or a war movie. So that stuff is very much alive. It's just that in television, what worked for us in terms of the marketplace was this more intimate stuff, which, by the way, I do love for sure. It's just that I haven't really forsaken my childhood love, they just haven't found the right venue yet. You know, we did a pilot last year for ABC set in the 1200s. But ABC declined to order it.

Longworth: What was the name of it?

HERSKOVITZ: It was called *The Castle.*

Longworth: And they didn't want it?

HERSKOVITZ: They didn't want it.

Longworth: But we're in a five hundred-channel universe now, I mean, somebody would grab it.

HERSKOVITZ: Yeah, but it's a very expensive show.

Longworth: Yeah, but what is the cost of living in the Middle Ages anyway?

HERSKOVITZ: (*Laughs.*) Unfortunately, we needed a few *modern* purchases in order to depict it.

Longworth: Early on in your career you wrote for *The White Shadow.* I especially liked the episode where Coolidge's house burns down and he moves in with Coach. It was great.

HERSKOVITZ: Oh, thank you. That was fun.

Longworth: And yet it goes back to this theme of you looking at relationships, and of people having to live under one roof together, and get along. Now, am I reading too much into all of this, or are you just damn good at writing about relationships?

HERSKOVITZ: (*Laughs.*)

Longworth: Because Ed said you didn't know a damn thing about basketball, so—

HERSKOVITZ: I didn't know anything about basketball when I started it, so I had to learn. Basketball was the one sport I never played as a boy. I played football and baseball. I never played basketball, so I had to learn. I'm now a fan of basketball.

Longworth: But my point is that show wasn't about basketball.

HERSKOVITZ: No, it wasn't. It was about relationships, absolutely. By the way, one of my closest friends is Josh Brand, who was a story editor on that show and that's where I met Josh. I was hired as a freelance writer. I came in and did what I was asked to do, which was to write relationship-type stories. I'm good at that. I can do that, and it's no coincidence that my career has reflected that.

Longworth: Let's move forward to *Once and Again,* and a question that I also put to Ed. The show is about divorced people starting over. If half of all marriages end in divorce, then do you have a built in audience, or do the folks who identify with the themes of the show not want to relive the trauma?

HERSKOVITZ: I've learned not to approach these questions that way. And I'll tell you exactly what I mean. When a show is a hit today it has, what—a twenty share? That means that 80 percent of the television audience is happily watching something else at that moment. So, a hit is a very limited item in a certain way, and I think it's terribly hard to analyze what makes people want to watch something if you're only talking about 20 percent of the population doing it anyway, you know what I mean, because a very small minority of the population is going to watch your show. So who are they and why are they watching? I don't know. I think that some percentage of people who have been divorced, or who are the children of divorce, will be turned off by the idea of a show about divorce, and some percentage will be turned on by the idea.

Longworth: Because it'll be therapeutic.

HERSKOVITZ: Yeah, or just because it's about them. Forget the therapy, just narcissism, the fact that people are interested in seeing themselves reflected. So I can't possibly in my own mind gauge quantitatively how many will be turned off and how many will be turned on. And we've never been able to figure out why that is. Why is it that *thirtysomething* was a marginal hit, but *My So-Called Life* was not. I have no idea.

Longworth: And *My So-Called Life* was also ahead of the curve.

HERSKOVITZ: *My So-Called Life* was demonstratively ahead of the curve. That's the one I look at and say, "Yes, I really was ahead of my time, and I can prove it."

Longworth: So what's going to happen with *Once and Again* when *NYPD* regains its time slot? Doesn't that frighten you a little bit?

HERSKOVITZ: I think that networks rarely shoot themselves in the foot on purpose. If the show performs really well, it's not in the nature of a television network to take a hit show off the air for three months so that everyone can forget about it. They just don't do that. They follow self-interest more closely than that. It is my belief that they see this show as a more important asset than they saw *Relativity* or *My So-Called Life*. They look at this, and they look at Sela Ward, they look at Billy Campbell, they look at the subject matter. They look at the way it's done, the response, all of that. And they say, "This is an asset." I felt that with *thirtysomething*. I didn't understand what that meant in those days because I was new to the game, but as I look back on it, we felt just a sense that this corporation valued this asset and was going to do well by it. My feeling is that if the show performs, we're not going to be off the air for three months.

Longworth: Back on the relationship theme, I wanted to ask you something about *thirysomething*. It's my understanding that your wife and Ed's wife were writers on that show with you guys. Wasn't that pretty unusual for that time, or any time, to have two married couples contributing to one show at the same time?

HERSKOVITZ: Yeah, I would say it was unusual. The whole thing was unusual. Ed and I learned early on how to handle the combination of the personal and the professional. In other words, you're my friend, I love you, but this isn't good enough. It has nothing to do with our friendship, but you have to make it better. And we've said that to each other so many times, it was easy for us to say to other people. Sometimes it blows up in our faces but most of the time it worked.

Longworth: Were your wives writers before that, or did you bring them in and have them help you with some ideas about these *thirtysomething* characters?

HERSKOVITZ: Well, actually, the answer to that is very interesting. Ed's wife had just become a writer a year or two before, had written a brilliant screenplay that was sold, wrote on spec and sold it. And had sort of immediately proved herself as a writer. My wife had been told since the age of seven that she was going to grow up to be a writer and had been terrified of the whole concept of writing and had basically spent most of her adult life avoiding being a writer because she felt she couldn't possibly be good at it, whatsoever. And when we were just beginning the series *thirtysomething*, she told me she was writing—she had written a couple of scenes from an episode she had sort of made up in her mind. And I was so astonished to hear this. My mouth dropped open. But I knew enough to just say, "Oh, that's very nice," because if I ever put any pressure on her, she would go in the opposite direction. Then, like a couple of weeks later, she said, "I've written some more and

I think maybe you should take a look at it." It was just amazing to me that she just did this kind of on her own with no expectation that she would work for the show. For her, it was tiptoeing toward being a writer. And at this time we had just hired all these outside writers, we were just starting, we were in a panic. Scripts were coming in that weren't any good, nobody understood what the show was about. And I read these twenty-five pages that my wife had written completely on her own, and they were brilliant. They were just great.

Longworth: And had Ed's wife already given him ideas about the show too?

HERSKOVITZ: Well, with Ed's wife it was more straight forward. We just asked her if she wanted to write for the show and she said yes. But with mine, she did it on her own, we read it, and it was great. So then it was easy after that and we just hired her. [Marshall is divorced from his first wife, Susan, but Ed's wife, Liberty, still works with Bedford Falls and writes for *Once and Again*.]

Longworth: In New York you also said something to the effect that you like writing for television because, unlike film, it allows you to write over time. Does that have to do with why insiders talk about television being a "writers medium" and film a "director's medium," and is that why you prefer to work in television?

HERSKOVITZ: That's a good question. When they say TV is a writer's medium, they don't just mean that. I think what they mean is even more political than that, that writers rule in television. That the most powerful people in television are writers who've become producers, and that the script is at the center of the enterprise in television. That's what I think they mean by it's a writer's medium. Now, included in that is some of the things that writers enjoy in television. One of them is you can write stuff over time.

Longworth: Right, and if Ed's written *Glory*, you can see what a great character Denzel played, but once the film ended, even if his character hadn't been killed, you don't know what else happened, and that was it, it was over. With a *Glory* TV series, for example, Denzel's character would have gotten married and had kids. So again, do you prefer working in television over film because of that freedom?

HERSKOVITZ: No, I wouldn't say I prefer it. I would say I love that freedom in television. I love that opportunity in television, but it's only one of many things as a writer that I might respond to. There are things as a writer I can only do in movies and I can't do in television. And those things are important to me. You know, I've always wanted to tell epic stories like I said. It's very hard to tell an epic story on television.

Longworth: You also have more freedom in film to deal with sex than you have in television. Since *Once and Again* deals with sex, are you anticipating having to fight any battles with Standards and Practices?

HERSKOVITZ: I think that when it comes to sexuality on television, partly because of what happened in the culture with Clinton and everything, that so many of those barriers have come down. I'm pretty amazed at what I see on television now. I think there are certain limits that are just not going to be broached in the next ten years on broadcast television. You're not going to see frontal nudity, you're not going to see people saying fuck and shit, you know? But I think it's gone in the direction of more permissiveness on television, not more censorship if anything.

Longworth: By the way, do network Standards and Practices people ever say fuck and shit when you're meeting with them in private?

HERSKOVITZ: No, they tend to be pretty upright people. They tend to be very sober.

Longworth: And they display no frontal nudity in your meetings?

HERSKOVITZ: Well, generally not, you know, once in a while it slips. (*Laughs.*)

Longworth: So you think it's more permissive?

HERSKOVITZ: Yeah, but I think violence is taking the heat right now. And by the way, I think this is really good that we're finally making a separation between the two. I mean, we've been talking about it for thirty years, but I think the culture is finally saying, "Oh, yeah, there's a difference." And as a culture we made the wrong choice. We said, "Oh, this thirteen-year-old boy can't go into that movie because it shows breasts, but he *can* go into this movie where it shows people's heads blown apart. Oops, maybe it should have been the other way around."

Longworth: It sounds as though you believe we've lost our way. In fact, at the Museum of Television and Radio in New York, you said, "The things that used to hold people together in a matrix have eroded." What did you mean as it relates to our culture?

HERSKOVITZ: What I believe is the stuff that knits people together—marriage, family, community, church—has eroded, and the need for individual freedoms has expanded, so that you have people today (for whatever reason, we don't understand), they're more prone to do unethical things. They're more prone to abuse their children. They're more prone to get drunk. They're more prone to work for the CIA and sell secrets to the Russians.

Something has happened in the culture where it's become almost compulsive for people to have their individual freedom at the expense of what I call the matrices, the things that connect people. Those are the things that have eroded, and you can certainly see this in the black community. If you look at black communities, and to me, that's a microcosm of the culture at large, it's not about color. What you have is—if you're a young black man, you have almost no role models anymore for how to live growing up in most inner cities. The majority of black men are either dead, in jail, or in some way destroyed by society by the time they're forty years old.

Longworth: OK, so you're a big shot TV producer—so why isn't *Once and Again* about two black people who have been divorced? You don't have to be black to write about black people do you?

HERSKOVITZ: No, you don't have to be, but it would help, though if you're going to write about the black experience in any way, it would help to be black or to have grown up around black people in a more significant way than I did. I don't think I could do a good job writing about black people. I could fake it for sure. But you know what? I just don't want to. I don't want to write a show about old people. I don't want to write a show about people in Greece, you know? I don't want to write a show about a family in Brooklyn. I just don't want to. (*Laughs.*)

Longworth: But did you feel compelled to add black characters?

HERSKOVITZ: No. And by the way, we're going to have two recurring black characters, but that's not what the NAACP is talking about, they're talking about regulars. And they're right. I just think our show doesn't pertain as well as other shows. In other words, the main characters on our show are all family members. It's about a man and a woman who fall in love. Yes, we could have done an interracial romance. One of these families could be black and one could be white. We just didn't feel like doing that. It's not the same as a show about four friends in their twenties. It's so much easier to make that diverse than to say two people fall in love, and this is the story of them and their families.

Longworth: So getting back to the matrix, what are *you* as a producer doing now to try and effect change. What responsibility are you going to take?

HERSKOVITZ: I take that really seriously, I do. In other words, the work we do is in some way, I think, trying to elucidate how people relate to one another. And one of the by-products of that, I think, is to help people relate to each other better. It's not our primary aim, but it's a responsibility we take seriously—that the reason people abuse each other and kill each other and harm each other is because they don't understand how you relate to another person, how you really connect to another person. And it's our aim to throw light on that. And if we can show how families can handle divorce and separation, and the trauma that it causes their children, then maybe we can help people avoid that trauma and handle it better.

Longworth: Thanks for doing the interview.

HERSKOVITZ: Thank you.

Longworth: And by the way, I plan to keep your photo by the phone, which shows that I've been at this much too long.

HERSKOVITZ: (*Laughs.*)

Longworth: If I need a psychiatrist, could you help me? After all, you portrayed a shrink on an episode of *thirtysomething*.

HERSKOVITZ: I certainly did. So you better pay attention to what I say, 'ause I played one on TV. (*Laughs.*)

Longworth: Will you show up as a therapist on *Once and Again?*

HERSKOVITZ: No, I want to play some other part this time. I don't want to play a shrink.

Longworth: What part do you want to play?

HERSKOVITZ: Some terrorist or something. (*Laughs.*)

6

DAVID MILCH | phi beta cop

David Milch. COURTESY OF PARAMOUNT PICTURES.

TELEVISION CREDITS

1982–87	*Hill Street Blues* (NBC)
1987–88	*Beverly Hills Buntz* (NBC)
1988	*Home Free* (NBC)
1990	*Capital News* (ABC)
1993–	*NYPD Blue* (ABC)
1995	*Murder One* (ABC)

WW WW WW

It reads like an agent's pitch for a TV movie: A street-smart kid runs numbers for the mob, gets expelled from law school for a brush with the law, later returns to the same college as a teacher, moves to Hollywood to write about crime, is a devoted husband, loses a fortune betting on the ponies, nearly dies from clogged arteries, spends time in rehab for drug abuse, and wins every major award in his industry.

What great drama! But it comes with one disclaimer. It's not fiction. It's the story of David Milch, one of the most respected writers in the history of television drama.

David's story began in Buffalo—not exactly the epicenter of crime and adventure, yet some members of his extended family also weren't what you would consider nine-to-five people. In *True Blue: The Real Stories Behind NYPD Blue* by Milch and Detective Bell Clark, Milch said, "A number of my uncles and greatuncles wound up in the rackets. . . . Great Uncle Nate managed the Latin Quarter in partnership with Lou Walters [Barbara Walters's father] . . . [and] my Uncle Natey was managing [Piping Rock Casino] for Meyer Lansky."

Meanwhile, young David had a ringside seat. "From the time I was seven, it was my job to write down the bets my uncle would call, and cryptically recite them into the telephone." Milch's father escaped any involvement with organized crime. "The plan was for him (my father) to attend college and follow a more reputable course."

The older Milch complied, and ended up in medical school. Dr. Milch went on to have a distinguished career as a surgeon, and even served as chief of staff at a Buffalo hospital. David's father also "operated" at the horse track.

In *True Blue*, Milch continued, "My dad owned a few inexpensive claiming horses, and my strongest memories from childhood come from the week we'd get to spend together in August at the track in Saratoga. . . . I remember, on my first day at the track, my dad slipping me a twenty dollar bill and whispering to me (since I was not permitted at the betting windows) that Max the waiter would run my bets. I won three of nine races, but I kept all the tickets."

Milch's experiences at the track with his father would later have a profound influence on his life and career. His father's drinking problem and involvement with horses would manifest themselves in the writer's own addictions to gambling, drugs, and alcohol, the latter of which he began in high school, and which blotted out most of his memories of college, first at Yale, then at the prestigious Iowa Writers' Workshop.

In an article for the February 1998 issue of *Written By* (with Susan Bullington Katz), Milch admitted, "I was a drunk. I was a drunk all through college, and I was good and drunk out there in Iowa. . . . [F]or example, [once] I didn't get back to my apartment for six months, so that will sort of give you an idea of the kind of life I was living." Still, Milch managed to graduate from Yale first in his class. [A] lot of people are what are called 'high functioning addicts.' . . . I was one of those."

After graduating from Iowa, Milch sought the refuge of Yale Law School as a means of deferring his draft status for the Vietnam War, but he was later expelled after an altercation with police.

Fortunately, David's mentor at Yale, Robert Penn Warren (*All the King's Men*), went out on a limb for his protégé, urging the university to take Milch back, this time on a teaching fellowship. In the same article, Milch said, "I learned how to be a man. Mr. Warren was a person of great decency, and honor, and kindness . . . his example was something for me at a time when I didn't really believe in very much . . . or have a sense of . . . what I was about."

Milch worked at Yale for six years and never taught a class under the influence of anything other than Warren's intoxicating wisdom. And David's perseverance was rewarded when opportunity and college roommate Jeff Lewis came knocking at his door. In 1982, the year of Hollywood's writers' strike, Lewis approached Milch about coming to work on *Hill Street Blues*. Cocreator Michael Kozoll had just left the show, and, because of the strike, Steven Bochco was prohibited from reading Guild members scripts, so Milch was signed to a three-script deal. His first outing was a home run. Titled "Trial by Fury," the show won an Emmy, a Humanitas, and a Writers Guild award. It also won the respect of playwrights, authors, and academia.

Hill Street Blues went on to win twenty-six Emmys, and everyone lived happily ever after. Well, not exactly. Bochco was fired from his own series after the fifth season, and Milch's newfound status was no ally to his personal weaknesses. Milch, in *True Blue*: "By the time Steven had left in 1986 . . . MTM began paying me a lot of money. . . . I didn't squirrel much of this money away. I used most of it to buy racehorses."

After the demise of *Hill Street*, David created his own show in 1990, *Capital News*, starring Lloyd Bridges as a Ben Bradlee-esque newspaper editor in the nation's capital. In their *Complete Directory to Prime Time Network and Cable TV Shows*, Brooks and Marsh note, "Although producer David Milch said, 'I'll go to my grave denying that the series is based on *The Washington Post*', it obviously was. . . . The giant newsroom looked like that of the *Post* [where] co-creator Christian Williams worked for 13 years. *Post* staffers were interviewed and their work habits studied in developing the series, and several of them actually worked behind the scenes on the show" (p.158). *Capital News* lasted only four episodes.

Meanwhile, the Bochco machine was running out of hit shows. *L.A. Law* was on its way out of the top twenty-five. *Cop Rock*, a police drama set to music, also came and went in 1990. *Doogie Howser* was in its second season, but far from a ratings success. *Civil Wars* went on the air in 1991, but would last only two seasons, and *Capitol Critters* opened and closed in 1992. David and Steven were due for a big score, and hoped to have it with a new show called *NYPD Blue*, which Bochco envisioned as a groundbreaking program in its realism and in its inclusion of adult language and nudity.

Today, despite ongoing cast changes, *NYPD Blue* is still strong after seven seasons, and is regularly rewarded with statuettes. In 1993, however, Milch nearly lost his chance at writing the series at all, when ABC, Congress, and the American Family Association drove Bochco to the brink with threats of everything from major rewrites of the pilot (ABC) to a citizen boycott (American Family Association and the Reverend Donald Wildmon) to preemptions (fifty-seven ABC affiliate TV stations refused to carry the premiere episode). However, time heals, affiliates came back in droves, and Milch kept his job.

Still, the stresses of readying a new series took their toll on Milch's health, and as *NYPD Blue* settled into its first season, doctors discovered blocked arteries in his heart. A balloon angioplasty fixed the problem and served as his wake-up call.

As *NYPD* progressed, it became clear that Milch was basing much of the Detective Andy Sipowicz character on himself and on how he dealt with everything from chemical dependency to learning how to be politically correct in a world with ever-changing social rules.

If *NYPD Blue* offered David a familial outlet through Sipowicz, he may have turned to another project for sheer nostalgia. In 1997 Milch created the Emmy-winning but short-lived police drama *Brooklyn South*. Ken Tucker wrote in *Entertainment Weekly* (December 18, 1998), "That show felt like Milch's attempt to revive the spirit of Bochco's breakthrough, *Hill Street Blues*, but it was an ensemble piece that never jelled."

As the new millennium opened, Milch had signed a long-term deal with

Paramount that will make him financially secure. A father of three, he has his wife and soul mate, Rita, by his side, and still teaches writing workshops as often as time allows, offering young people the same kind of support that he was afforded years ago. In *True Blue,* he stated, "Whatever happens, I've got no complaints. I've gotten the chance to do honorable work, and to love and be loved."

Longworth: It seems that the men in your family, just like Sipowicz's character, provide us with a great dichotomy. Your dad, who was very compassionate and very well respected, also drank and gambled. You, as an innocent youth, ran numbers for your uncle, and later, you get into trouble with alcohol and drugs. Still, you've been awarded all these great honors, you've accomplished so much. Are you attracted just by your nature, then, to stories and characters that seem to always teeter on the edge between hero and villain?

MILCH: I think stories choose you rather than you choosing stories. I guess that might be a way of saying yes. Except that I don't think that I have to go out of my way to find those stories about people who are self-divided. I've never met anyone who wasn't. And it's a distortion, and I think oftentimes what television as well as other kind of storytelling does is to posit as a whole being what is really simply a trait, and that's how you get sort of simplistic storytelling.

Longworth: Right, but shouldn't we still have some kind of resolution to where that line is drawn, in other words, as was noted by John Sumser in his book *Morality and Social Order in Television Crime Drama,* in the nineties, the heroes and villains of TV crime drama are not clearly definable because no one wants to take responsibility for their actions, i.e., the era of Bill Clinton. Where the story itself is at fault, rather than the characters.

MILCH: That's not very good thinking. You can say that of every period, but it's just not true. A true moral relativism is unwatchable. The moral sense is, I think, indigenous to humans, and because characters who lose their moral sense are finally unrecognizable, you can't have too many of them. A truly amoral story—nobody's going to watch that. What this gentleman is saying is that because characters don't conform to his sense of morality, they are amoral, and that's certainly up to him. But our series is intensely about the question of how to be and that's what governs all of the stories.

Longworth: You mentioned in your book that your dad would take you out to the track when you were just a boy, and he could point out to you which guys were phonies. Are you somehow driven to write characters and dialogue that is not phony? I ask that because, historically, the easy way out with cop dramas is to turn in a script that's full of cliché language delivered by cliché characters. Even when you look back at the *Madigan* series in the seventies, it was very well done but was full of clichés. Do you catch yourself avoiding that pitfall? Are you constantly trying to look for what's *not* phony?

MILCH: No, you're trying to look for what's human. To me, what is phony is inauthentic behavior. What makes a phony at the racetrack is someone who is using his behavior to satisfy an inner need to "fix" on the way he looks, or how he's taken, or the feeling he's trying to get. And his commitment is to "fixing" the way an addict fixes, as opposed to being responsive to the actual stimuli of the moment. That's a phony. But that's also a human being, and I love writing about phonies. I love the way people lie. But for me, the obligation is to get it right, to get the phoniness right. And I work very hard, we do so many drafts because to me, getting the speech right is simply a way of getting the character right, and if I don't get the character right then I'm not doing my job.

Longworth: Well, then, aren't *you* a big phony, because isn't it sacrilegious to have spent your Humanitas prize money from the Catholic Church to buy a racehorse?

MILCH: Let me catch you up on that. That's a very interesting story. I won the Humanitas prize again just a couple of weeks ago, and I said of Father Kieser [the administrator of the prize] when I first met him, there was a look in his eyes. You'll probably recognize it, when someone feels that they know something about you that you don't know yet about yourself? And people who had that look in their eye always pissed me off. And I said in my acceptance speech that I had always gone out of my way to try and antagonize Father Kieser, and that after I had won the Humanitas prize for the first time with the first script that I wrote, I won it again the following year, and I made sure to tell them on the podium that I had used the money from the first prize to buy a racehorse. And that was all an effort, which I couldn't understand in myself, to sort of reject that look in Father Kieser's eyes, which said he knew something about me that I didn't know yet about myself. And this year, a couple of weeks ago, what I said was that I was grateful to have lived long enough to have come to understand the thing that Father Kieser knew about me all those years ago, which was that the shadow I felt, I and my characters had to live in, was cast by God's loving hand.

Longworth: And Kieser's reaction?

MILCH: Actually, he wept. I don't think it's the appropriate setting to talk about the arc of my own feelings and beliefs. But certainly if you watch the last season of *NYPD Blue*, that [arc] has been reflected in those episodes. So yes, I think it was honest to say what I'd done with the money, but the phoniness was to think that it somehow would be able to keep me from and protect me from what it was that Father Kieser knew I was afraid to believe. By the way, I sold my best horse yesterday. I'm feeling a little sorry for myself. (*Laughs.*)

Longworth: Why are you getting out of the horse business?

MILCH: Because it was, as you say, it had to do with sort of keeping my memory of my dad alive in an unnatural way, and actually in kind of a destructive way.

Longworth: Owning horses didn't give you any pleasure?

MILCH: It gave me a kind of compulsive, anxious release. (*Laughs.*) I wouldn't call it pleasure exactly. You know, they had a Writers Guild tribute to Steven [Bochco] a couple of years ago, and there were pictures taken of me, and it always strikes me as I look at those pictures, because I seem like a normal person (but) I lost a million three hundred thousand dollars that afternoon.

Longworth: That afternoon?

MILCH: Yep, about an hour before, two hours before.

Longworth: Now, is that the most you ever lost?

MILCH: In an afternoon, yeah.

Longworth: So you were into this gambling thing big time.

MILCH: Well, I'm an addict, you know. And one is too many, and a thousand isn't enough. And those compulsions usually develop around what are essentially anxious or traumatic settings.

Longworth: I'm looking at a photo of you, Tom Fontana, Diane English, and a few other folks from the early 1980s. It looks like it was taken around a swimming pool.

MILCH: Maybe at a Humanitas luncheon or something.

Longworth: And the caption mentions—

MILCH: "The Buffalo connection."

Longworth: When did you all first meet?

MILCH: I never met anybody from Buffalo until I came out here [to L.A.]. (*Laughs.*) You know, Tony Yerkovitch, who is also a Buffalonian and who created *Miami Vice*, was a *Hill Street* writer before that, we had exactly parallel family backgrounds. His dad was a chief of staff, surgeon at one of the Buffalo hospitals, and my dad was the chief of staff, surgery at another Buffalo hospital, and Tony and I never met either before we walked into a room at *Hill Street*. (*Laughs.*)

Longworth: Did you join *Hill Street* before or after the famous sheep story?

MILCH: I was there for the famous sheep story. In fact, I think I might have had something to do with the famous sheep story.

Longworth: How was that resolved with Standards and Practices?

MILCH: The sheep story? You know, in a way, I have led a privileged existence in terms of my connection with the networks and the Standards and Practices of the world. As I say, my relationship with Steven has been I do the writing, then he, at least at the beginning of *NYPD Blue,* would be responsive and edit. That stopped midway through the first season. So, in a case like that [the *Hill Street* sheep], I wrote it, and he fought the other battles. (*Laughs.*) The thing is, I tend to be so irrational in those kinds of conversations that I'm just not useful. (*Both laugh.*) So he doesn't let me have them. [For a description of the episode in question, see chapter 12, Steven Bochco.]

Longworth: Speaking of controversy, when something flows from your pen, do you write down in the margins "David Caruso shows his butt" and then, once you write that down, almost like a stage direction, do you say to yourself, "Aw, geez, we're going to get boycotted by fifty-seven affiliates"? And do you know there's going to be a shit storm? Does all that go through your mind?

MILCH: No, not if you're any good.

Longworth: Why?

MILCH: Because your obligation is to the character and to the reality of the situation, and before you sit down to write, you have presumably integrated, internalized, and neutralized all of those outside considerations. Those things are supposed to go on *before* you sit down and write, because if you allow all that extraneous stuff to go on while you are actually trying to realize the scene, the scene is going to suck. It's going to be what most—well, I'm not going to talk about what other television is, but you have to sort of owe a single allegiance when you're writing, and that's to the materials, it's not to the way the materials are going to be received.

Longworth: But you want them to be received. You want them to be seen.

MILCH: And as I say, there is a prior process that goes on before you begin to write in which you internalize and make a decision about the conventions of the show, and then having made that decision, you try and forget it because your initial conception of the characters has been responsive to those concerns. And what you try to do is strike a balance, so that whatever the conventions you're going to obey, you can believe completely that within those conventions, you can be true to your characters.

Longworth: Steven had told me that you guys went through eighteen drafts of *NYPD* before you came up with the first shooting script. Is that true? Why so many? What was it you guys were hung up on?

MILCH: That was at a time when people felt the hour [drama] form was dead, that it was a dinosaur. First of all, we had not worked together for about five years, and so there was that process of sort of reacquainting ourselves with the other's work process and sensibility. And, for the most part, I would write, and Steven would edit and make suggestions. And we were both feeling our way toward what it is that we felt was at the core of a series concept that would engage the audience. And that's an intuitive rather than a calculated or necessarily logical process.

Longworth: Sure, but to the casual viewer, your process appears seamless, not labored. Which kind of show, then, is easier to construct, a *Hill Street* or an *L.A. Law*, for example?

MILCH: Well I'm not prepared to speak for either of those shows because I joined *Hill Street* in the third year, and I didn't have anything to do with *L.A. Law*, but it would amaze me if that weren't exactly the same process, you know? Just on an ordinary episode of *NYPD Blue*, you will note probably ten drafts.

Longworth: I didn't realize that.

MILCH: Well, I'm a very sort of intensive revisionist. *(Laughs.)* Every morning I look at all the materials.

Longworth: Remind me not to let you get a hold of the Constitution.

MILCH: Yeah, but I think if you go back, you'll find *that* went through a lot of drafts. *(Longworth laughs.)* And it's just a kind of figuring out what it is that's exactly at the emotional center of the scene. So we have a great tolerance for that. And I do think that because we were sort of pushing at the margins of what an hour show could or couldn't do on network television—there was that. And Steven was very much the kind of point man for that "pushing out."

Longworth: Twenty years ago, writers might have had to come up with twenty-two story lines for *Rockford*, whereas today, on ensemble shows like *NYPD*, Bochco noted that you might have to come up with seventy to a hundred story lines in one season. Because of that, is there quicker burnout for writers? How about you?

MILCH: No. I think the question of burnout is a more subtle and complicated one. What will burn you out is, I think, what *ER* does, which is a commitment to a kind of overwhelming multiplicity of story lines as a goal in itself to suggest the atmosphere of a hospital. And that kind of assault on the sensibility—the feeling that you have to maintain one pitch I think, as opposed to letting stories find their own pitch—that could burn you out, I suspect, I mean I'm not sure because I don't write that show, but it seems to me that when you do a show like that, you are subordinating a sort of normal, creative process to a single premise, which is "pace makes the race," and so I would think that might be exhausting, just writing with any single premise.

Longworth: In your book, you noted that your college professor and mentor, Robert Penn Warren, had said, "The secret of any story worth telling is what we learn or fail to learn over time." If you believe that the modern TV drama format distorts this ability, then how do you reconcile writing fast-paced, multilayered stories with Warren's advice?

MILCH: Well, what you have to do is find other ways to suggest the weight of time. Mr. Warren's aphorism that the secret subject of any story worth telling is "time," he was talking about the subject of the story, he wasn't talking about the structure of the story.

Longworth: Oh, I'm sorry, I misunderstood.

MILCH: But I think what I said in the book remains true, which is that the commitment essentially to telling a story in a twenty-four-hour period, and that really harkens back to the Aristotelian idea of proper story structure. You have to find ingenious ways of acknowledging that the secret subject of the story you're telling *is* time. That's why you have to owe a loyalty only to your characters and your story because that's hard (*Laughs.*), and if you're letting yourself be confused with how many black people need to be on the screen, instead of trying to identify and commit to the deepest rhythm of the story, and to see how that subject resonates—the subject of time—you can get very easily distracted.

Longworth: In researching old articles about *Hill Street* and now *NYPD*, I came across a lot of laudatory prose about how great these shows are, and in many reviews, the authors and critics wrote about the scripts as literature—literary masterpieces.

MILCH: Yeah.

Longworth: Will we eventually have library archive shelves, where we'll see stacks of videotapes alongside the stacks of books, thus giving scripts like yours the same status as books?

MILCH: I would say that the likelier outcome is that you won't see any more libraries (*Laughs.*), and that the only path to which people have access will probably be electronic. So the question isn't will television and films sort of survive as literary documents to be studied, but whether anything else will. And that's not to say that they are equal to or better than literature, it's simply to say that seems to be the drift of the culture. But as to whether the work that we have done will come to be respected as much as, say, literary efforts in previous centuries, I don't know. I am proud of the work that I've done. I had a choice as to the venue in which I would write. And as is always the case, the reasons that I wrote for television were very complicated. But I've said elsewhere that television does not demand honorable effort, but it doesn't preclude it. And I regard my efforts and those of my peers, the ones, sort of the group you are talking about, as honorable and respectable.

Longworth: But what prompted you to go into television writing [as opposed to other forms]?

MILCH: As I say, our stories choose us, and probably our occupations do. I was so sociopathic, and so self- divided that nothing, that no form of literary activity which did not reinforce its demands in a very practical, continuous, coercive sense would have done for me. I wouldn't have been able to write. I had tried for years, but television with its sort of insatiable requirements was the only—[well,] the first year I worked on *Hill Street,* I secretly lived in Las Vegas and I flew in every morning to work on it. But the fact that I had to fly in every morning and work, any opportunity I would have had to screw up I would have taken, and it was only because television had to have the scenes every day that I was able to sort of neutralize all of my character defects sufficiently to function at all. And thank God I'm finding some other ways to do that now.

Longworth: As a winner of the prestigious Humanitas prize, you were obliged to be the speaker for a gathering of the Paulist Fathers of the Catholic Church, which was attended by professional writers. The topic you were assigned was "The Challenges and Pitfalls of Portraying Human Values in Entertainment Writing." You told the gathering that it wasn't difficult for you to portray Sipowicz in your writing because you could identify racist impulses in yourself. What was that all about, and were you prepared for how much controversy that was going to create?

MILCH: You know, I guess I should have been because anytime you address a charged subject, you're going to release some of that electricity. And that process of releasing electricity doesn't have to be sensible, it's just electricity. It seemed to me the most painfully obvious fact about anyone in our society is that he or she has racist feelings. That's not to say that he or she is racist, but certainly I am able to draw on the fact that racism is based on fear. We have been trained to be afraid of "the other," whatever the other is. Anyone with whom we're unfamiliar, a mythology develops as a way of dealing with our unfamiliarity.

Longworth: Then you were speaking in a universal sense [during that public appearance].

MILCH: Absolutely. No one, white, black, yellow, does not have fear within himself or herself that will sometimes express itself as a racist fear. I heard Chris Rock crack a joke, and he was saying, "When I'm at an ATM if a white guy comes up next to me, I go about my business. If I see a brother coming up next to me I put my hand over the ATM machine." (*Laughs.*) Now, that's a racist reaction. And it's based on fear. So, in drawing a character, what I was trying to explain about Sipowicz was, I'm able to draw on those experiences and fears in myself, and simply present them in a different proportion for the character of Sipowicz.

Longworth: But you were talking a moment ago about when you write something—are you prepared to go through the problems you're going to go through? To know that 27 percent of the stations will boycott you, for example.

MILCH: In the same way, that question was put to me when I was teaching the Humanitas Masters seminar. I was a teacher before I came out here, and I regard that as a very serious and sort of a holy business. And I'm not going to bullshit if someone asks me a question. I have to assume that they're asking it with good intentions, and I'm going to try and answer it the same way, with honesty. And after that, what other people think about me is none of my business.

Longworth: Well, there's a political side to all of this too. The NAACP is threatening to boycott the networks because out of twenty-six new shows slated for the 1999–2000 season, there are no lead black characters on TV. Maybe what the NAACP is saying is that there's just a bunch of "Sipowiczs" in suits and ties at the networks. What's your obligation as a writer/producer? Are you compelled to pitch a new show with black characters? Do you feel you have that responsibility?

MILCH: I don't. I don't feel any responsibility at all. That's not my job, which is not to say that I don't portray a heterogeneous society in my work—I do. A significant proportion of those characters are minorities. But for me, it's putting the cart before the horse in an unhealthy and racist way to make a decision based on race. I mean, decisions based on race are racist, and I'm not going to do it. And I'm not going to be blackmailed by some guy who's looking to raise the enrollment of NAACP by getting a high-profile issue. That issue is nonsense. It's just pure nonsense.

Longworth: Let's tackle one other issue that will continue to be on people's minds, and that is the rise in violence today, particularly teen violence. Following the Columbine High School massacre, the networks actually adjusted their schedules, in one case preempting an episode of *Buffy* and even telling Fontana and Levinson to air some episodes of *Homicide* out of order. Are you sensitive in any way about the things you write for *NYPD Blue* that might be misconstrued, might be influential—that could add to the problem?

MILCH: You know, anything might be misconstrued. And I guess I would go back to the original answer and I would try to apply what I'm about to say to the last question you asked me, which is, before you begin to write, you try to internalize a whole set of variables, as an antecedent to writing. And in that preliminary process, I definitely take into account being racially diverse and what might the effect be on a particularly sensitive portion of the population. But that is a preliminary process that cannot be allowed to go on simultaneous with the act of writing. Because then you're writing by a kind of an internal committee instead of being—submitting yourself to the world of the imagination, which is the only world you owe any responsibility to as a writer. As a producer, before I begin to write, I take all of those things into account. But for me, I feel our show has internalized and set a standard about the treatment of violence long before any of this, which is, if you portray violence, you portray its consequences, and you portray them with exactly the scope and scale that humanizes the experience, and shows how extreme a form of behavior is. We never revel in it. We don't extend it. We don't sensationalize or trivialize or brutalize it. So having said all of those things as going on before I start to write, once I start to write I don't give a fuck . . . I'm going to be true to the situation. But I hope that that prior process will sort of make me someone whose vision is acceptable and will not cause damage to a particularly sensitive kid.

Longworth: So where do you want to go from here?

MILCH: That's a real good question. I just signed a deal with Paramount, but I do not feel—I don't have to write this way anymore in order to be able to write. So I'm feeling my way into the alternatives, because the way I write television is a very exhausting process. Only if you have to do it the way I used to have to do it, do you really want to do it that way.

Longworth: So do you want to do movies?

MILCH: Well, I have a family that I want to spend—I want to be a better husband and a better father, and I've tried always to sort of pass my gift on, I've tried to teach even during these years, organizing courses of my own, but in the deal I signed with Paramount, I made contractual provisions that there would be ten students continuously that I will be teaching while I do my work, so I'm just feeling my way into it.

Longworth: When does that start?

MILCH: That starts in March [2000].

Longworth: So have you decided that there's a point where you're going to sever yourself from Bochco?

MILCH: Well, he's going to be at Paramount also, but we are not contractually bound, as I am contractually bound to him now. And if circumstances move us in that direction, perhaps we will collaborate.

Longworth: But you guys seem to get along well.

MILCH: I think professionally we are a great complimentary organism, I think we complete each other. Steven is not a writer primarily, and, essentially, that's all I am.

Longworth: What's the last innovative thing you're going to do with your life in terms of TV? What's the next leading edge?

MILCH: I think I know. But you're never sure until you do it, so I'd rather not talk about it. But I'll make a promise to you. I think I know the thing I'm going to do next, and I'll send you the first draft, and then you can see how many drafts it goes through. (*Laughs*.) OK?

7

JOHN MASIUS | Man of Principles and Providence

John Masius. COURTESY OF JOHN MASIUS.

TELEVISION CREDITS

1978–81	*The White Shadow* (CBS)
1982–88	*St. Elsewhere* (NBC)

1989	*Dolphin Cove* (CBS)
1989	*Nick & Hillary* (NBC; revamped version of *Tattingers*)
1990	*Ferris Bueller* (NBC)
1991–92	*Brooklyn Bridge* (CBS)
1992–93	*L.A. Law* (NBC)
1993–94	*Touched by an Angel* (CBS)
1996–99	*The Single Guy* (NBC)
1997	*The Visitor* (FOX)
1999–	*Providence* (NBC)

ΛΛΛ ΛΛΛ ΛΛΛ

In *St. Elsewhere*, a doctor's wife is killed in an accident, and he is left to raise his autistic son, who seldom speaks.

In *Dolphin's Cove*, a man's wife dies, and his daughter is so traumatized that she cannot speak.

In the original pilot for *Touched by an Angel*, Roma Downey's character had died in an accident and her first assignment as an angel is to care for an autistic girl who won't speak.

In *The Visitor*, a World War II pilot is presumed dead, only to be resurrected fifty years later, having emerged from the Bermuda Triangle unscathed but pursued by evil forces.

In *Providence*, a widower is having trouble coping with the death of his wife, and now finds himself caring for his three adult children, and they for him.

Over the past twenty years, these compelling stories have shared some common themes, among them, suspension of life and disbelief and dealing with death and disability. It is also no coincidence that all of these plotlines are from the heart (and heartbreak) of the same man—John Masius, one of Hollywood's most talented storytellers, and one of the most deeply principled men in show business.

Although most celebrities lend their names to popular causes by coordinating their wardrobes to the ribbon color of the week, John Masius ("Maysh" to his close friends) has lived with the kind of adversity that most of us would only know about watching *Oprah*.

Maysh has come a long way since his early days waiting tables. Today he is "king of the world," with his trend-setting megahit *Providence*, and, over time, he has found a comfort zone in which he can better appreciate his personal and professional blessings.

Matt Blank, president of Showtime, was Masius's college roommate and best friend, and they were best man at each other's wedding. Matt explains John's complex and often misunderstood persona. "John would always question people, question honesty in relationships. And I think maybe one thing people didn't like about John is that he is one of the most honest people you can meet, and that's something I knew from day one. If he didn't like you, he'd tell you, and that bothers some people. To me, it always made him endearing . . . the honesty and the way John expressed his beliefs probably took away from his career. And I think what John has learned in the past couple of years is to try and channel that honesty into his work, and to kind of accept the institutions of networks and production companies as being what they are, and not letting that get in the way of the honesty in his work. I think that he's at a place now where the excellence of his work allows him to be a different kind of player out there. There's more balance in his view of the work he produces, and the people he works for. He's a very sensitive person. I think when people sometimes confuse John's honesty for hostility or for a need to be difficult, I think his honesty is a function of that sensitivity, and that's where it comes from."

John comes from the suburbs of New York City, where he was born on July 30, 1950. His father, William, sold insurance and specialized in pension plans; his mother, Barbara, was a homemaker and avid bridge player. John also has a sister. His maternal grandmother, Stella, most influenced his view of the world. Stella was married to Daniel Auslander (the namesake of Norman Lloyd's character Daniel Auschlander in *St. Elsewhere*), and she provided young John with a lasting image of a strong woman—the kind he would later write for and about. "She was kind of the 'Auntie Mame' in my life. She was an artist, and she was a painter, and sculptor, and she lived in New York City, so she was always dragging me to museums and to the theater."

Although having been exposed to various cultural offerings, Masius loved *The Three Stooges*, and was a huge fan of *Rocky & Bullwinkle*. Go figure. Later, he attended Scarsdale High School, where he began to show some promise for and interest in writing. "I loved to read. I got advanced placement credit for writing out of high school, so I placed out of freshman English [at the University of Pennsylvania]. So, at that point, I realized I didn't have to take any more English courses. Writing's very difficult for me. It's very hard. I don't jump at the prospect of doing it—like homework. For me it's like having an exam paper due, and I've always been a pretty good procrastinator. You don't get the paper in, and your 'incomplete' turns to an *F*."

So creative writing and a career in television weren't even on John's radar screen. Instead, he pursued a more traditional academic major. "I got a degree in economics, and I was a finance major. But I knew nothing, I learned nothing, I did nothing. It was a weird time, 1968–72. I was trying desperately not to get drafted. So I did as little as was required. One of my more memorable nights in college (I was a sophomore) was the night of the national lottery for the [Vietnam] draft. Live from Washington they were pulling out the Ping-Pong balls, and I'm sitting in a room with a lot of people, and they're leaving one at a time. It was really weird."

John went on to do quite well in college, and not just with academics. Matt Blank recalls: "John was always very popular. He was always one of the good-looking guys, and the girls loved John. He always had a good social life."

Masius left Penn and went to UCLA to get his M.B.A. After that, he made ends meet by waiting tables at a Los Angeles restaurant. There he first waited on Bruce Paltrow, who subsequently put Maysh to work as a gopher at MTM. Several years later, Paltrow was producing *The White Shadow,* and promoted John to the position of writer/producer. Comparing his two "careers" (waiter vs. writer), Masius told *Entertainment Weekly,* "In a lot of ways, the jobs are similar—except tips are better as a producer."

In 1982 Masius joined Paltrow, Mark Tinker, and Tom Fontana in producing *St. Elsewhere* (Josh Brand and John Falsey left after the first season). During *St. Elsewhere*'s six-year run, Masius won two Emmys and a Humanitas.

MASIUS: We made the best show that was ever on television, and there was a price to be paid for that.

Longworth: Meaning?

MASIUS: As much fun as Tommy and I had, and as much laughs as I had with Bruce and with Mark, there were a lot of damaged relationships, but that's life I guess.

Longworth: Who specifically do you mean had relationships damaged?

MASIUS: A lot of people aren't talking to each other.

No matter the effect on relationships, *St. Elsewhere* had an enormous effect on the way television portrayed medical drama and health care issues. Also during *St. Elsewhere* Masius began dating Ellen Bry, who portrayed Nurse Daniels. The couple was careful to handle their relationship in a professional manner, as Ellen recalls: "People think it's all nepotism and playing favorites . . . so if anything, John went overboard the other way. It would have to be up to other people to come up with story lines for me. I didn't try to increase the size of my part, you just don't do that, especially when you have a romantic involvement with someone. It's not appropriate."

Ellen left the show as a regular at the end of the third season, and later she and John were married. As *St. Elsewhere* ended its six-year run in 1988, the Masius' first child, Hannah, was born. A year later, Masius tried his hand at a short-lived series, *Dolphin's Cove* (for CBS), which lasted only eight episodes.

As a new decade dawned, John and Ellen's lives would begin to unravel. Son Max was born in 1990, and his younger brother, Sam, was born twenty-one months later. Not long after Sam's birth, Max was diagnosed with autism. That led to a battery of tests on Sam, who was also discovered to be autistic. It was an eerie twist of fate in which Masius's writing of the autistic boy in *St. Elsewhere* had foreshadowed his own personal adversity.

Understandably, then, the early 1990s were difficult for John and Ellen as they cared for three children, two of whom were severely disabled. John worked on *Ferris Bueller* (NBC), which starred an unknown Jennifer Aniston and lasted less than one season. He also wrote for *Brooklyn Bridge* (CBS), and won his second Humanitas in the process. He and *St. Elsewhere* pal John Tinker were then called in to breathe new life into *L.A. Law* for the 1992–93 season. It was, to say the least, a bad experience all the way around.

Bob Thompson, in his book *Television's Second Golden Age*, says, "The pair injected some of the playfulness of the *St. Elsewhere* intertextual style into the mix . . . but the results were rejected by viewers and critics alike. . . . [C]onsensus was that the show's delicate balance between the elements of legal drama and soap opera had gone out of whack in favor of the latter. Tinker and Masius were gone by January '93. Masius told *Entertainment Weekly* he 'found the cast [of *L.A. Law*] to be incredibly mean-spirited . . . we were caught in a show that, quite frankly, was on its last legs.'"

By 1993 Masius was filling up with anger and resentment from the one-two punch of personal tragedy and professional disasters. Turning inward, John created *Touched by an Angel,* but the original pilot, though filmed in its entirety, never aired. John was fired because he was unwilling to compromise his vision. (He is still listed on the credits as creator, and still receives residuals from the series.)

Over the next few years, Masius would punch the clock and pay the bills by working on series such as *The Single Guy* and a sci-fi drama, *The Visitor,* both of which bit the dust quickly. Commenting on *The Visitor,* John told *Entertainment Weekly* (January 9, 1999), "The 'sci' part was bad, but the 'fi' part, I got."

In 1997, fate stepped in, and NBC asked John to develop a new family drama. At the same time, the network also had a deal in place with actress Melina Kanakaredes. Masius came up with *Providence*, had an in-house star waiting in the wings, and the rest is television history.

At first, *Providence* was universally panned by the critics. *Entertainment Weekly*'s Ken Tucker wrote, "In *Providence*, a plastic surgeon gives her life a 'face lift', but the sappy new NBC show doesn't quite cut it." NBC's Don Ohlmeyer had been around long enough, however, to know a hit when he saw one. "The more you read the critics and see what they were yammering about, you see that what they were yammering about was exactly why the show had a chance to succeed. People get too concerned about what the critics say. There's about four or five critics in this country that I used to read religiously because I knew if they hated the show, it had a good chance to succeed. And if they liked the show, you knew it had no chance. They're so totally disconnected from the public psyche."

The public psyche tuned in to *Providence* week after week. Not long after its midseason premiere on January 8, 1999, *Providence* was averaging 16.9 million viewers—a 55 percent increase over *Dateline*'s numbers the year before.

More important, *Providence* gave Hollywood the courage to explore similar themes on commercial television for the 2000 season (*Judging Amy, Family Law*). Meanwhile, Masius's new show about a strong woman character drew millions of disenfranchised women viewers back to Friday night television.

Like *St. Elsewhere*, *Providence* focuses on medical issues every week, but, to paraphrase Showtime's Matt Blank, "It's really about humanity."

By July 1999 *Providence* was hotter than the summer weather, and NBC Studios quickly signed Masius to a three-year development deal.

So, the brutally honest man from New York City, the one who never gave up on his vision, the award-winning, under-appreciated writer/producer, has gone from *waiting* tables, to *turning* them on the industry.

Bob Thompson, in *Television's Second Golden Age*, when describing the writers (such as Masius, Milch, and Fontana) at the old MTM Studios, noted, "These people saw the work they did as better than most of what was on TV. They went on to create characters who, like themselves, might have been perceived as highly talented people, working in a world run by idiots." Today, the idiots are still in charge of the world, but Masius has learned to live with them, and with himself.

Longworth: We are living in an era of empowered women, so by rights, *Providence* should be written by a woman. Yet, here you are a man who is able to write great women's roles, with stories about women, and that attract a lot of women viewers. How is it you have this ability? According to your buddy Matt Blank, he says it's because you were a real ladies' man in college.

MASIUS: (*Laughs.*) I don't know. Basically, I love women, I just never really thought I understood them. I've always been attracted to strong women. I was surrounded with them growing up.

Longworth: By the way, your grandmother's namesake might have shown up in *St. Elsewhere*, but you didn't have a female lead on that show in her honor.

MASIUS: Well, as Tommy [Fontana] probably told you, *St. Elsewhere* was always about fathers and sons. And truly, I don't think we did service to the women. For me, I became interested in father-daughter relationships when I had my own daughter. Those seemed to be the most unresolved relationships among women who were my peers, and it was something that I just decided to explore later on.

Longworth: So the relationship between Mike Farrell and Melina on *Providence* is coming at a time when you're ready to explore that theme, is that what you're saying?

MASIUS: Well, my relationship with my daughter has grown, I mean, she's only eleven—it's truly the relationship with a woman I've always wanted to have.

She's always glad to see me, she loves me unconditionally, and she laughs at all my jokes.

Longworth: We'll return to *Providence* later, but first, I'm curious. How is it that you were able to jump from gofer to writer at MTM?

MASIUS: Paltrow thought I needed a new car (*Both laugh.*) and so he let me write a script, and that's how it came down. It was a *White Shadow* episode about the Harlem Globetrotters.

Longworth: I was expecting a really emotional answer, and instead it just came down to you needing a new car.

MASIUS: Yeah.

Longworth: I think there's always been sort of a quirky spiritualism to your work, dating back to *St. Elsewhere*, and on up to today with *Providence*, in which the lead character's dead mom is on the show every week. Now, having talked with Ellen, hearing what a great father you are, and how you guys later dealt with the autism, your faith has obviously been tested in ways that a lot of people's faith isn't. How would you say that this kind of spiritualism has evolved, and how has that affected what you write?

MASIUS: Well, I was brought up a very Reform Jew. I didn't have a very strict religious upbringing. A lot of the *St. Elsewhere* stuff was pretty much just dealing with the idea of life and death, and Tommy and I just sort of trying to come to grips with our short time here, and what it all meant. The thing that's even weirder to me is that I spent all this time on *St. Elsewhere* writing about autism, and then got two autistic kids. I really didn't have a sense of what I was writing, because it was just kind of in the abstract. It was a fictional life. You just pick up the paper and you read stuff, and it's like it's something that happened to someone else.

Longworth: And yet, when you tried to incorporate what had really happened to you, by writing about it in the original pilot of *Touched by an Angel*, CBS ultimately fired you.

MASIUS: The *Touched by an Angel* pilot was the first time that I wrote about what it was like to be a parent of a disabled child. The network [Jonathan Levine at CBS] wanted to do something with angels but didn't know what it was. I said, "OK, I'm going to try to put it out there about what it is to be a special needs parent, and what it is to deal with that." That's all I wanted to do. And at that time, I was pretty angry at God, because truly, I still don't really understand what kind of God does terrible things to small kids. And the other thing that I couldn't handle was people, in their urge to comfort us, would say, "God doesn't give you more than you can handle," which Ellen and I just found incredibly disturbing. In the *Touched by an Angel* pilot, the funny part was having network meetings where executives were trying to tell me what angels could and couldn't do. (*Laughs.*) You know, the dog talks, but what languages does he really understand? It was completely stupid. But I had this back-story where the Roma Downey character, Monica, was originally a mother in the 1920s, and she died and became an angel because she saved her daughter in a runaway carriage accident. And in the course of the [first] episode we see her back in the twenties. We see her with her family, we see her singing a lullaby to her daughter, and then we see the accident. Then the play gets kind of resolved—back on present-day earth her daughter is still alive, and she, as an angel, now goes to visit her daughter [who is now] in a nursing home, and in her eighties. She had had a stroke, broke her hip, and she's given up hope, so Roma [Monica] sings that same lullaby to her "elderly" daughter. It's pretty moving stuff. But at the same time, the Angel of Death shows up [played by Michael J. Pollard], and the mother [Monica] says, "This is my daughter, she's suffered enough, why can't you take her with you?" And Michael says, "No, no, Monica, I'm just a messenger just like you, and besides, God doesn't give you any more than you can handle." To which Monica replies, "That's a lot of crap." And it was for that that I was fired, because I refused to take that line out.

Longworth: So, did you ever complete filming on the original pilot?

MASIUS: Oh, yeah.

Longworth: But it never aired?

MASIUS: No. That was the other great irony. Here's the *St. Elsewhere* connection. David Morse played the father. Ellen played the mom. What really annoyed me was what the show evolved into. And, once again, this is also me dealing with my own stuff, vis-à-vis my family and my kids. The show became so fundamentalist, i.e., if you believe in God, God will take care of you—that you are not responsible. And part of the evolution of the spirituality of *Providence* is that "no, you *are* responsible. You can make changes. You are responsible for your life. And you can effect change within your life." And that's pretty much the major decision Syd makes in going back home, rather than leaving it up to some other force. According to Martha Williamson, you could climb to the top of the tower at the University of Texas, or those boys that blew away all the people in Littleton, and well, it's just God's will. On the other hand, as I look at the world (and this is the other thing that I realized), when you have disabled kids, your whole set of what's "normal" changes, and your priorities change. It isn't about whether they'll go to Harvard or will they get married, it's will they speak, will they be able to take care of themselves on any level? But when I hear people complain about Little League coaches or something, that stuff is as real to them as my stuff is to me, but I look at it differently now. Originally, I said, "I'd give my left nut to talk about Little League, and what that means, you know? But now, this is who I am, this is what I do. I can't imagine my life any differently. I adore my kids, and it's part of who I am. And frankly, *Providence* wouldn't have happened without it.

Longworth: Playing devil's advocate, though, I might say to you, "OK, you didn't want to bend on *Touched by an Angel*, you wanted it more realistic not fundamentalist. But *Providence* is not exactly dark—it's upbeat, even though it's realistic. Would you have liked to take *Providence* in a little different direction, but you knew it would be a losing battle with NBC?

MASIUS: Well, here's the other thing that's also different. I'm dealing with parents who are very old, who are pretty infirmed right now, and it's a difference—

Longworth: We're in the sandwich generation.

MASIUS: Yeah. And also, I'm three thousand miles away. I mean, one of the things about being out here is that there are a lot of people who are really disenfranchised, talking about "what if" and "if I could." And did I want to change *Providence?* Well, it's fiction but it's the fiction that I wanted it to be. Honestly, I am not the guy now that I was when I was writing some of the fiction on *St. Elsewhere,* which is OK. But I think *Providence* also has an integrity to it, and a truthfulness to it, that, regardless of whether people find it soapy or sappy, the fact is, as you said in the beginning, it's touched a nerve. *Providence* was not done by mistake. I knew what I was doing. I didn't realize I was going to get into the national spotlight—that I was going to so strongly hit a nerve, but I knew this was the show that I put together very carefully.

Longworth: Since you brought it up again, has America caught up with Masius, or has Masius figured out how to bend to America? You now have a show that fundamentalists can watch, and Jews can watch, and atheists can watch. Have you not really changed your convictions all along? And the people who didn't watch *St. Elsewhere,* the people who didn't appreciate the writing you did on *L.A. Law*—have those folks caught up, and it's now time for them to appreciate what you're doing? Or have *you* changed so much that they now appreciate what you're doing?

MASIUS: Well, I didn't consciously change. I mean, it's just evolving as a person. When I was doing that other stuff I was, I don't know, I didn't have a family. I think family changes everything just in terms of how you approach your work, what is the legacy you want to leave—to be able to sit down and watch the show with my kids. I don't know. I once made one of these cavalier statements that "critically acclaimed doesn't pay the mortgage." But I'm also pragmatic about supporting and taking care of my family. At the same time, there have been times when I've done stuff that was the "wrong pair of shoes" for the season. And I can't explain why this is, but on the other hand, I'm not going to pretend that it was just dumb luck.

Longworth: In *Providence,* what's the "ghost mom" vehicle for? Was that inspired by your Grandmother Stella, who is in some way still watching over you?

MASIUS: First of all, that character was not supposed to come back as a ghost mom. She cracked wise for the first two acts of the pilot, and then she was mourned for the second two acts. She tested incredibly, highly. But what happened, in terms of "the darker voice," what it became was two things. Tommy [Fontana] and I always used to talk about how death ends a life, but doesn't end a relationship. I mean, that wasn't our original line, but as it played in the history of *St. Elsewhere,* no relationship is ever "over." And this woman was such a force in this household, for her to be gone created a void. But I needed a device that would send up Syd. Whenever you got a sense that she was clean as a whistle or holier than thou, that there was this voice in her head that was a little cynical, acerbic, and would pull no punches. Also, the dad comments about his relationship with his late wife every now and then. She was always critical, because he lived down in that basement, or she would say he never wanted to "come to bed with me." I mean, it was more based on just the idea, the whimsy, and having the fantasy on the show, more than on any specific person, although the voice was very similar to those that I heard around my mother's bridge table for years.

Longworth: What about the scene where Syd catches her fiancé in the shower with another man, which then prompts her to leave L.A.?

MASIUS: The network went insane.

Longworth: Now, obviously, it's not as shocking as what you see on *Oz*, but . . .

MASIUS: The only difference is that the two men would be bleeding rectally on Tom's show. (*Both laugh.*)

Longworth: Why did you do that?

MASIUS: Honestly, I needed something dramatic to spin Syd around and get her back East. But I also did it just to send up every agent-client relationship I know.

Longworth: That's funny.

MASIUS: And actually, if it had been really truthful, the one thing that was wrong about that scene is that we had the client scrubbing the agent's back, and we should have had the agent scrubbing the client's back. (*Laughs.*) That was the one we'd change if I had it to do over.

Longworth: And yet, you have all these sensitive women who love *Providence* who didn't find it offensive for two men to be in the shower together. So you must have hit on the right formula.

MASIUS: (*Laughs.*) Women basically think men are pigs and will do anything, so they were rooting for Syd. And timing is everything. If her mom hadn't died, the show would have been called *Brentwood*, she would have come back and lived with the schmuck agent, probably married him, and who knows where her life would have gone.

Longworth: With *Providence*, do you write part, all, or some of every episode? How much do you have your fingers in every episode?

MASIUS: This is one thing that evolved from the *Elsewhere* days. I'm now a firm believer in that writing credit should go to the person who writes it. I don't buy into four or five people putting their name on a script. I'm now a firm believer in pride of authorship. And so someone starts out knowing that they're going to get the "written by" credit. Bobby DeLaurentis and I break all the stories, I will punch up a script at the end. But I find most of the time that the true value of television is in the editing bay. I know it's all about writing the scripts, but it's still a visual medium.

Longworth: But you're not comfortable enough to turn the product over to someone else entirely?

MASIUS: I don't think it's rocket science. I think people should be allowed to write until they can't elevate it enough. And then, you've just got to take it over and give it a boost. And frankly, some stories work when you break them, and some don't, and with a new series, it's always an evolving process. I'm a firm believer in delegation—the ability to surround yourself with people you know and trust, otherwise you turn into David Kelley and I don't know where the future is in that.

Longworth: Is *Providence* a six-day, seven-day production schedule?

MASIUS: It's eight days. But truthfully, I don't understand why it can't be done in seven.

Longworth: How many shows are coming up?

MASIUS: They wanted us to do twenty-four, but we're only going to do twenty-three.

Longworth: Gee, what a tough problem to have.

MASIUS Yeah.

Longworth: Now, I read somewhere in a magazine article that you shoot in a former munitions factory?

MASIUS: Yes, we do. It's out next to the Van Nuys airport, but we're moving out of there because the building's for sale. But it was really pleasant. I truly enjoy not being on a studio lot. You're kind of undisturbed and you're focused. There's not a lot of people running around.

Longworth: When the initial reviews came out for *Providence* and a lot were either negative or skeptical, did you momentarily think you had misread something?

MASIUS: No, I knew the show was good. You see, I knew from the people who had seen it that they were moved. I also knew how well it had tested. It was the highest testing pilot that NBC had that year, and Melina was the highest testing character either comedy or drama.

Longworth: But how did you know going in that it would work?

MASIUS: I just knew. And then when I cast Melina, I really knew. And when we shot twelve days on the pilot, there wasn't one day of dailies that I didn't like. It was one of these things that truly, from the beginning, has been an incredibly pleasant, delightful experience.

Longworth: You know, I couldn't really get into the show until the second or third episode. I couldn't get comfortable with the characters at first because I had never met them before.

MASIUS: Of course, that's part of it. But the thing that Bobby and I did by design in the first six episodes is taking baby steps. All the stories are self-contained. There's no big character jumps. All it is, is you're trying to get vested in these people, see if they're good at what they do. And care about them, so if you miss the first one, or the second one, and you like the third one, and you jump into the third one, you're not lost.

Longworth: I immediately bonded with Farrell's character because my wife and I adopt animals.

MASIUS: And the genesis of that was quite frankly—I had a dad who could roll around with our pets but not with us.

Longworth: So it's OK that I didn't get all of it the first time?

MASIUS: Yeah. Listen, I've been on shows where because you're so "inside" making them that you think everyone has all the knowledge that you do, and they spin out of control. But it was by design that you could jump in anywhere and feel comfortable, where there were no arcing stories—everything was self-contained.

Longworth: There must be a lot of pressure on producers like you, though, to make new shows a hit right from the beginning. I didn't like *Dallas* the first season, but then I got into it because they left it on the air. You need time to get to know the characters, and so forth. But in today's environment of having to have big ratings early on, there must be a lot of pressure.

MASIUS: Well, the other thing that we had really going for us is that we had great promotion. But as the NBC Promotion Department says, "We can promote you, we can get you up to the plate, but after that it's up to you."

Longworth: Yeah, I was wondering, did you sleep with somebody to get that promo schedule?

MASIUS: No, Don Ohlymeyer was a huge fan of the show. The first people that were incredibly moved by this is anyone that was trying to deal with any father-daughter relationship.

Longworth: But suppose everybody had been like me the first night, and it was going to take several episodes to—

MASIUS: But you're a guy.

Longworth: Well, that's true, last time I looked. But seriously, you guys have got to be under the gun to grab as many viewers the first couple of episodes—

MASIUS: This is the other thing too, which was Olhmeyer's genius—was that he knew somehow that there was an audience on Friday night at eight o'clock that was untapped. It was all about going home, and truly, once again in terms of the national . . .

Longworth: Psyche?

MASIUS: Psyche—it was one of those things.

Longworth: But when you talk about network schedules and the luck of the draw . . . when they moved *Chicago Hope* up against *Law & Order*, that really pissed me off. I mean, they could have counter-programmed and put on *Rocky & Bullwinkle* up against *Law & Order*, or—

MASIUS: I'd still watch *Rocky & Bullwinkle*. (*Laughs.*)

Longworth: But from the cartoon to the sublime. On the award you received for *Brooklyn Bridge* . . . you went from the "humanitas" of that, to the "inhumanitas" of your experience with *L.A. Law.*

MASIUS: Yeah.

Longworth: We don't have to get into that too much.

MASIUS: No, I have no problem talking about that.

Longworth: What you did was good, but I guess it wasn't good for the people who wanted things to stay the same.

MASIUS: Here's the thing, and I'm not saying anything that John [Tinker] wouldn't agree with, because he was there. We were given a license to "shake up" the show by the studio. But the reality is Bochco didn't want to shake anything up, nor did anyone on the show. And on one level they were right, because they were Emmy-award winners three years in a row, and we were the new guys coming in. But we weren't coming from a bad place, and we were treated like we were.

Longworth: What was it they didn't like that you wrote?

MASIUS: They hated everything we did. (*Laughs.*) No, they hated it from the opening bell when we tried to do a show that was done on the day of the L.A. riot, "L.A. Lawless" it was called. Bochco hated that.

Longworth: After *L.A. Law* do you ever wish that you and John Tinker had taken Barry Levinson up on his offer for you guys to do *Homicide*?

MASIUS: No. It just wasn't economically or physically viable, because, at the time, they only ordered like four episodes, and they were shooting in

Baltimore, and my family was in L.A. I think in the first three years they only did like twenty episodes. No, I have no regrets about that at all.

Longworth: Do you ever just write for pleasure?

MASIUS: No, I only write for cash. (*Laughs.*)

Longworth: Which would you rather receive, a Humanitas or an Emmy, if you could only have one?

MASIUS: Honestly, I would prefer a Humanitas, because it is about family values. I'll be amazed if we're not nominated, I'll be really amazed. I don't know if we'll win or not. I'd be truly amazed that [Father] Keiser would not give the show a nod. The Emmy thing is not even within the realm of possibility.

Longworth: But if it were, what does it mean and what does a Humanitas mean really?

MASIUS: Well, Tommy and I were always the Humanitas—

Longworth: Brothers?

MASIUS: Whatever—and finally we won one, so they had to give us like a lifetime achievement award. We got nominated twice in one category for the first time—the first time any show had ever done that—and we lost, and then had the ability to do it again. So finally they had to give us one.

Longworth: It was the only "humane" thing to do.

MASIUS: (*Laughs.*) Exactly. Humanitas is weird because it is kind of inhumane. First of all, it's weird that they give cash to people who certainly don't need it. (*Longworth laughs.*) But it's that whole idea, it's weird. Humanitas is a really special luncheon because it honors writers writing. And the Emmys is about something else. At least you feel at Humanitas that your work is being read. It isn't on the Emmys, but at least with Humanitas you're being acknowledged for the material, and at the Emmys they're just watching the shows.

Longworth: Earlier you mentioned that critical acclaim doesn't pay the mortgage. At what point does a big shot producer become wealthy from a new show? How many episodes do you have to have in the can for syndication, and at what point do you know if a show has made it? What's the formula for knowing that both you and the show are financial successes?

MASIUS: Well, I would say you really know it when a show goes into syndication, and that depends on a couple of things. And this is the great Hollywood dilemma, the definition of profit, and the definition of ownership, and creative bookkeeping. But a true barometer is how well it sells in syndication, so that whatever deficit that the studio is claiming exists is either true, or like "come on, guys" and it's wiped out. In this climate, you pretty much know after a couple of years. But in terms of seeing the money—that could be a long way off.

Longworth: Why, then, aren't guys like you doing more half-hour dramas—half hours sell better than hours? Why not a half-hour *Providence?*

MASIUS: Obviously, the half hours syndicate better than the hours for a multitude of reasons. But half-hour single-camera shows are very expensive. We were doing *Brooklyn Bridge* in five days. As far as storytelling, having done half hours—*Ferris Bueller, Brooklyn Bridge,* and doing a half-hour *Single Guy*—it's hard to tell a story in twenty-two minutes, so that you feel you're really connected. It's a weird hybrid. And even under the best of circumstances, somehow I think the audience feels cheated. It's either not funny enough or dramatic enough. They're not really sure what they're watching.

Longworth: Tell me a classic TV show that you wish you had created, and then give me one from today.

MASIUS: You know what? I'm not very much of a TV watcher now, except for *Sportscenter* (ESPN). If I could have created one show? *Sesame Street.* Absolutely. I just think it's amazing. And if I could be producing one show that's on the air now that's really fucking cool, I like *The Larry Sanders Show,* I thought that was one of the best shows I've seen.

Longworth: So what's next for you? Are you going to be content to nurture this *Providence* thing, or are you going to go off and do three other projects?

MASIUS: Honestly, truly, I've got so much going on in my other life that for me to do more than one thing is truly [undesirable]. This was kind of my last shot, and I'm sure it'll give me the opportunity to have other shots now, but no, I don't take this for granted, and I'm not going to pretend that it was an accident. It was a combination of hard work, fun, and luck. I love the people I work with. *Providence* may not redefine the medium, but we're having fun.

Longworth: Well, thanks for taking extra time on this.

MASIUS: Sure, thank you for the questions—they were really good.

Longworth: Hey, John. Suppose there were never any credits on TV shows, how would somebody know if they had just watched a Masius show?

MASIUS: (*Laughs.*) They'd get some laughs. And they'd probably be moved. And they'd be twisted up a little bit emotionally. They'd be manipulated. I'd fuck with their heads. (*Laughs.*)

JOHN WELLS | The Thirteen-Million-Dollar Man

John Wells. COURTESY OF JOHN WELLS.

TELEVISION CREDITS

1987	*Shell Game* (CBS)
1987–88	*Ohara* (ABC)

1988	*Just in Time* (ABC)
1988	*House and Home,* aka *Rough-House* (CBS Summer Playhouse)
1988–90	*China Beach* (ABC)
1991	*The Nightman* (ABC movie)
1992	*Angel Street* (CBS)
1994–	*ER* (NBC)
1994	*Mystery Dance* (ABC)
1998	*The Adversaries* (NBC)
1998	*Trinity* (NBC)
1999–	*Third Watch* (NBC)
1999–	*The West Wing* (NBC)

⩗⩗ ⩗⩗ ⩗⩗

There's an old saying about living in Virginia: "If you don't like the weather, just wait a few minutes." The implication is that you're never allowed to adjust to one climate, because it will change to another very quickly.

It must be no coincidence, then, that John Wells is from Virginia, where he learned early on about the value and nature of frequent changes in climate and scenery. Today, his television programs reflect that lesson. Whether it's *ER, The West Wing,* or *Third Watch,* quick pacing is his trademark, and viewers are never allowed to settle into a particular zone for very long. In Janine Pourroy's book *Behind the Scenes at ER,* Wells comments, "We usually have anywhere from nine to eighteen stories running in any episode. We wanted the pace to move in a way that would hold the audience's interest."

The fictional talk show host Larry Sanders (HBO), when tossing to a commercial break, always admonishes viewers with the catch phrase "no flipping." When you're watching a John Wells show, however, the warning is moot, because John gives us neither the need nor the opportunity to flip.

Although his fast-paced programs keep us wondering where we are at any moment, Wells knows exactly where he is at all times. In fact, John has a habit of being in the right place at the right time. Whether it's landing in a college class being taught by a script reader from Columbia studios or getting Steven Bochco to critique his early teleplays or being hired by Warner Brothers without ever having a script produced or being tapped by Steven Spielberg and Michael Crichton to produce *ER*, John has always seemed to be exactly where he needed to be to have a shot at success.

Sure, there have been script rejections and failed pilots along the way, but the luck of the Irish is with John. In many ways, he is like the Old West gambler who somehow always gets invited to sit at the high-stakes table. The tribute to John, though, is that once he gets to the table, he has the skills to stay in the game and win the pot.

Enough with the analytical introductory remarks. If John were editing this chapter he would have already moved on to the biographical scene. So here goes.

John Wells was born in 1956 just outside Washington, D.C., in the town of Alexandria. His father was an Episcopal rector, his mother, a schoolteacher. He has one sister (Ann, now an occupational therapist), and a younger brother (Lew is the producer of *The West Wing*). Growing up, John and his siblings were taught the value of a good work ethic. "My mother, my parents were children of the depression, and my mother felt it was important that we had jobs (chores). So I always had a job from the time I was eight or nine years old. Some of it was pretty silly, just doing the traditional Norman Rockwell stuff, from being a paperboy to selling lemonade on the street. We were always engaged in some activity to make a living from the time we were little, and that's made all of us—all three kids—concerned about money and managing it. Being sort of anal-retentive people, who get upset if their checkbook isn't properly balanced."

There was also time for fun in the Wells household, as the children were exposed to a variety of recreational and cultural activities. John recalls: "My father was very interested in the arts, so we spent a lot of time at the theater, ballet, opera, and symphony. And then, just a lot of outdoor activities, biking, camping . . . there wasn't a television in my house until I was about eight years old. Our viewing was restricted for many years. My father felt it was important that we read and experience other things. But, you know, by high school, I rebelled against that, and I was watching an awful lot of television." Questioned about the shows he was restricted from watching, John responded: "Well, it wasn't so much censoring of material, just the number of hours that he would allow you to sit and watch [TV]. My father was famous for talking about the boob tube, so he didn't want us sitting there very much. Also, what I remember is that when he wasn't at home, you could watch a little bit of television. (*Laughs.*) So before he got home from work, we'd watch *Gilligan's Island* and *McHale's Navy*. Then we would watch certain programs in the evening—news programs and *The Defenders*. I remember we watched *Profiles in Courage*."

Later, the Wells family moved to Colorado, where his mother, now retired, still resides. "I went to high school out in Denver at a place called Cherry Creek," John recalls, "then I worked a year in dinner theater, and in rock and roll as a roadie. Then I went to Carnegie Mellon [formerly Carnegie Tech] as a production design student. I became a graduate directing student at Carnegie after I finished my production design work. Then I went from New York to Los Angeles to the USC Cinema Department, called the "Peter Stark" program. We were required to take a writing course there, and we called it "Writing for Dummies." I don't remember what the official title was. It was mainly just a scene structure class. And the guy who taught the class was a reader over at Columbia [Jim Boyle], and [he] read a few of the things I had done, and really encouraged me to keep doing it. So I took a shot at it, and wrote a few screenplays and really enjoyed it."

The writing paid off, and after a few scripts had circulated around Hollywood, Wells landed a job with Warner Brothers, where he wrote for a number of television series. One of them, *China Beach* (1988–90), gave John an opportunity to try his hand at mixing drama and action with romance and realism. In one episode ("The Interview"), he wrote a story that called for filming real Vietnam War veterans. Though *China Beach* never broke into the top twenty-five, it won critical acclaim. For a while however, after its cancellation, it seemed as if good reviews might not be enough to sustain Wells. In a town where the official motto is "So, what have you done for me lately?" John hit a dry spell with his program pitches. True to form, though, he once again found himself in the right place at the right time.

Michael Crichton's script for a feature film titled *ER* had been gathering dust since 1974 when, twenty years later, good friend Steven Spielberg resurrected it—this time as a television pilot. Spielberg was familiar with Wells's work on *China Beach,* and, suddenly, John was sitting at the high-stakes table again, ready to play. NBC's Don Ohlmeyer recalls the beginning: "I looked at the first act [of the pilot] and I turned to Warren Littlefield and said, "Warren, they're [the audience] either never leaving or they're never coming back," because it was the most intense twenty minutes I had ever seen. And at the time, the biggest fear in this country was health care . . . it's interesting how the national psyche turns, but that was the number one fear on every survey. And my concern about *ER* was could people be drawn to watch? And I said to John, 'We're going to do a promotional campaign about compassion; I hope that's how the show turns out.' And John, with *ER*, touched a nerve in this country. It created a place that was in the back of people's minds. It was,

'Please, God, if I'm in a car wreck, let there be a place like *ER*, and let there be a doctor like Dr. Greene, who gives a shit whether I live or die'—as opposed to *Chicago Hope*. Both shows are very well done, very well acted, very well written, but *Chicago Hope* was about rich doctors driving around in Mercedes, talking on a cell phone. *Chicago Hope* was what people were afraid of and *ER* was what they weren't afraid of. That's where the national psyche was at the time."

Ohlmeyer's predictions were right on target. From its premiere in September of 1994, *ER* assumed ownership of NBC's 10 P.M. Thursday time slot and was an instant success, both in ratings and revenues.

In *ER*, John was able to mix a number of genres together—action, mystery, drama, comedy, romance—and all interwoven at breakneck speed compared with the traditional hour drama. Wells had arrived, and with each new story that he wrote, the other players around the high-stakes table were forced to fold or settle for a loser's share of the pot. In fact, *Chicago Hope* could have been a top-ten show all along had it not been pitted against *ER*. For the 1999–2000 season, David Kelley's attempt to resurrect the program was aided by CBS's decision to finally move *Hope* to another time slot. Moreover, while most shows tend to lose steam after a few years, *ER* just kept getting better with age. Wells's bosses were impressed with his ability to turn out quality week after week.

In her book *Behind the Scenes at ER*, Janine Pourroy quotes Steven Spielberg: "I have a very strong relationship with John in that I'll read the treatments, and then the scripts, and I'll give him my ideas. He's free to use them, and he's free to throw them away. I'm never insulted when nothing is used, and I'm always very pleased when something gets in there."

Despite the rapid pace of *ER*, Wells managed to display real humanity in real terms and real time. Pourroy quotes Wells: "We didn't do a *single* episode about Benton's mother's death. Benton's mother's death takes *eleven* episodes, because that's the way things really happen. They're painful and slow, and one day's good and one day's bad, and those things in our lives take a very long time. We didn't do an episode about Greene's marriage falling apart, because marriages don't fall apart in a day . . . we use the reality of the medicine to carry through to the reality of the personal stories. We follow the characters as they live their lives in real time, and I think that heightens the sense of realism on the show." And Don Ohlmeyer adds: "I remember an episode [number five, 'Into That Good Night'] where Alan Rosenberg played a guy who was waiting for a heart transplant, and he ends up dying. And every time I watched it,

I cried. And I kept watching it, over and over again, 'cause I didn't quite understand why it was touching me that way. And finally, after the seventh time, it dawned on me. In the scene at the end of the show where the heart doesn't arrive, and he knows he's going to die, you look at those scenes and you would like to think that no matter who you were—from the nurse, to Dr. Greene, to the guy who's dying—you'd like to think that you had the content of character to act like they did. With that dignity, with those human qualities. And it was like this fabulous life lesson that you were watching."

Everybody was watching as *ER* stayed at or near the number one spot every week. Then came the now famous (and historic) deal in which NBC agreed to pay 13 million dollars per episode for *ER,* and suddenly, Wells had hit the jackpot. The luck of the Irish was on his side once again. Ohlmeyer continued: "All the stars in the universe had to line up right for *ER* to get what it got, which wasn't 13 million, but it was close enough, so that's in the ballpark. But you had to have a situation where *Seinfeld* quit, *ER* was the number one show, NBC wasn't going to have football the next season—I mean, you had to have like nine things, nine of the stars and moons aligned—ABC and CBS had to say they would pay 15 million an episode for it. All of these things had to line up in a row for that to happen. So it had nothing to do with worth, it had to do with what the marketplace was for that particular day. And if the deal was done six months earlier or six months later, [the show] wouldn't have gotten that [much]."

Wealthy, respected, and successful (at the dawn of the new century he was named to *Entertainment Weekly*'s list of the hundred most powerful people in Hollywood), Wells, as most genius workaholics tend to do, began to look for new projects. He struck out with *Mystery Dance* in 1995 and *Trinity* in 1998, but in 1999 he and his partners unleashed two new dramas, *The West Wing* and *Third Watch,* both sporting the trademark Wells pacing, both drawing rave reviews, and both turning in respectable numbers for NBC. Of course, *The West Wing* was somewhat of a gamble. With many Americans having just had their fill of Monica and Bill, the show could have been passed over as a political tabloid. Still, Wells was optimistic.

WELLS: "I think there's a tremendous pent-up desire in this country to believe in our leaders" (*Newsweek,* September 1999). Perhaps that's why so many people believe in John Wells—he's a leader. Like most leaders he's always on the go, always busy. That's why he and I agreed to conduct his interview over several sessions on his car phone during his morning drives to the studio. Before the first session, I had just viewed the *West Wing* pilot, so the similarity of John's life and schedule to that of the fictional President (code name "Potus," for President of the United States), wasn't totally lost on me.

Longworth: Your assistant, Shelagh O'Brien, told me she was patching me through to you, and I had this image of presidential urgency, as if I should send you a pager message saying "Potus needed for interview."

WELLS: (*Laughs.*)

Longworth: By the way, are you the Potus around your office?

WELLS: (*Laughs.*) No, I don't think so. I don't get nearly the deference. Nobody addresses me as Mister before they talk to me, that's for sure.

Longworth: (*Laughs.*) How about at home? Are you the Potus at home?

WELLS: No, that's definitely not the case. I'm the lone male involved in a world of women.

Longworth: How many daughters?

WELLS: I have one daughter, and my wife, and my wife runs her business out of the house, so it's all women.

Longworth: Before we get to your career, I'm curious about one aspect of your education. Of all the producers I've talked with for this book, you're the only one who started out with an interest in production design. Do you consider that a big leap to where you ended up, or an advantage in preparing you for your career today?

WELLS: Well, you know, I really always wanted to produce. I don't know where I got that idea, but I did early on and there really isn't any place to go as an undergraduate student in, say, learning how to produce. Production design was the closest thing—it actually, I should say, was production-/-design, so we had stage management courses and theater management courses, and then we also had costume, set, and lighting design courses.

Longworth: What was your first big break in television?

WELLS: There were so many of them. I had been writing for three or four years and sending my stuff to Bochco, who was doing *Hill Street* at the time, and after they fired him off of *Hill Street,* he had a little bit of time, I guess he caught up on his reading file, because he called me up and said that he had read one of my pieces—gave me a lot of notes, a lot of encouragement, and that was very helpful.

Longworth: How would you describe your relationship with Steven, and do you stay in touch?

WELLS: I can't say that we're personal friends. He's been a tough critic, and also very supportive when he likes the work. You know, I would actually say that Bochco is the entire reason that it even occurred to me to write any television. I was out at USC in the fall of 1980, and that spring, *Hill Street Blues* came on the air, and I just thought it was the best thing I was seeing in film or television. And it really encouraged me to write for television. All of us know each other, we all run into each other at the same events. And we exchange writers, and talk, and argue, and, in a sense, it's a healthy competition. I don't consider myself as competing with Bochco. I have a lot of peers, people that I hang out with, and everybody is just trying to raise the bar in a field that I think we really love. And so, I think it's very competitive, but I also think of it as very healthy.

Longworth: But back to Bochco and your scripts.

WELLS: He then recommended to me that I read a pilot that was being done at Twentieth at the time called *Moonlighting*, and I liked the pilot very much. So I wrote him back, and then Glenn Gordon Caron and the guys over at *Moonlighting* had me in a bunch of times to pitch and that was where I really learned how to sell something. I got hired over at Warner Brothers in 1986, just out of the blue. I was making optioned screenplays for five grand, and my agent, Jeff Stanford, called me up and said, "You're never going to believe this, but some guy at Warner Brothers called up and wants to pay you $150,000 a year." And I thought he was kidding me. And I've been at Warner Brothers ever since.

Longworth: And that was just to develop scripts?

WELLS: That was one of these overall deals that they used to do a lot more of then than they do now. There was so much money in hour television in the mideighties, you know, with *Rockford* and *Magnum P.I.*, and everything was still syndicating in the afternoon, *Scarecrow and Mrs. King*, so they were making money hand over fist with hours. So even low-level writers in the country who had some talent got these overall deals.

Longworth: Just for the record, did you actually write an episode for *Moonlighting?*

WELLS: I wrote them, just nobody ever produced them. Really the experience over there was my being able to go in and pitch, and they were really very nice to me, very supportive, taught me a lot, but my first script that I got that was actually my first television screen credit was on a show called *The Shell Game* over at Warner Brothers.

Longworth: What do you think about Warner Brothers cutting that script development deal with advertisers? Is that a good thing for young writers, or could it start a dangerous trend toward content control by advertisers?

WELLS: I think it has the potential of being both. Certainly you return to a lot of what business used to be thirty years ago. The danger is that advertisers will get too involved in the type of programming they want to do, like Hallmark has done, but that's worked out pretty well for them, so.

Longworth: How did you get to *China Beach?*

WELLS: I did a bunch of shows for Warner Brothers as a staff writer. I was on a show called *Shell Game* and a show called *Just in Time.* I was on a show called *Ohara* with Pat Morita and then I was doing pilots for them. I had written a comedy pilot for Warner Brothers, for an executive at Warner Brothers named Scott Kaufer. Scott was also developing *China Beach,* even though he was the comedy vice president, and he recommended me for it. John Young hired me and we hit it off.

Longworth: What was your role on *China Beach?* How much responsibility did you have?

WELLS: We did fifty-six episodes over four years, and I was there for the last three years. The first year they did a pilot and six. Then my responsibilities increased as I was there. I came on as a producer, and was the co-exec by the final year that I was there. You know sometimes you just find a show where you really click with the material and with the people, and I really learned how to produce a show there. It was a great experience. It was a very difficult show to do, extremely ambitious. They never really thought we were ever going to last. We had a lot of latitude. Like Tom Fontana and John Masius in the three or four years of *St. Elsewhere,* one of the reasons the show was able to be as adventurous as it was was that there was no pressure to succeed. They just thought they were going to be canceled every year. And we had very similar experience on *China Beach.* The assumption was that we weren't going to make it every year so we just took a lot of chances. And we really did some great work that I'm very proud of.

Longworth: Since you mentioned *St. Elsewhere,* I want to read you a quote from Bob Thompson's book *Television's Second Golden Age* in which he comments:

"*ER* quite shamelessly ripped off story ideas . . . that *St. Elsewhere* had done years ago, and much of the grim 'depressing' feel for which people had blamed *St. Elsewhere's* low ratings was present in many episodes of *ER* . . . but the new show had . . . more pretty faces and an audience fifty percent larger than *St. Elsewhere's.* Its hit status was greatly helped by its hyper-kinetic pacing . . . in retrospect, the leisurely *St. Elsewhere* looks like *ER* unplugged."

WELLS: You're looking for a comment from me?

Longworth: Yes.

WELLS: I've never heard that quote before. I can't tell you that I watched a lot of *St. Elsewhere*. As far as shamelessly ripping off, I've never had a single conversation on *ER* with anybody who said, "Hey, they did this story on *St. Elsewhere* that we ought to do." You know all these genre shows—they build upon each other. Stories that were used on *St. Elsewhere* were used on *Dr. Kildare* which were also used on *Marcus Welby* . . . there are just so many stories that you can do. In the same way if you're doing cop shows, you get into the same kind of cop shows. I mean, there just aren't that many of them.

Longworth: You can have the cop going after the drug dealer, or the cop shaking down the prostitute—

WELLS: Right, so there just aren't that many situations. I would say that certainly what ER was doing was trying to make a show that was realistic in the setting. And there's a huge difference between the rhythm from the hospital ward and that of an emergency room. All you have to do is go and spend some time there. It's just a different rhythm. I mean, we didn't set out to make a really fast-paced show; we set out to make a show that was realistic to the setting we chose, and that gave it a much greater pace.

Longworth: You mentioned *Dr. Kildare*. Bochco and I were talking one day about how in those days twenty-two episodes of *Kildare* meant twenty-two stories. Today *ER* has many more.

WELLS: Yeah, on *ER* we traditionally have twelve to fifteen.

Longworth: So then, does that tend to burn out writers faster?

WELLS: Well, I think it tends to burn out story material faster. (*Laughs.*) It just brings you back around to that point I was making before where you discover that you are going to hit all the same material, particularly because over ten years of *Dr. Kildare* or twelve years of *Ben Casey*, they only were doing twenty-two stories per year. And you're doing many, many more stories, so there aren't that many medical stories to do, or cop stories to do. You're trying to find ways to change the situation with this person, with that person, and just trying to shuffle the pieces over the board and see if you come up with something interesting for the character. The difference in the kind of storytelling that we're doing now—and this began with my knowledge of *Hill Street*—is that the emphasis went off of the guest star and on to the lead character. And that, for me, was the huge innovation of *Hill Street*. Because before, these shows had always been where an interesting guest star came in, and our steady, knowable, central character responded in some steady, knowable way. So you would see the woman who came in and she had cancer in the first act, and you proceed through it with Dr. Welby. And we don't tell those kinds of stories anymore. The stories are about the characters, and I think that's one of the reasons why the shows [today] don't have the same kind of fourteen- to fifteen-year life span many of them had in the past because you *do* start to get to the point where you've moved your central characters around on that chessboard in every possible configuration. And it just starts to get ludicrous. Whereas a show like *Law & Order,* which is really not character based at all in the sense that you don't know anything about your lead characters, you really don't understand their life, but what you're interested in is the plot. And I think that's why that show can go fifteen [seasons], and it's why *N.Y.P.D. Blue*'s only got a couple more years in it, and *ER*'s probably got three more years in it—very different kinds of storytelling.

Longworth: I know you've been doing a lot of interviews and most of them focus on your success, but I'm always interested in what it was like to fail. I read that after *China Beach* you had pitched something like five pilots in one year and that none of them were picked up. What were you thinking when the fourth or fifth one didn't fly? Were you saying, "Maybe I'll think about a different career"?

WELLS: I don't think there were ever four or five in one year, but certainly over several years, there were an awful lot of them that never made it. It's the ratios that I always like to talk about. If out of every five projects you do, if one of them is really successful, and two of them are pretty good, and two of them stink, you're actually doing pretty well.

Longworth: A good batting average.

WELLS: Yeah, that's a good batting average. Most of the time you are doing shows, pilots, writing them or producing them. You're doing scripts that become short-list series. I think almost everybody has a pretty good batch of unsuccessful materials. I don't really get depressed by it because these things are so difficult to do well. There are so many factors involved in doing them well that you've got to have a terrific script, you've got to have the right people making it. You've got to have the right idea at the right time and the right time period, the right cast.

Longworth: You weren't wealthy and famous when those pilots didn't make it, yet you didn't have any doubts about where things were headed?

WELLS: No, you know what? I have an old line where a third of the way through every script I've ever written I turn to my wife and say, "I've finally realized that I'm absolutely untalented." I think that's the process of being a writer, you never get over that feeling. But people who do these things are very much like any other entrepreneur. You really just have to believe that you can't fail, and that you're doing the right thing, and sooner or later it's going to work. You have to have sort of a stupid ability to continue to accept tremendous failures to get very far.

Anybody who's reached the point I was when I was doing four or five pilots, you know it's not like you're just starting your career. You're already at a point where you've got a certain amount of success, and you're just hoping that you can get this thing together and you're doing other stuff at the same time, you know, movies or you've got another series. And even to get to the point where you have an opportunity to be on staff of a show, you had to have had such ridiculous, foolish confidence in your ability and the thought that you have any talent at all. And again, everybody's telling you that you don't. And frankly, I don't remember making pilots that failed being nearly as difficult as writing scripts when I was living in a four hundred dollar-a-month apartment, building houses during the day, and waiting—hoping that somebody, anybody, would just tell me they liked it, much less want to pay me money for it.

Longworth: Were you being paid to develop those pilots or did you do them on your own time?

WELLS: No, I was being paid to develop them. It's a very foolhardy exercise trying to do pilots on spec.

Longworth: You told me your dad was an Episcopal priest, and I grew up in the Episcopal church too, but as I sit here today in the Bible belt South I can't help but wonder as I watched last night's episode [Roscoe Lee Brown as an elderly minister who knew Peter as a boy and ends up conducting a prayer session with Benton and Jeannie] if there was a lot of spirituality to that. Has your life come full circle with influences on your writing?

WELLS: I think that's right, I think you become, no matter how hard you rebel against it in your late teens and twenties and early thirties, you do become who you were raised to be. I think it's very difficult to fight that. We try to put spirituality and religious beliefs into shows not out of any attempt to proselytize. But to not show spirituality and religious beliefs in at least some of your characters is, I think, not presenting a very accurate picture of the audience—the people who are actually going to watch the show.

Longworth: You once commented that when you first read the original *ER* script [which Chrichton had written nearly twenty years earlier], you described it as a "pointillist painting," and saw that you wanted to take it into a different direction. What kind of changes did you want to make, and how would it have been different if they had hired John Doe instead of John Wells?

WELLS: Well, I don't know if I can speak to the last part of that question. I would say that we had to craft it so that it was obvious why it would be a series, and not just, say, a two-hour movie of the week. We needed to lay in a few more elements that were going to leave the audience wanting to come back and see what happens to these people. The basic structure of a two-hour film or any film is sort of a beginning, a middle, and an end on a character arc. And what you're trying to do in pilots, and then in the series, is to do the beginning, some of the middle, and end at the end, so that people feel like "Gee I gotta come back next week and see what happens."

Longworth: We were talking earlier about the multiple story lines in each show.

WELLS: They change from show to show. We've had as many as thirty and as few as nine or ten.

Longworth: Obviously, then, it's driven by having such a big ensemble cast. I saw a photograph of you at the office standing in front of a white marker board with multicolored marking pens, and the caption indicated that you were outlining character development. Was that a publicity shot, or do you really stand there and do character development at the board?

WELLS: Yeah, absolutely. We have a bunch of four by eight dry erase boards and a lot of colored markers. And we track characters through all the episodes, so we can keep track of where they are. And I've sort of traditionally always done that on shows that I've worked on. So, yeah, absolutely, we track them all through the season and say, "Geez, that doesn't make sense, or we're doing too much of this, or that's going to get depressing."

Longworth: And you keep a record of those?

WELLS: They're permanently up on the walls in the conference room.

Longworth: It has been said of you that you're a very organized person. If that's true, where did you learn your discipline skills? Fontana credits the Jesuits for his disciplined writing regimen, but you're not Catholic, so what's your story?

WELLS: Well, I'm almost Catholic, you know, as an Episopalian. (*Laughs.*)

Longworth: That's what they tell us.

WELLS: My mother is a retired schoolteacher and she put a tremendous amount of emphasis on organization, study habits, how you're going to organize your day. She's just a very organized person, and she instilled that in all of us. My brother is a producer and a very good one. My sister runs a large therapy department, a geriatric facility. So, we've all got jobs that requires sort of multitasking, and I think that all comes from mother. And a certain kind of educational background, that's the way we were brought up. But I think it's not far off from Tom Fontana's Jesuits. There's a sort of a general sense of "Idle hands are the devil's work," that you stay busy, and make sure that you're focused, and that you're useful. I think the thing certainly in my house has been seen as the greatest failure of parenting would be children who grew up not in some way useful.

Longworth: Before you and your siblings came along, everything on television was live. You're the only modern-day producer that has really attempted a live broadcast of an hour drama, harkening back to the glory days of the fifties. And yet, I got the sense from the audience that television has gone so far in the direction of slick postproduction that a lot of *ER* viewers were sort of ambivalent about what they saw because it wasn't as slick. What's your take on that?

WELLS: We knew going in that there wasn't much of an experience to be had by the audience. Not like a live performance where you don't know the outcome, like a sporting event. So to the audience I think it was only moderately successful, but what was successful about it was a sense of "Gee, I wonder if they'll screw up," and sort of feeling as if you were in on something, that you were watching something that you could talk about the next day. But we knew that going in. I mean, to the viewers it's not going to look all that different. All it was going to do as you suggested was be minus some things. Minus a full score, minus the kind of editorial work we can do to really jazz it up. But we went into it to do it more for the cast and the crew. We really did it for ourselves at a time when we needed a new challenge, and it just completely reenergized the company. And that also is one of the responsibilities of keeping these shows running is you need people to be excited about what they're doing. You have to be a good boss in the way that anybody in any kind of a job setting has to be a good boss.

Longworth: Before we leave *ER* I can't not ask about the 13 million-dollar-per-episode deal, because historically, readers and students need to know, plus I also have other producers commenting on it as well. So here goes. Back in the summer of '99 there was a week during reruns when *Law & Order* actually tied *ER* in the ratings. *ER* costs 13 million, *Law & Order* costs 2 or 3 million per episode. Is *ER* 10 million dollars better than *Law & Order*?

WELLS: Well, let's put it into this kind of perspective. During the first four years of *ER*, NBC never raised the license fee from the pilot—the nego-tiated license fee. Also, you should know that 13 million dollars is not the real number. It's less than that. It's been widely reported as 13 million, but it's not. During those first years, NBC, because of what they were paying Warner Brothers, was making just under a quarter of a billion dollars net profit—that's after costs, license fee, and everything else on *ER*. So, in the first four years of *ER*, they made over a billion dollars in profit, and that's not including the fact that *ER* turned Leno into the number one nighttime show, that we brought huge business into all the O&Os [TV stations owned and operated by a net-work] for their late newscasts, and the promotional time for other series that came out of the value of *ER*. So the question you have to ask isn't "Is it worth—is it that much better in some sort of quantitative sense than *Law & Order?*" but what kind of money has *Law & Order* been making for NBC? It is a pure economic question, and has absolutely nothing to do with quality. But the reality of the profitability of these series is such that *Law & Order* has done, and is going to continue to do, extremely well in its syndicated run and its stripping into basic cable. And that's where Universal is going to see most of their profits. But the audience for *Law & Order*, not in straight numbers but in demographics and in advertising value, is much, much less. It's widely pub-lished—you can get the figures for what they get for a thirty-second spot, and what the demo is because it's who's watching it, and how much the adver-tisers want to reach them. Do the comparatives on the profits, and remove any kind of qualitative things out of it, and you'll see that the math is absolutely perfect. We've done all this research. *N.Y.P.D. Blue* is getting a price exactly what it should be getting compared to where *ER* is, compared to where *Law & Order* is, compared to where *Homicide* was, as far as an economic venture. But it has nothing to do with quality, it's only business.

Longworth: As we began the new millennium, racial diversity in televi-sion programming is once again an issue, but not a new one. There were commission reports in the early 1970s and another in 1991. The NAACP is looking for minorities in leading roles who are role models. Now, certainly you have Eriq LaSalle in a leading role, but shouldn't you make him a hospi-tal administrator instead of a surgeon, for example? Do you feel that you as a producer have a responsibility to respond to these concerns by making an effort to change or add roles to become more compliant?

WELLS: I would certainly disagree with the general premise of your point, but if you're stating that Benton as a character should not be a compli-cated, tough, irascible, frightened, difficult guy because he's a black character, I'd say that it is an extension of prejudice, frankly. What we need is to show everybody in every way. We don't need every felon that appears on television to be black, and we don't need every hero that appears on television to be black or Hispanic or Asian. What we need is true diversity, which is showing everybody as human beings in the workplace—how they are. Sometimes they're good guys, sometimes they're bad guys. But you get into something where we simply start saying, "Oh, well, if you're going to put a black character in this show, the black character has to fulfill an ultralateral purpose for the community," I think is just to further the discrimination. In fact, that is a discriminatory practice. We have Gloria Reuben who plays Jeannie on *ER* and couldn't be sweeter, more compassionate, more empathetic. Should we have done that with Benton, and not made him the other kind of character? I would just say it makes for uninteresting drama, then nobody's watching, then we don't change any of this.

Longworth: How did you come up with the idea for *Third Watch?*

WELLS: I got interested in the subject matter from spending a lot of time in the emergency rooms in *ER,* and spent a lot of time around paramedics and firemen and cops, who come in and out of the *ER* and started feeling "Well, there are all these stories that we can't tell because they're outside those doors." And I just kept collecting them and then it seemed the appropriate time to try to do it.

Longworth: Now, whether it's *Third Watch* or *ER,* have you ever had problems with Standards and Practices? I noticed on the pilot for *Third Watch* one of the paramedics called someone a "jack off."

WELLS: He says "jag off."

Longworth: OK, but isn't that sort of pushing it? Anyway, have you ever had anyone from Standards and Practices come down during the years you've been working on *ER* and suggest that you need to change a phrase or a story line?

WELLS: Sure, with language. Not so much with story line, occasionally, but that usually has to do with health care issues. On *ER* it's because they're concerned that we in some odd way provide a lot of health care information to the viewing audience more than anybody else does. So they'll get concerned if they think we're not being balanced in a portrayal of a health care situation. But, sure, on language. You know the problem that we're increasingly having is that—and I think you and I talked about this the other day—we really don't compete with the other networks as our only competition. We compete with cable, so I've got to compete for viewers with *The Sopranos* and every movie that's on HBO or Showtime. That's a viable option to the viewing audience. We are constantly fighting the battle, saying, "Look, if Bochco said it on ABC, we have to be able to do it," but I can't go back and say, "Oh, my show is actually a show from the mideighties, or the early nineties. We're in those battles all the time. The network, they're genuinely concerned about how far can they push it and not lose advertising. And, at the same time, knowing that you could get beat to death on the other side by cable and by what other people are putting on the air. So they're very conscious of it. It's not just "Oh, we won't let you do this because we're prudish"; it's "How far can we push it to compete with cable, and at the same time not alienate advertisers and some audiences?"

Longworth: For the record, you never called a person from Standards and Practices a "jag off."

WELLS: No, I haven't. In fact, I haven't had a male Standards and Practices representative for eight or nine years. They almost all tend to be women with advanced degrees in sociology.

Longworth: You mentioned your brother Lew earlier, and that he was producing *The West Wing*.

WELLS: Lew also produced *The Grifters* and *Soul Food* and a lot of pictures. I'm very lucky to have him. He's a year and a half younger than I am. It's the first time we've worked together in fifteen years. We both had to get to a point where we were established enough in our careers that we could do it noncompetitively.

Longworth: So you're doing three shows at once, and probably have ideas for others in your head. You're constantly working. I remember earlier you talked about the time your family spent together when you and Lew and Ann were growing up.

WELLS: This is going to be a question to make me feel guilty, right?

Longworth: That's right, this is a combination of an Episcopal and Jewish question.

WELLS: (*Laughs.*)

Longworth: Isn't it sort of ironic? You are a very successful person, and you had a great, supportive childhood, spending all this quality time together, limiting the hours spent on TV. Now, ironically, it seems that you're spending all of your time on television. Do you have any time for your family, and if so, what kind of fun, quality activities do you do together?

WELLS: I don't have nearly as much time as I would like to have. The advantage of doing television is there are cycles to it, so there are nine or ten months that are very busy, and then I'm able to take a whole month off with my family every year. But it's a real challenge, and when you enter into any kind of career I think you have to accept that you're really going to be struggling to fit everything in and to be the kind of parent or husband that you want to be. I think that's the sad reality of any job. It applies to being a CEO of a company, it applies to heading a law firm, you know, any job in which you've got seven or eight hundred people working for you, and, in the case of the three shows this year, we're spending about 220 million dollars on the shows. Anytime you're in those kinds of circumstances, it's going to be very demanding, and still get everything you want out of your home life and your business life.

Longworth: Yeah, but how much is enough? Nobody in the business has accomplished more than you have during the past few years. Why not just retire and let Lew run things at one show and Lydia [Woodward] at another, for example, while you and your family go off fishing for about ten months? You don't need the money, you don't need the headaches. Have you thought about early retirement?

WELLS: Yeah, but the thing is, this is what I really love doing. It never crossed my mind that I was going to make a lot of money doing this. I didn't set out to try and make a lot of money. I was hoping to make a living. And so it's one of those things that when the dreams of what you hope you will accomplish in your life actually come true, it doesn't mean that you don't still love what you're doing, and why you started doing it in the first place. So I think the balance is, and something I struggle with all the time, is "How do I find a happy medium where I can enjoy other things in my life at the same time that I am being fulfilled in my work life?" And I don't think that's an experience that's unique to me. I mean, I think that many people who are successful in their careers struggle with the same thing.

BRENDA HAMPTON | Friend of the "Family"

Brenda Hampton. COURTESY OF BRENDA HAMPTON.

TELEVISION CREDITS

1989	*Sister Kate* (NBC)
1990	*Lenny* (CBS)
1993	*The John Laroquette Show* (NBC)
1990–94	*Blossom* (NBC)

1994	*Daddy's Girls* (CBS)
1995	*Mad about You* (NBC)
1996–	*7th Heaven* (WB)
1997–98	*Love Boat—The Next Wave* (UPN)
1999	*Safe Harbor* (WB)

〜〜 〜〜 〜〜

On balance, the 1990s were good for the city of Atlanta. The Braves, dubbed "America's Team," dominated their league. The Coca-Cola Company rebounded from introducing Classic Coke. And Brenda Hampton set the standard for how to write about families on television.

True, some of the TV families she crafted early in the decade were somewhat dysfunctional, but as the new millennium dawned, Hampton had found a niche writing about the happy American home, and, later, creating her own in real life.

Brenda Hampton was born August 19, 1951, in Atlanta, Georgia. Her brother is four years younger, and her sister, four years older. "I worshiped my older sister. I still do. I just held her in very high esteem growing up. If only I could be her. She was beautiful and popular, and wonderful, and I would have given anything to have been my older sister when I was growing up. Right now she is a stay-at-home mom, but her sons are twenty-two years old—they're identical twins."

Brenda's parents still live in Atlanta. Her mother still manages the house, and her father is retired from two different careers. "He was an electrical engineer with AT&T, and he was a television repair man . . . so, I have family in the 'business.'" (*Laughs.*)

Fortunately for Brenda, the family television set was always in good working order. "I liked *Leave It to Beaver, Father Knows Best, The Donna Reed Show, The Andy Griffith Show.*"

[Longworth] "So now we know why you did *7th Heaven.*"

[Hampton] "Yes. But I also liked *Mr. Ed* and, later on, *The Mary Tyler Moore Show* was one of my favorites."

By her own admission, Brenda and her siblings were good kids, just like the fictional Camden clan on her current hit TV show *7th Heaven.* "I don't think we ever got into serious trouble, but as teenagers, we had strict curfews, and we would be grounded if we broke them."

Hampton attended East Atlanta High School, and then went to the University of Georgia (class of 1973), where she nurtured her writing skills.

HAMPTON: I always wrote, and when I went to the University of Georgia I was looking for a major that didn't require a foreign language. So I picked journalism. (*Laughs.*)

Longworth: You weren't preparing for the global market then?

HAMPTON: (*Laughs.*) No. I had taken Latin in high school and I didn't want to take more of it in college and I didn't know another language."

Longworth: Not too much demand for journalists to broadcast in Latin.

HAMPTON: I was looking for a major that wouldn't require a foreign language, and there wasn't a requirement for it in journalism, so that's how I got into it.

For Hampton, however, the road to a career in television writing didn't begin immediately after graduation nor did it begin in Hollywood. Instead, the government and her community came calling first. "I started out in 1973 working as a technical writer for the U.S. Navy down in the Bahamas. I did that for about a year. And then I went back to Atlanta, and I was a substitute teacher for about six months. I taught reading at an inner-city school. This was a school where the federal government had put a lot of money into a reading lab, and I think they were having trouble for a long time getting teachers at that school who were certified in reading. But, in the meantime, I filled in, and when the teacher came, I helped her."

Buoyed by the navy and nurtured by her hometown, Hampton was ready to venture outside traditional support systems and try her wings in television, so she migrated first to New York, then to California. For much of the 1980s, Brenda found success in writing humorous speeches for corporate executives and jokes for stand-up comics such as Roseanne. She was also married to a comedian for ten years (he is deceased). By 1993 Hampton had established herself as a writer/producer, and found work on a number of television series, including *Sister Kate, Lenny, Blossom, The John Laroquette Show, Daddy's Girls* (which she also created), and *Mad about You.*

Blossom's family was quite dysfunctional compared with the *7th Heaven* bunch. *Blossom*'s dad was divorced, one brother was a recovering drug addict, and the other a skirt chaser.

Daddy's Girls starred Dudley Moore as a divorced dad whose wife had run off with his business partner. He was left to care for his daughters, one of whom was played by a pre-*Felicity* Keri Russell.

Mad about You was the most successful show Brenda worked on, and it led her to be noticed by Aaron Spelling, who hired her to apply her "family skills" to hour dramas. To date, she has created three shows for Spelling, including the short-lived *Love Boat: The Next Wave* (UPN). But her signature show is *7th Heaven*, the story of the Camden family, led by Stephen Collins (a minister) and Catherine Hicks (a "supermom"). Though the show is broadcast by the WB, whose numbers are weak compared to the big-three networks, Brenda's creation was a hit with young and old people alike. Critics also came around to liking the show. *TV Guide* even sported a cover with the banner, "The Best Show You're Not Watching." In fact, *7th Heaven* was the WB's first show to break into the top fifty, and by February 1999, nearly 13 million viewers tuned in to Hampton's TV "family."

While some right- and left-wing groups and Congress were railing against violence on TV, *7th Heaven* was getting thumbs up from all corners. The National Fatherhood Initiative even named Collins's character as the top dad role model on TV (he tied with *Promised Land*'s Gerald McRaney).

Noted family authors Richard and Linda Eyre told *TV Guide*, "*7th Heaven* tries to portray a model family in a way that is believable and identifiable. The effort is noble, and the program succeeds more than it fails."

TV Guide critic Mat Roush (March 1999) added that "the slow but steady rise of this show is one of the happiest surprises in a season [1998–99] that could really use some upbeat news."

Bob Thompson, director of Syracuse University's Center for the Study of Popular Television, observed, "All of us who watch it [*7th Heaven*] think of it as our little secret."

Aaron Spelling must have known the secret would spread. In *TV Guide*, March 6, 1999, Spelling said, "There were a lot of people in my company who said, 'Why are you doing this show? It'll never sell.' But they were wrong. You've got to gamble sometime."

In 1999 Spelling and the WB gambled on another Hampton drama, *Safe Harbor*, which starred Gregory Harrison (*Trapper John, M.D.*) as a small-town sheriff and single dad. In *Soap Opera Weekly*, Hampton said, "I would compare it to the *Rockford Files*. It's a comedy/mystery show about the sheriff of a small town and the crimes he solves."

In the September 10, 1999, edition of *Entertainment Weekly* she added, "I'm aiming for a *Northern Exposure* with kids. It's a small town with odd ball people—good people, but odd people."

Safe Harbor didn't have safe passage. Before its launch, the entire pilot was reworked and partly recast. It's no *7th Heaven*, but then, what is?

Today, Hampton is a devoted wife and mother who is dividing her time between her real life family and her TV families. She has a great sense of humor, loves a good joke, and has an infectious laugh. As I learned during our interviews, she is deeply rooted in traditional values, and is an activist who shows no sign of wanting to cut back on her use of television as a forum for promoting the sanctity of family life and individual freedoms. In July of 1999, after the Columbine High School shootings, Brenda was asked by *TV Guide* to join a distinguished panel in a roundtable discussion of how television might affect violence in America. Reacting to threats of TV censorship, she commented, "Detroit and Toronto have the same TV lineup, yet the rate of violence in both cities is vastly different. So how much is the media really influencing these kids?"

In a recent episode of *7th Heaven*, she had the Camden women railing against "gender apartheid" in Afghanistan.

Somehow, for a woman who avoided foreign languages in college, Brenda Hampton has done very well at telling dramatic stories and promoting important causes through a universal language—television. In doing so, she has also proved that, perhaps, the best family value of all is communication.

Longworth: Here I am pushing fifty, and the highlight of my week is going to the grocery store to buy bran cereal. I get home to read over the dietary fiber rating, and what do I see on the back of the box of Raisin Bran but . . .

HAMPTON: *7th Heaven!*

Longworth: Yeah, a contest to meet the Camdens!

HAMPTON: *(Laughs.)*

Longworth: First of all, why are you intruding on my bran cereal, and second, who are you marketing this show to, me or to kids?

HAMPTON: That's a Warner Brothers promotional item. And I think they're just trying to promote the show any way that they can, but you would have to ask them what audience they're trying to reach. It's on all Post cereal boxes.

Longworth: That's great.

HAMPTON: Yeah.

Longworth: It's almost like you've arrived, right?

HAMPTON: Uh, I think so. That may be the mark. That and the *TV Guide* cover. *(Laughs.)*

Longworth: I was reading an article that reported on some teenage focus groups that had viewed *7th Heaven*, and they thought it was a bit unrealistic on one episode for Matt to willingly accept his grounding without some bitching and moaning.

HAMPTON: Yeah, well not at *my* parent's house. (*Laughs.*) If you don't want to go by the rules, you get your own place! They were blue-collar people, Dad working two jobs to support us. It's like, I think you would accept those kind of things. (*Laughs.*)

Longworth: Did you have to do chores?

HAMPTON: Not a lot. My mom grew up on a farm, and because she worked very hard, she was determined to let us enjoy our childhood.

Longworth: At what point did you display a talent for writing?

HAMPTON: I remember having a poem published in my grandmother's church bulletin. (*Laughs.*)

Longworth: That was a big thing.

HAMPTON: That was a big thing for me. And I always liked to write.

Longworth: What was the name of the poem?

HAMPTON: "Spring." (*Laughs.*) And I'm sure it started with "Spring has sprung," but I don't have it in front of me.

Longworth: And you were how old?

HAMPTON: Eight.

Longworth: Do you still have a copy of it?

HAMPTON: I have it somewhere. I have a copy of a lot of my writing from that time on.

Longworth: Well, if your name was in the church bulletin, that was a pretty big deal, because here in the South, we use the church bulletin for two things—seeing whose name is in it and using it as a fan in the summertime.

HAMPTON: That's right. (*Laughs.*)

Longworth: How big a role did organized religion play in your life?

HAMPTON: I don't know if I want to get into a discussion about religion. (*Laughs.*)

Longworth: The only reason I'm asking is because of the nature of *7th Heaven*—

HAMPTON: I don't consider it a religious show.

Longworth: What do you consider it to be?

HAMPTON: A family show. We've only mentioned the word *Christian* one time and that was in reference to "Hooey," the imaginary playmate. So while many people have grabbed on to it as a religious show, I think we've been very evenhanded in giving information that all religions can agree on.

Longworth: Oh, I agree. In fact, I brought it up because, in reading the *TV Guide* review, Matt Roush commented that the show is not preachy, that it's not holier than thou. I wondered, Is it hard not to slip into that preaching mode when you're dealing with certain types of family issues, and the father happens to be a preacher?

HAMPTON: No, because he's actually based on a friend of mine who was a minister of a church in New York. And, if I ever call him for advice or have a social conversation with him, it wouldn't sound religious.

Longworth: That sounds like the Episcopal priest I knew growing up, who would come to the house, take off his collar, and have a beer.

HAMPTON: Yeah, this guy, Eric Camden, even though he's in this family, they live their religion, but I would never present a religious belief on TV and try to talk people into it, because I think that's a different kind of television. I don't think that's entertainment.

Longworth: And since you've also taught school, would you say your role as a writer for *7th Heaven* is more teacher than preacher?

HAMPTON: No, not even that. Because some people are looking at this as some kind of parenting documentary, (*Laughs.*) which is very funny because I only adopted a child about eighteen months ago, and no one else up here has a child, so we are making this up. (*Laughs.*)

Longworth: So what you're telling me is that you're not qualified to be producing your show. (*She laughs.*) Then you need to stop immediately!

HAMPTON: I'm not qualified to tell anyone how to raise their children, and the thing that we do is hopefully present a story or an issue that parents can talk about with their kids when they turn the episode off. But we're not trying to tell you this is the way to raise kids. We're saying these two people raise their kids this way, and you're free to comment on it.

Longworth: What kind of feedback have you received from real people, real parents?

HAMPTON: It's so positive. People are so excited that they have role models for parenting, and I hate to tell them "I'm not that person."

Longworth: Do they ever say that you've helped them with a particular family dilemma?

HAMPTON: Yes. We got a letter recently from a mom who said, when the news broke about Columbine, that she sat down to talk to her two boys about it and they said, "Well, Mom, don't you remember we watched that episode of *7th Heaven* where the girl got into the gang, and it was so hard for her to get out? We would never do anything like that." So we get these wonderful letters from people. We had a little girl who turned in her father for abuse because, until she watched *7th Heaven*, she didn't know it was against the law.

Longworth: That's kind of sad in a way, but it's good that the show addressed it.

HAMPTON: She didn't know that she could do something about it. She went to a school counselor the next day. She assumed that since he was the parent and she was the child, he could do whatever he wanted to. So we get wonderful letters from people.

Longworth: You know, of course, that the TV shows you liked growing up never got into those kinds of issues. Now, you could say, "Well, that's because it was the fifties and early sixties," and yet, your show is kind of parallel to those in the sense that there's a warmness and a sense of family. So, I guess they dealt with the issues they could deal with, and you're dealing with the ones you can deal with.

HAMPTON: Well, we certainly discuss current topics and we have a very political show coming up in episode three here, but once again I think what we've done is present a story that will indeed set off some discussion when the hour is over.

Longworth: Marshall Herskovitz told me recently he was disturbed at how Congress was trying to blame Columbine on Leo DeCaprio's *Basketball Diaries*, and yet, they didn't bother to praise him (the actor) for his heroic role modeling in *Titanic*.

HAMPTON: The most annoying thing about it to me is we still refuse to talk about the one thing that caused those shootings in Columbine and that is mental illness. We have yet to talk about mental illness with this incident. And this is just amazing to me.

Longworth: Why aren't we doing that?

HAMPTON: I don't know because it's easier to simplify it and talk about guns. It's so much easier to blame someone as if we could assign blame and then we'd all feel better about it because we found the problem. But mental illness is a much harder thing to assign blame with and we talked about it on the gun episode of *7th Heaven*, if you have a kid who's troubled, do you really want to arm them? We just asked the question. And that was long before Columbine.

Longworth: Do you see part of your mission as a producer, as a writer, as a creator, as a mother, to do programs that are going to benefit people, or are you just trying to entertain people for an hour?

HAMPTON: We do something in between. We try to entertain and remain harmless. It's so much harder to remain harmless than to try to help people. I think it's very dangerous to try to help people when you don't know who they are or what their problems are. So we try to remain harmless, but at the same time, provide an hour of entertainment that has some substance to it.

Longworth: Jessica Biel, who plays oldest daughter Mary, commented that she and her young costars on the show are nowhere near as bright as the characters they play. So that set me to thinking. Are the Camdens a reflection of most families, or are they a portrait?

HAMPTON: No, I think they're no one's family. They're a family that people don't mind spending an hour with. (*Laughs.*)

Longworth: Do people want to be like them?

HAMPTON: I don't know. I don't know if people want to be that good or not. (*Laughs.*)

Longworth: The only criticism I've read about *7th Heaven*, and it's not really a criticism, was in *TV Guide*, who thought your characters resolved problems too quickly.

HAMPTON: See, I don't think that's true at all because we rarely—we have the beginning of a resolution, like with the cutter girl, the beginning of the resolution. She was sent to treatment that specializes in teenage girls who are cutters. We didn't get into that which solves the problem. It was just the first-step to solving the problem. We do a lot of first step kind of resolutions. You know, we only have the hour to tell the story. Each episode is self-contained, so we have to do something storywise that gives you some closure.

Longworth: Well, since you mentioned the confines of the hour, would you ever consider serializing multiple story lines over several episodes, where maybe one story is resolved in the hour and the others are carried over?

HAMPTON: Well, you have the issue of syndication, and foreign syndication, and not knowing if the episodes will be shown in the order they're shown here, so we *do* that. Some stories start in one episode, and you see a piece of that story later, but we do need to make each story pretty much self-contained unless we do a two-parter kind of episode.

Longworth: You have a great sense of humor; you wrote for *Mad about You* and other shows, but many of the producers I've interviewed say they wouldn't want to write a comedy show.

HAMPTON: Well, see, I wrote comedy first. I wrote jokes for a lot of comedians, and I wrote half hour before I got into hour, and I actually think *7th Heaven* is a pretty funny show. I only have half-hour comedy writers writing it.

Longworth: Since you've crossed over from comedy to drama, and, as you say, there's comedy in your drama, which genre is easier for you to write?

HAMPTON: I like the hour format better because you have longer to tell the story. And as a Southerner, I'm a storyteller and I like to tell that story. In a half hour you want to tell a story and you want every other line to be a joke. It's very challenging to write that, but I like doing that too. I like sitting at a table of comedy writers and pitching jokes, which is fun.

Longworth: With *The Andy Griffith Show,* which both of us loved, the writers didn't write jokes, they created stories and situations.

HAMPTON: We have a lot of jokes in *7th Heaven.* We don't have a laugh track so they may go right past some people, but (*Laughs.*) there's some really good jokes in there. I think the kids get the jokes. We had a runner, in fact, in the Christmas episode that made me and the other writers laugh, and I don't think anyone got it all. It was the whole stupid runner about Simon asking the guy from New York a hundred questions about *Cats* [the musical] and if it was based on a poem. Kind of silly, more than jokes, but it made us laugh every time, but I sat in a room with other people here who didn't get it at all. (*Laughs.*) It doesn't matter, sometimes we put stuff in there for 1 percent of the audience who'll look at it and laugh.

Longworth: *7th Heaven* is such a great family show I'm going to assume you've never had any arguments or problems with WB's Standards and Practices folks.

HAMPTON: I have problems with them all the time. (*Laughs.*)

Longworth: You do?

HAMPTON: Yes, because they annoy me—they send me a memo almost every week that if we're shooting in the car, we have to fasten the seat belts, and that just bugs the heck out of me. Anyone in this business knows that if the kid's in the car, the seat belt is on. Also they got into this big thing with us last year 'cause we had Mary say she was going to open up a big can of "whup ass"; (*Laughs.*) this made us laugh because it was, for her, so far over the edge because she was fighting with Matt, and she was so angry that she said that. And it's such a mild term. And they got all upset that our audience would be upset about Mary saying "whup ass." Well, we didn't get a phone call or a letter on it. It just made people laugh.

Longworth: So, while Bochco says he's caught flack for trying to describe oral sex, you've got problems with "whup ass."

HAMPTON: I know, see it's a totally different thing. They think that [the network censors] know our audience and they think that our audience is religious right-wing conservatives, and I'm telling you we hear from all kinds of people who watch the show, and I think that's a large segment.

Longworth: How did you come to meet Aaron Spelling?

HAMPTON: My agent called one day when I was working at *Mad about You* and asked if I would like to have a meeting with Spelling television on a blind pilot pitch, where you can come in and pitch anything you want. So I pictured myself saying, "Dear Diary, today I met Aaron Spelling," so, of course I wanted to do it because he is a legend in this business and I was very excited. So I came up with a pitch so I could go over and talk to him. I had no idea it would ever go anywhere, I just wanted to meet Aaron Spelling.

Longworth: Was the pitch about—

HAMPTON: *7th Heaven*. That was the first meeting. I came into his gigantic office and he had a lot of people in there, but he pulled up a chair knee to knee with me and goes "Whatcha got?" And when I started pitching he was so enthusiastic and made me so comfortable that I probably did the best pitch that I've ever done in my life.

Longworth: Did the other people stay in the room?

HAMPTON: Yes, but he was totally focused on me, and it was just the two of us talking really, and he's just the greatest.

Longworth: That's kind of amazing when you think of it.

HAMPTON: Yeah, because he's done x-number of hours of television, which means he's heard ten times that number of story pitches. (*Laughs.*)

Longworth: So you expected him to say what?

HAMPTON: "Very nice meeting you, thanks for coming up." (*Laughs.*)

Longworth: Well, he's a Southern boy, too.

HAMPTON: He's from Texas, yes.

Longworth: So, maybe that's why you hit it off.

HAMPTON: We didn't get into anything personal, it was just strictly business, I mean, that was it. There was no chitchat.

Longworth: What kind of a person is he in general?

HAMPTON: He's a family man. I rode to the press tour with him just day before yesterday and it's an hour over there and an hour back. And he talked about nothing but Tori and Randy. (*Laughs.*)

Longworth: Aaron seems to be the only studio head to raise the glass ceiling for women producers.

HAMPTON: Well, I don't think it has anything to do with that specifically. I think that the man is brilliant. And man, woman, or child, if you came in and pitched a good show to him, he would jump on it. So he absolutely does not discriminate because of age, race, gender—it's all about the work. "Can you do the work?" And I think he's great at recognizing who can do it, and he's a brilliant storyteller. I jumped at the opportunity to work with a man who's been so successful.

Longworth: Here's a guy who's done everything from *Johnny Ringo* to *Love Boat*. It seems that he's always been able to reach everybody, not just certain niche audiences.

HAMPTON: I don't know how he knows. He knows a good idea when he hears it. (*Laughs.*) I'll go up and pitch six episodes at once. And on *7th Heaven*, there are about five stories on each episode, so I can pitch thirty stories straight out from beginning to end. And when I get finished, he can tell you, "You know, that comic runner you have in episode two really plays into the subtext of episode five." And he can fix it in the verbal pitch, so we do no rewriting. Once he knows what I'm writing, he doesn't come back at the outline stage and say, "Oh, I thought we were doing something else" or "This story doesn't really work for me or "I thought this would be different." He fixes it in the room when you pitch it to him, and I can't tell you how many days, weeks, months that saves you over the long run. He's so good at it that it just makes our lives so much easier on this show because we're not doing a lot of rewriting.

Longworth: Is Aaron like a father figure? What kind of relationship does he have with his associates?

HAMPTON: I don't know what kind of relationship he has with everyone else, but I can tell you this, I wouldn't be a mother if it weren't for Aaron Spelling. When I met him I was trying to hide the fact that I was single and trying to adopt a Vietnamese child, because I was afraid he would think that I couldn't do both things. And one day after a screening of the pilot he said, "I want to talk to you about something personal, can you come in here?" And I'm like, "Oh, no, he found out, he found out." I came in and he said, "I heard you're adopting a child," and I said, "Yes, but I come from a blue-collar family, I work very hard, I know I can do this and adopt a child," and he looked at me like I was crazy. And he said, "No, no, no, I just wanted to know if you needed any help. Do you need any money? Do you need a lawyer? Do you need us to fly you over to Vietnam? Is there anything we can do here to help you out?"

Longworth: I'll be damned.

HAMPTON: And the man didn't even know me. We were still in the pilot. It wasn't like this was a reward for doing a good job. We were still in the middle of getting the pilot done. And he provided an office for my child care. That's not in my contract. He told me anytime my kid needed to come to a screening with me, or a meeting, that she was welcome at any Spelling function at any time. So he has made it so easy for me to be a mom.

Longworth: That's neat.

HAMPTON: And like I said, this was not negotiated between an agent and Spelling television. This was just Aaron Spelling offering it.

Longworth: Well, I've heard stories that he treats all of his work family that way—men, women, everyone.

HAMPTON: Yeah, he's a gentleman. He has always been very nice to me and to my daughter, Zoë, and to my husband, Tim Bui.

Longworth: Let me shift from father figure Aaron to something we touched on before, which is Eric, the father figure on *7th Heaven*. As you know, the National Fatherhood Initiative came out with their survey, in which they studied one hundred network TV shows, and found that only fifteen had fathers of young kids, and of those, only four portrayed fathers in a positive manner. Stephen Collins's character, Eric, received the highest marks of anyone. I'm sure that makes you feel very good, but on the other hand, what does that say about where we are in television right now?

HAMPTON: I don't know. (*Laughs.*) I don't know where we are in television right now. (*Laughs.*)

Longworth: We're back in *Pleasantville* with your dad the TV repairman.

HAMPTON: I guess people like the way Stephen portrays a father. I have a wonderful father myself, and I like writing dads. I like writing the new one in *Safe Harbor*, and I like writing Eric Camden.

Longworth: Are there any issues you would never tackle in your shows? That no matter how topical, or how much you thought you could help people by addressing it, is there a certain line you wouldn't cross, a certain topic that you won't broach?

HAMPTON: Well, it all depends. We never approach a story with the issue in mind first. It's always "Here's the story and within that story is an issue." We never start with "Well, let's do an episode on this or that." We don't do it that way.

Longworth: If you should get feedback from WB that they think something you wrote might negatively influence kids, would you be flexible in reworking the scenario?

HAMPTON: We've never gotten a note like that, and I think we are infinitely more responsible than anyone who might be giving notes on our scripts.

Longworth: Another issue that's out there today is one of racial parity as it relates to lead characters on network television programs. Is it your responsibility as a producer to, for example, write in a role for a new black character, so that you'll have a black leading character? Is it your responsibility to rush out and hire three Asians and two Latinos and insert them into *7th Heaven* because of pressures from organizations?

HAMPTON: We've been doing the "right thing" on *7th Heaven* for four years, and doing family television with something entertaining, and with values for families to watch, and no one has cared (*Laughs.*) until the show got successful. And now people care. And on that show we've had an African-American family that I would love to spin off, and there has been no interest in having me spin them off. So I've been interested in bringing some diversity into the shows that I do, for a long time. And on the new show, *Safe Harbor* [before anything was said by the NAACP], we could not find identical twelve-year-old twins, which is what I wanted. So I made the suggestion that the youngest son have a best friend, and that the two of them think they are twins, and we should cast that friend as an African-American.

Longworth: The "cosmic twin" you refer to in the pilot script?

HAMPTON: Yes. But now, I have heard reports (*Laughs.*) in response to the NAACP's request that I have gone so far as to replace a Caucasian twin with an African-American, which makes me sound insane. (*Laughs.*) I didn't do that. It was a creative solution to a casting problem, and it came up before the request from the NAACP. Also, we added an African-American cast member to be a series regular on *7th Heaven* this year. The African-American family's oldest son is John [Chaz Lemar Sheppard], and we made him Matt's roommate for next year. Those stories we started breaking last January because we had finished with last year's scripts and had moved on to this season. So we've been trying to do the right thing to put some diversity on the screen for a while now, but I'm afraid the effort looks like it was only in response to this request, and it wasn't. I think I have been conscious of just how "white" television is for a long time. And I've become more conscious of that since I adopted a Vietnamese child and then I married a Vietnamese man.

Longworth: Well, next, the media will say that you did that just for publicity.

HAMPTON: (*Laughs.*) They could. And not only has it made me aware of how few Asians there are on television for her to watch, the Asians that are portrayed are so stereotypical that it is absolutely embarrassing to watch them with her most of the time. Now, on this new show we not only have this African-American kid who's playing the cosmic twin, we have a Cuban woman who's playing the deputy.

Longworth: So timing aside, your efforts have nothing to do with the current storm of concern.

HAMPTON: Right. It's not only the right thing to do, it's more interesting and more accurately portrays the American life on television to put diversity in the show.

Longworth: So why haven't you written to Mr. Mfume at the NAACP to let him know what efforts you've made?

HAMPTON: (*Laughs.*) Wouldn't you think he would have brought up the fourth episode of *7th Heaven,* when we did an entire episode on the burning of black churches? Does he know about our show? He hasn't mentioned the WB with any of his comments that I've seen in the paper.

Longworth: I think the NAACP has focused it's complaints on the big-four networks.

HAMPTON: Right. But you know what he ought to do? He ought to give the WB credit for doing something *positive.*

Longworth: You know, as I listen to you, and get to know your convictions and enthusiasms, I can't help but notice that Annie Camden is your alter ego. She's a great parent—she's a—

HAMPTON: She's closest to my sister, who can actually do [all those things]—minor plumbing repairs, painting, wallpapering. When her twins were six months old, I think she wallpapered her entire house.

Longworth: So you still deny that Annie is really you?

HAMPTON: You know, there's a little bit of me in all of them, but there's also a little bit of other writers in all of them because we've developed these characters over the years. And there's a little bit of the actors in them. I don't want to say it's just me, because it really is a mix of people.

Longworth: We were speaking of the WB earlier. A few weeks ago, the story broke that WB had signed an agreement with its top advertisers to underwrite the development of eight new "family scripts." Given your background and the opportunities you would have appreciated, is this a good thing for young writers, or is there a danger that advertisers could begin to exercise content control?

HAMPTON: Ever since they did that, we've been joking that I can't take phone calls 'cause "I'm on line three with Dave Thomas about his new bacon cheeseburger." (*Laughs.*) I mean, we're comedy writers, and this is very funny that they'd make this deal. It's nice to have advertiser support, because that's what keeps us all on, but I can't quite understand why advertisers are having to pay networks to develop family-friendly programming. If there's support for it, they will develop it. I don't know why they have to give them any money. Advertisers didn't give the WB money to develop this show.

Longworth: Would you have liked for them to do that?

HAMPTON: No, no. I don't want any government or advertising involvement. I don't even like network involvement. (*Laughs.*) I don't want anybody bothering me. It's a clean show, I try not to get any notes. (*Laughs.*)

Longworth: Let's go back to *Safe Harbor*. It's the story of a widower and his children. He's a small-town sheriff in Florida, and in the pilot episode I loved how you surprised me with making one of the good guys a villain. Even though it is a so-called family show, are you going to have a police mystery in each episode?

HAMPTON: Well, that was part of the creative discussions between me and my network, (*Laughs.*) because I like the heavy detective—the heavy sheriff story. I like that this is a guy who may have to walk away from a dead body and then go deal with the kids' math homework. They [WB] would like a lighter story—more small town, Andy Griffith, and I think that's fine. I hope to do a mix of them, because I think if we only have him do funny, crazy small-town things, he wouldn't have much substance to him. To have him do something that's real sheriff work gives the character some reality, and allows us to do those other funny shows.

Longworth: I also noticed in the first episode that young Jeff spouts out some philosophy about how mental illness, not weird clothing, is the cause of school violence. And I'm thinking Brenda says she's not a preacher, but she sure is preaching to us here!

HAMPTON: (*Laughs.*) Has no one connected these tragedies to mental illness?

Longworth: No, you're the only one.

HAMPTON: Is this the last discussion we're going to have? Is everybody going to talk about everything else before we finally get to mental illness? I thought this was a topic that was out of the closet that we could talk about in this country.

Longworth: But you have no credibility with me anyway because you married for publicity.

HAMPTON: (*Laughs.*)

Longworth: But in that kind of a scene in a family drama, you really are an effective preacher without hitting people over the head.

HAMPTON: It just amuses me that I'm going to try and play both sides of politics in the show, so that both sides are represented. So sometimes they'll be saying things that absolutely aren't my philosophy. In one show the kids were complaining about having to do artwork in school because art is a complete waste of school funding. Now, I don't believe that at all, but it was a funny thing for the kids to say. (*Laughs.*)

Longworth: Finally, let's talk about your family. You work eight hundred hours a day, so when you *do* have a few moments free, what kinds of things do you and your daughter and husband do together?

HAMPTON: Well, first of all, I don't work those hours, and my kid and husband are at the same office area. They have a schoolroom here, and she's in independent study with the L.A. school system. So, when she takes her little snack break, she comes into my office and has a snack, and we usually talk about whatever I'm doing or whatever she's doing.

Longworth: And your husband?

HAMPTON: He's her teacher, that's how I met him. I brought her over here and then I hired a teacher for her to translate when I had her in private school, and that's how I met him. He was the teacher and he still teaches her. So I see them all day long, and I come in around nine-thirty and she rides in with me. They do school all day, they leave an hour before I do, about six in the evening. And when I go home, we all eat dinner together. My husband's a wonderful cook. And then Zoë and I spend the evening watching TV or reading.

Longworth: What do you and Zoë like to watch?

HAMPTON: Her favorite show is *Drew Carey,* which would sound a little risqué for a twelve-year-old girl, but you do have to remember that she comes from a very different background, and she has heard and seen a lot. And we're very open about what we talk about. She finds Mimi on that show to be hysterically funny. Also, Drew was once very nice to her at an awards ceremony we went to, and she's never forgotten it.

Longworth: So what shows *do* you like?

HAMPTON: I also love *Drew Carey*—that would be one of my favorite shows.

Longworth: I know you're an accomplished comedy writer, but what dramas do you like?

HAMPTON: My daughter occasionally watched *Buffy* and *Felicity,* but we've only seen them three or four times.

Longworth: Finally, let me get you to pull out your crystal ball. We both grew up watching the same kinds of TV programs—family shows, the kind that you've created. As we move through this new millennium, what's the television family going to be like ten years from now? Will the values of *7th*

Heaven be obsolete, or will the value structure be pretty much the same as it is today? Do you have any idea where we're headed?

HAMPTON: No, because I think there's such a fragmented audience now that there is something for everyone on television, and I am all for that. I haven't had the opportunity to watch *The Sopranos*, but that would be my kind of show, I would love to see it, it just seems that I am busy with something else at the time. Before I got my kid, I would go home on Friday night and put on the Independent Film Channel and I'd still be watching it Sunday night. (*Laughs.*) A&E *Biography*—love it. I watch all kinds of television. I think just because it's a family with family values doesn't mean that each person in the family doesn't watch all kinds of television.

Longworth: Well, if A&E ever does a biography on you, what conclusion will it make about you at the end?

HAMPTON: The woman is mad. (*Laughs.*)

10

ED ZWICK | Man of Action

Ed Zwick. PHOTOGRAPHER, DANA TYNAN.
COURTESY OF THE PHOTOGRAPHER.

TELEVISION CREDITS

1976–80	*Family* (ABC)
1983	*Special Bulletin* (NBC movie)
1982	*Paper Dolls* (ABC movie)

1982	*Having It All* (ABC movie)
1987–91	*thirtysomething* (ABC)
1989	*Dream Street* (NBC)
1994–95	*My So-Called Life* (ABC)
1996	*Relativity* (ABC)
1999–	*Once and Again* (ABC)

MW MW MW

America loves action. Evidence the rise in popularity of professional wrestling, and the NFL's supplanting of baseball as the national pastime. Ask anyone watching a football game and they will tell you that sports such as baseball and golf are just too slow. There's no "action."

In an interview about the making of *The Dead* (Independent Film Channel), the late John Huston commented on the similarities between directing period dramas and action pictures. "Action," said Huston, "doesn't have to be a car chase . . . action can be one's mind, in one's thoughts."

If that's true, Ed Zwick is the world's greatest writer, producer, and director of the action genre. Like his longtime partner, Marshall Herskovitz, Ed has made a career out of exploring personal thoughts and telling stories about the human condition—stories about people trying to come to terms with who they are, and how they fit in at home, at work, and in society.

Time magazine's Michael Krantz characterized Ed and Marshall's work as having "explored the quiet dramas of everyday life." What is truly amazing, though, is that Ed has done extraordinary things with ordinary topics.

In fact, before the ink was even dry on the notes for this chapter, Ed and Marshall's latest effort, *Once and Again*, had taken the nation by storm, and had already begun to establish a discernible trend away from mindless sitcoms and banal teen shows, and toward thoughtful adult dramas. This shouldn't surprise anyone who knows Ed's work or his gift for anticipating public tastes.

In the 1980s, *Special Bulletin* was the prototype docudrama. It raised eyebrows but it also raised consciousness. Meanwhile, *thirtysomething* not only reflected yuppie life in America, but it also helped influence changes in lifestyle and fashion. In the 1990s, *My So-Called Life* set the standard by which nearly every subsequent teen drama would aspire to.

Even Ed's films have gone against type to bring a new way of thinking into the mainstream. *Glory* proved that white Americans would pay to see a Civil War movie that featured a predominantly black cast. In *Courage under Fire*, he not only made the Gulf War more personal, but he also reminded us that women can be heroes too. In the Oscar-winning *Shakespeare in Love*, he proved that the Bard was bankable.

Yet, with all of these trend-setting, award-winning efforts to his credit, Ed's (and Marshall's) television programs have never broken into the top twenty, and only one even made it past a single season. So, before the premiere of *Once and Again*, reviewers and industry insiders offered backhanded raves along the lines of "It's great, but is America ready to embrace a show about divorce?"

It was a mistake to doubt "action" Ed. *Once and Again* not only has become a pathfinder for new millennium adult dramas, but it has also become so perhaps at the expense of what were considered television staples—half-hour comedies and cop shows. In fact, *Once and Again*'s early performance almost pushed veteran *N.Y.P.D. Blue* out of its perennial Tuesday night time slot, causing an open feud between Steven Bochco and ABC.

All this hoopla over a show with no "action"? Hardly. Harkening back to Huston's quote, we realize that *Once and Again* is *full* of action. Moreover, we should all now come to appreciate Zwick's contributions to society, and his ability to shape popular culture.

Ed Zwick is a quiet, compassionate, deep thinker, and he writes about quiet, compassionate, deep thinkers. Oftentimes, his work has been unsettling to those of us who either refuse to think outside the box or do not wish to confront our inner feelings. So, if Ed's visions have stepped on toes, or occasionally caused the television industry to spin on its axis, he has meant no harm. He's just creating "action."

Whether it's African-American heroes in the Civil War, or women heroes in the Gulf, or teenage heroes coping with day-to-day life, or married heroes learning how to stay together, or divorced heroes adjusting to change, Ed Zwick knows how to portray "action" on all levels.

Visit an Ed Zwick soundstage and listen carefully as the camera begins to roll. You'll probably hear someone whisper, "Lights! Camera! Think!" Now, *that's* action.

Edward Zwick was born October 8, 1952, in Winnetka, Illinois, to Alan and Ruth Zwick, who divorced when Ed was young. Ruth died in 1983, before Ed became successful in television and films.

Zwick began directing and acting in high school, then trained as an apprentice at the Academy Festival in Lake Forest. After graduating from Harvard, Ed was accepted as a directing fellow at the prestigious American Film Institute in 1975. His short film *Timothy and the Angel* won first place in the student film competition at the 1976 Chicago Film Festival. It would be the first of many awards and honors Zwick would receive in his career. His AFI film also helped him get noticed in Hollywood, where he landed a job as a writer for Spelling/Goldberg's highly acclaimed drama *Family*.

Leaving *Family*, Ed went on to direct a number of television films and pilots. In 1983 he teamed with fellow AFI alum Marshall Herskovitz to write and direct *Special Bulletin* for NBC. The docudrama, about antinuke terrorists who threaten to blow up Charleston with a nuclear bomb, won four Emmys and a host of other honors for its groundbreaking portrayal of how television news covers a major event. The movie also helped launch Ed's dual career in films and television.

Zwick's motion picture work has included *About Last Night, Glory, Legends of the Fall, Courage under Fire, The Siege,* and *Shakespeare in Love;* the latter brought him an Oscar for Best Picture in 1999.

Although Ed's achievements in film may overshadow his other work, his imprint on the small screen has been enormous. After his stint on *Family* and then at the helm of *Special Bulletin,* he and Herskovitz (under their Bedford Falls banner) cocreated *thirtysomething,* the seminal 1980s drama about young, affluent, married couples and their introspective lives.

Once characterized by the press as "the show you love to hate," *thirtysomething* was also described by author Jane Feuer as having created "an aesthetic out of yuppie guilt." In her book *Seeing Through the Eighties,* Feuer also accurately opined that the show eventually took on "art status" among TV critics. She cited *New York* magazine's Claudia Weill, who wrote, "It's very unusual television. Ed and Marshall encourage you to turn every episode into a little movie." She also quoted *Los Angeles Times* critic Howard Rosenberg, who observed, "These are filmmakers making a pit stop."

Thirtysomething was a landmark show that perhaps changed television drama forever, but the Bedford Falls boys weren't done breaking ground just yet. In the 1990s the pair created two excellent TV shows, both of which were ahead of the curve and neither of which caught on with mainstream audiences. *Relativity* and *My So-Called Life* received rave reviews but low ratings. Then in 1999, Ed drew on his experience as a child of divorce (and Marshall on his as a divorcé) to create a show that audiences would embrace. *Once and Again* was launched in the fall of 1999, but it was risky for ABC for two reasons. First, Ed and Marshall hadn't produced a TV hit in more than a decade, and second, how could the network be sure that people would watch an hour about divorced people trying to date again? ABC's gamble paid off, however. As a bonus, *Once and Again* seemed to be attracting female viewers who had grown disenfranchised with network fare. ABC cochairman Stuart Bloomberg told the *New York Times* (October 14, 1999), "Hallelujah! Forty year olds are sexy!" Zwick added, "There is obviously a hunger on the part of audiences that might have felt ignored."

Even CBS's Leslie Moonves admitted his surprise with the success of shows such as *Once and Again, Providence, Judging Amy,* and *Family Law.* In the same *New York Times* article, he said, "The fascination with youth . . . on network television is probably overdone this season. Suddenly, some of the shows that appeal to baby boomers have a great deal more appeal than Madison Avenue first thought."

Poor Madison Avenue. Like Hollywood, they just follow the trends and go where the action leads them. Trouble is they didn't realize that "thinking adult" dramas such as *Once and Again* are full of action. You just have to know where to look.

Ed *does* know, and that's why he has won every major award in the industry. So what do you give a man who has everything? For my part, I'm calling Hasbro to see if they'll issue an Ed Zwick commemorative action figure. It may not sell as well as the professional wrestling dolls, but I bet it will last a lot longer. Real action figures always stand the test of time.

Longworth: Before we get going here, tell me about your educational background.

ZWICK: I went to New Trier High School, which is a very good, progressive high school, and graduated in 1970, then went to Harvard. I graduated Harvard, Magna in English literature, and got a Rockefeller Fellowship, then went abroad. I was essentially going to observe itinerant French theater troupes like Peter Brook and—

Longworth: That's it! This interview is over! First Marshall, then Milch, now you. You guys are just too intelligent!

ZWICK: (*Laughs.*) I'm sorry.

Longworth: But there you were—a distinguished scholar, traveling abroad. Were you thinking, Gee, I'm going to go through this academic phase, and then I'm going to direct movies?

ZWICK: That's a really good question because you know, the truth is like any middle-class kid, you're scared of that contingent life, the artist's conditional adventure, and you might romanticize it, but when it gets right down to it. . . . I also applied and was accepted to the law school [at Harvard], but the funny thing is, at the moment that the acceptance came, my life changed, because I knew I couldn't do it. I knew I wouldn't want to do it. I knew it wouldn't kill me, but it might kill my spirit, and so, I chose to take this fellowship instead.

Longworth: But the writing you did in college opened some doors.

ZWICK: In college, I wrote for *Rolling Stone* a little bit, and also for *The New Republic*. And when I was working for *The New Republic*, through a series of odd circumstances I got to correspond with Woody Allen. He had these pieces he was writing for *The New Yorker,* and they didn't publish all of them, so Woody started giving us some pieces. Now, by the time I was in Paris [for the fellowship] things started to happen. I knew Woody Allen was making a movie there, so [one day] I was literally walking down the boulevard and I just walked up to him on the street and introduced myself. (*Laughs.*) I asked if I could hang out on the set of this movie he was going to do, and as it turned out, I ended up becoming kind of an assistant to production, to him.

Longworth: What film was it?

ZWICK: It was *Love and Death.* He was just very kind to me during the process, and allowed me to do things that are so presumptuous, things which I would never do now, knowing what a director is and what's on his plate. You know, when to look through the camera, etc. I ended up working on the film for several months; he [also] gave me some silly little part in it. He was just very kind to me.

Longworth: Did you get paid?

ZWICK: I did, actually, although they didn't have to pay me much, you see, because I had this fellowship, so one of the appeals was that I spoke some French and I was cheap labor. The point is, though, I, like every kid in college in the 1960s and 1970s spent so much of my time in movie theaters, but I had directed theater, so I really thought I would be working in theater. I thought the movies were somehow forbidden meat, because I didn't have the technological expertise. I don't know why, it just seemed mysterious. And then to work on a film, and see this literary man able to translate those ideas, opened a window to me, and I went, "Oh, wait a second. Maybe I could do this!" So what I did, rather than going back to New York, I applied to go to the American Film Institute and I got accepted.

Longworth: Wait a minute, you had experience on one film, and you're basically just a gopher—

ZWICK: Yeah. So how did I get accepted to film school?

Longworth: Yeah. I mean, no offense, but . . .

ZWICK: No, no, no, it's a fair question. What I sent them in my application was reviews of plays that I had directed while in college and some in summer stock. I sent them pieces that I had written as a journalist from *Rolling Stone* and *The New Republic,* and even sent them some songs that I had written—a kind of weird résumé of somebody aspiring to be an artist and, as yet, unfocused.

Longworth: An everyman.

ZWICK: I don't know about that, but they were willing enough to interview me and then they accepted me.

Longworth: What a great success story.

ZWICK: It was nice, and I got very lucky for several reasons. There was an artist in residence there named Jan Kadar, a great Czechoslovakian director, who directed [*The*] *Shop on Main Street.* Nina Foch was teaching there too. She was a wonderful teacher. But most of all, it was where Marshall and I met. We met the first day of film school, and this kind of recognition took place, warily at first, I have to say. But it very quickly flowered into something of a friendship. In that particular film school, you are directly in competition with everyone else because it *is* a conservatory. There are twenty-five people there at the end of the first year, and only six or seven of you will be asked to make films, so you're very directly in competition, and yet you're obliged to collaborate.

Longworth: That's weird.

ZWICK: Exactly. Think of the contradictions—to shoot for each other and act in each other's films and to help with props and set. So it's a very interesting enterprise, and a real crucible.

Longworth: So did both you and Marshall make the final cut?

ZWICK: We both did, yeah. And so did a guy named John McTiernan, who was our collaborator, and a guy named Ron Underwood—a bunch of us who have gone on to become directors from it.

Longworth: Do you remember what the first collaboration was in film school between the two of you?

ZWICK: Oh, gosh. I think I might have done sound for something he directed. He wrote and directed an adaptation of . . . *Where Are You Going, Where Have You Been.* I think he might have acted as a director of photography for me once, and I actually acted in something he directed.

Longworth: What was that?

ZWICK: I don't want to even reveal that because it might see the light of day. (*Laughs.*) [Marshall revealed that the film was titled *Cambridge Nights* and that Ed's performance was very good.]

ZWICK: It was actually a story about one night during the trashing of the ROTC building at Cambridge in May of 1970, during the bombing of Cambodia. It was about these kids, one of whom wants to go into Cambridge and protest, and the other of them who wants to get laid. (*Laughs.*) And the one who wants to get laid ends up being the hero of the protest, and the one who wants to be the protestor ends up getting laid. It was kind of fun.

Longworth: (*Laughs.*)

ZWICK: The truth is, in that crucible was formed a friendship. But collaborations didn't become serious for many years, actually. We each felt we had to go our separate ways, and as we would have these things happen to us, triumphant or disastrous, we would always bring them back to each other, and tear them apart and mull them over. It's been my experience that it's actually very hard to learn something in school. Only years later do you tend to understand what you have learned. At the film school there's no mentorial or hierarchical structure for a writer or a director as there are in the crafts, and we still needed some shaping and training. As we left AFI, I think we became each other's teachers, really.

Longworth: So tell me about your "wilderness period."

ZWICK: Well, these things never seem to take a straight course. By the time we finished our film and put all of our money into it, it had taken, like, two and a half years. That started about September 1975, and by spring of '77, we're out of film school and showing our films. Nobody's particularly interested in hiring us, except that I got one job writing a screenplay for some "schmeisters" from Louisville, who wanted to make a film about the Kentucky Derby. I wasn't in the Writers Guild, so they figured they could have me cheap, and they wouldn't send me to Louisville, so I had to fake it with research. And I'm writing a script and they're paying me in cash weekly, (*Laughs.*) and once they get the script, they skip town, and that's the last that I hear.

Longworth: That's like a video we did for Ringling Brothers Circus about twenty years ago. I made sure we got the cash before we left the big top.

ZWICK: You were smarter than me. (*Laughs.*)

Longworth: So, anyway . . .

ZWICK: Well, also, I worked as a reader. I read scripts for United Artists. You read plot synopsis and analysis, and then they ignore you or take the credit for what you've done, and that was fine because I got paid twenty-five bucks a script or thirty-five dollars for a novel. I had to make money somehow, I had to pay the rent. And this went on for some period of time. By the end of '77, beginning of '78, my script for the student film came to the attention of a guy named Richard Kramer, who had graduated from Yale the same time I had graduated from Harvard. We knew a couple of people in common, but we had met out here and Richard read my script and had me in for a meeting. He had been brought up by a guy named Dan Wakefield. And Dan was doing a show called *James at Fifteen*. Well, Dan had just been fired, and Richard had been brought out to work on that show as a story editor on a ten-week deal. Then Richard suddenly knew he was going to get fired. So Richard read my script and he brought me into a meeting with the producers of the show [*James at Fifteen*]. They were so mean, so dismissive and disparaging to me and to Richard that we became fast friends. We went out to lunch afterwards and were drinking or God knows what, and commiserating about these fuck-heads, and Richard said, "You know what I'm going to do for you—I'm on my way out, so I'm going to send your script over to the producers of a show called *Family*." Now, Richard, it should now be noted, later became the first producer with us on *thirtysomething*. He then wrote, created, *Tales of the City*, and he has joined us on *Once and Again*. So that is a collaboration that is now more than twenty-two years old. [Anyway,] the script then came to the attention of Nigel and Carol McKeon, who produced *Family*, and to their story editor, David Jacobs. They had me in, and asked, "Have you ever seen the show?" And I, of course, lied and said, "Yes" (*Laughs.*) and quickly scrambled and found things and read scripts, and pitched them some ideas. And on the basis of the first script I wrote for them, I had this meeting, where David Jacobs said, "Well, we like your script, and I'm leaving."

Longworth: (*Laughs.*)

ZWICK: So Nigel and Carol invited me to take David's job. And David went off and did *Dallas* and *Knots Landing*. So I took David's job as a story editor on *Family*, and I was twenty-four, maybe twenty-five. I had a six-week guarantee, and then if I made it to the fourteenth week, I would get a bump in salary. And the deal I held out for was if I made it to the end of the season and if I was still employed, I would get to direct the last episode of the season, 'cause I wanted to be a director.

Longworth: Nice carrot.

ZWICK: Yeah. And so I made it. And I directed the show and it went well, and then Nigel and Carol announced that they were leaving the show. And I was the only one left standing. I don't think Len Goldberg and Aaron Spelling wanted me to become the executive producer of the show, but I did.

Longworth: And I remember up in New York you told me that you and Aaron didn't have a relationship.

ZWICK: No, but with Len I did. Len liked me. Len took to me and was very generous. So at twenty-five or twenty-six or whatever I was, I produced the last season of the show. And what I did was I hired all of my friends. I hired Richard [Kramer]. I hired Marshall. I hired a woman named April Smith. I needed the support and the collaboration of those that I knew, and that was the first really legitimate gig that I had. So now we're in 1979.

Longworth: But in the meantime, Marshall had broken away to do *White Shadow.*

ZWICK: Yeah, Marshall did anything he could fucking well do to stay alive. By the way, he didn't even know basketball at all. (*Laughs.*) He is now quite a fan, but, at the time, he literally couldn't have told you a jump shot from a jumping bean, he just didn't know anything. But that didn't stop him from writing *The White Shadow.* (*Laughs.*)

Longworth: Then came *Special Bulletin.*

ZWICK: Yes. There were other things in the process, and I'll spare you those, but what happened was finally, I had gotten to direct a TV movie for Len Goldberg and by virtue of getting the credibility directing a TV movie, I got another one. So suddenly, I had credibility as a director of long-form television. And then Marshall and I had this idea and we took it together to NBC to a man named Perry Lafferty, actually kind of a famous guy during fifties television, and he liked it. Of course, then *he* was getting fired.

Longworth: What is it about you and the people around you getting fired? (*Laughs.*)

ZWICK: Yeah, I think it's us. (*Laughs.*) But the good news was that he gave us the go-ahead to develop it, and then they all got fired. And we sort of existed under the radar. We developed a script without supervision. And we finished it, and we turned it in, and they went, "Oh, my God, what is this? We don't know what to do with this." But they liked it. And they said, "You're twenty-six years old, you can't do this, we need to put you with somebody who knows what they're doing." And they didn't have any deals with anybody in programming, but they had a deal with a guy from sports who wanted to do drama long form, but had never done it before. And so they hooked us up with Don Olhmeyer. And it was Don's first dramatic thing, too. We had already written it, but Don brought to it a very specific understanding about sports and how sports influences news, and so he became the producer of it with us.

Longworth: Did you know early on that you wanted to be able to float back and forth between television and major motion pictures?

ZWICK: Well, who knew? Nobody knew how it worked out here, and you thought you'd come out of film school and you'd be embraced into the bosom of the feature film world, and immediately you'd become Francis Coppola. It just didn't happen. What offered itself was television. I mean, I had had jobs writing movies for other people. In that interim period I did a rewrite of a movie called *Starman* for Michael Douglas, and I did other things. But I couldn't get a movie to direct. So, as it turned out, it was *Special Bulletin* that opened people's eyes in the film community to then say, "Oh, gee, maybe we'd hire him to direct a movie." It was actually the television work that then got me the opportunity to begin doing films. After some period of time, the film that I did, called *About Last Night,* was based on a David Mamet play called *Sexual Perversity in Chicago.* And that movie happily did very well. It was made inexpensively, and did very well at the box office.

Longworth: Was that the Rob Lowe picture?

ZWICK: Yeah. And you see it was in the wake of that movie doing well that Marshall had, in the meantime, made a deal for us to develop some television, because he just needed a job. So we developed *thirtysomething* in the wake of now suddenly having some viability in movies.

Longworth: This is really strange.

ZWICK: It's very strange. And we had no intention of going into television 'cause we now had finally gotten a hold of the grail, you know, the brass ring—movies. And so we did this TV show as a, I won't say it was a lark, but it was so odd and so different from what TV was like. We were convinced that nobody would let us do it, and if they let us do it, no one would watch it. And it was with a certain ignorance and a certain sophomoric spirit that we did it.

Longworth: An *L.A. Times* critic writing about *thirtysomething* said you and Marshall were "essentially filmmakers just making a pit stop [in TV]."

ZWICK: Well, it's interesting because after the show had been on for a year a half was when I left to make *Glory,* and Marshall stayed while I did that movie. And then I came back, and he went off to do *Jack the Bear,* and that began a process in which we would begin things together and then go off separately as the other held down the fort. And that happened again with *My So-Called Life,* and it happened again with *Relativity,* and it's been a thing where we engender these things together, but as time goes on, we feel we need

ED ZWICK | 165

someone present, but it doesn't [necessarily after a year or so] have to be both of us. And should *Once and Again* succeed, that will be our intention as well.

Longworth: Yeah, I was getting ready to ask, what's the relationship on *Once and Again?*

ZWICK: Well, we wrote this pilot together. We've written the first four episodes. We've written all the stories with the writers and the amazing thing is the staff that we have.

Longworth: But Marshall directed the pilot that I just watched. How do you guys decide who's going to direct each episode?

ZWICK: It's been interesting, it's never predictable, you know. The reason Marshall directed the pilot of *thirtysomething* is because that was the only way he was going to get to have a career as a director, 'cause he hadn't been able to direct yet. I was the only one who knew what a great director he was. I already had a career as a director and he didn't yet. So this we knew would become the springboard for him, so there was no question that he would direct the pilot for *thirtysomething*. But after that, it's been more of an ad hoc kind of process. There's no pattern, it's just what has happened, and now we'll both direct for *Once and Again*. I hope I'll find a movie I want to do, and I'll go off and I'll come back, and he'll find a movie he wants to do and he'll go off.

Longworth: That's interesting—it seems like you're really getting into this pattern of freedom, as it were, to collaborate and then go off and do your thing and come back.

ZWICK: Well, you know, we've had a partnership now for twenty-five years, really. We did our first treatment that we wrote together in 1975 or '76— I mean, nobody wanted to look at it, but we began working on it. But as men, sometimes you need to individuate as well. I think you need to have an autonomy and a creative self-expression.

Longworth: Almost like a good marriage—you have to have your own interests outside the marriage if the marriage is going to be—

ZWICK: Well, that's right. You can't be claustrophobic, and it can't be utterly symbiotic. It wouldn't thrive.

Longworth: I talked to Marshall about the relationship you two guys have, and how you try and stay out of each other's way, especially when one of you is directing, the other one doesn't come in and make suggestions.

ZWICK: That's a polite description. (*Laughs.*)

Longworth: Well, I was cleaning it up. My question, though, is what if one of you has a great idea that could help the product, but doesn't say anything because of the rule you have not to interfere.

ZWICK: I would say we'd probably interfere. I would say that there have been many moments in the midst of what might appear to be a—it's much more of a guideline than a rule. It's a guideline so as to promote an ease of commerce, but "passionate" always rules for us. And I would risk his displeasure in suggesting something if I felt it would really serve the enterprise. And however much he might be pissed off by my intrusion, if he believes it to finally be a good thing, he would end up welcoming it. I believe the same would be true in reverse.

Longworth: Yes, and for the record, his exact words were if you interfered, he would tell you to "fuck off"!

ZWICK: He would, but, by the way, what I would say is he would tell me to "fuck off," then he might likely do what I suggested. (*Laughter.*)

Longworth: Let's talk about the workplace relationships of you guys and your wives. All four of you worked together on *thirtysomething*, then, even today, your wife, Liberty, still works with you and Marshall on *Once and Again*. It looks like to me that you're married to two writers. So does that make you a bigamist?

ZWICK: It also means that I'm polymorphically perverse. (*Laughter.*) This has been the subject of conversation in my marriage. You know, the person to whom you reveal your innermost self is certainly a marriage, and so I'm not sure that one really reveals all of one's self ever to any one person. So I guess if there are two people in my life with whom I am truly intimate, that's not necessarily a contradiction.

Longworth: Is it true that when you and Marshall were preparing for a pitch meeting in which you still *had* no pitch, that it was your wife, Liberty, who helped you come up with the idea for *thirtysomething?*

ZWICK: In the time that we were coming up with the idea, and it was in the eleventh hour, we might have had this incubatory sense of talking about the world around us. But my wife is a very close observer of the foibles and emotional lives of our orbit, and she certainly encouraged us to believe that the things that we cared about in our personal life might also be the stuff of art. And she did say, "Look at this time, and think about when that happened, and think of how telling that was." So she was certainly at the heart of that decision. Those decisions are never made in a moment. It's not "Eureka!" But the show that we're doing now is the legacy of a ten-year conversation that followed *thirtysomething*. And *thirtysomething* itself was the legacy of ten years of conversations of writers and directors that had preceded it.

Longworth: And so, I guess there will be a "sixtysomething" TV show later.

ZWICK: Yeah, and a friend of mine said the rock band would be called "The Incontinentals." (*Laughter.*)

Longworth: Speaking of marriage and relationships, after viewing *Once and Again* for the first time, I'm thinking, 50 percent of the people who've been married have been through a divorce.

ZWICK: And the rest of the people are the children of divorce.

Longworth: So does that mean you'll have a built-in audience, or are you afraid that those who can relate to what you're writing won't want to be reminded of it?

ZWICK: I can't, and I refuse to ever try to operate in anticipation of some unknown embrace or renunciation. It would just so chill my process. I just have to do what I do and hope that it reaches people.

Longworth: But look, you know it's going to be a critical success. So that's why my question was so pointed toward the everyday guy who's been through a divorce.

ZWICK: It's probably more important about the everyday gal. I mean, "the suits," that's what they care about.

Longworth: They also care about content. Let's talk about Standards and Practices. How have those limits and mores changed from the time you were doing *thirtysomething* until today?

ZWICK: Oh, my God. It's a very different world, I think. There are still limitations. Ironically, one of the limitations that remains is what I believe is one of the most innocuous, which is language. I believe that content is obviously much more important than language in terms of profanity. The license that one has to explore topics and explore them in a way that would have been taboo less than ten years ago is enormous, and that's a cause for real celebration on our part, and also great abuse on others.

Longworth: But on *thirtysomething* you once showed two gay men in bed together.

ZWICK: Yes, and now it seems that the description of and the dramatization of homosexual relationships is something that is in the currency of the culture—certainly of the TV culture.

Longworth: Did you and Marshall catch hell for that incident? Did you lose ad revenues?

ZWICK: In fact, all of the advertisers threatened to pull out—pardon my choice of phrase. (*Both laugh.*) The network supported us and aired the episode and then capitulated and agreed not to rerun the episode. So they took a high road, and then a conciliatory road. It was interesting, they felt that they had stood up and done the right thing and yet they couldn't continue to pay a price for it that was financially punitive. They had already taken the hit for it. So they certainly didn't allow themselves to be browbeaten by those who protested, but neither were they willing to pay one nickel more in financial price than they had to for their good works. I remember a conversation—it might have been with Bob Iger—where he said, "I hope you guys can be OK with this, because we stood up for it the first time, and we're going to choose not to do it again." I think what they knew is that had they backed down the first time, we would have publicly excoriated them, and that would have been embarrassing to them, and difficult. But perhaps our willingness to not hold their hand over the flame was what he was talking about.

Longworth: Let's go from one extreme to another, from gay men in bed to family values. Are you encouraged by the deal the WB made with its advertisers to put up money to develop family scripts? Do you think that's good for the industry, or are you concerned that it could start a trend toward advertiser control of content?

ZWICK: That's very interesting, and it's a longer conversation having to do with what television has become. The combination of television program ownership by networks is, I think, much more to the heart of the future than advertiser control. I think that the notion of this vertical integration whereby the FCC allows them to own more programming and own more numbers of affiliates—that's where the future seems to be headed, more than advertisers controlling content, at least in my reading of it. I'm not a great scholar of it, but the trend that I see has to do with content being determined by these huge integrated companies who find several venues and outlets for their properties, and that that may have an effect, rather than—I don't see many more incursions such as the one you're describing from Warner Brothers. [*Once and Again* is the only Disney-owned program in the 1999–2000 ABC lineup, which some people believe is the reason *NYPD Blue* was nearly bumped from its time slot in favor of the new drama.]

Longworth: At the Museum of Television and Radio in New York, you said, "Ambivalence is one of the last great taboo subjects [on television]. People are terrified of inner conflict." If that's the case, why are you so attracted to those kinds of stories and formats?

ZWICK: It's almost as though it's a kind of litmus among people that the preoccupation with or the ennobling of the inner experience of life is a kind of defining characteristic of some people, and the resistance or the devaluation of that is another. In other words, I know many people, friends, who think that the point of life is to get on with life, not to spend too much time or energy examining either the past or the present interactions, and don't spend an undue amount of time scrutinizing that which might have motivated your behavior.

Longworth: It's too much work.

ZWICK: It's too much work, and it doesn't give them pleasure. It seems narcissistic to them. It seems oddly useless, and doesn't necessarily further their joy and experience of life. I don't judge these people or blame them, and I include some members of my family among them. It's just that there's another group of people for whom the examined life is finally the only one that they can be comfortable living. And I am a lifelong member of that particular club. I spend an undue amount of time thinking about these things, trying to look inward, talking about them with my friends and family. And I believe in the close examination of life and the interactions and dynamics and relationships between people, that there's an extraordinary amount of joy and riches to be mined.

Longworth: But a less-educated man could sit there, grab his beer, turn on the TV, and say, "Look, I might think about my navel every once in a while, but damn it, I don't want to watch a TV show about a belly button being thought about.

ZWICK: And, you know, God bless that man, because that guy has been just as seminally important to the creation of this country and its culture and to popular entertainment as anybody else. And I too, by the way, have made movies that are much less introspective—muscular in the way that movies are wonderful when they're muscular in the storytelling. And I just think, though, that, much scarier than vampires or icebergs or serial killers is ambivalence. I just know that the contradictory feelings that we have inside the dark corners, the shadow sides of our personalities, is something that is common to all of us, and when you are unwilling to acknowledge that aspect of your character, it can bite you in the ass. And there's some real value, and I would say political value, in talking about the inconsistencies and contradictions and frailties of people—that only with a willingness to do that can certain things in this society take place: things that involve empathy, things that involve a diminishing of the kind of hostility and violence that exists among people. I mean, there is a kind of deep politics involved in trying to learn, trying to write about, the dialectic of one's experience of life.

Longworth: You write, produce, and direct some shows and films that are introspective, while others have, as you say, muscularity. If someone were viewing a sampling of your work for the first time, and there were no credits on screen, when the viewing was over, how would he know that he was watching an Ed Zwick creation, keeping in mind that he might have just watched *Glory, Shakespeare in Love, thirtysomething,* and *The Siege* back to back?

ZWICK: I don't know. It's a hard thing to ask someone to describe their own work. But I do know that even in the pieces of scale that I've done in which plot has a strong role and historical period or context is central, I think more central always is a character or characters in some dilemma, sometimes moral, sometimes emotional with people who are forced to examine themselves in some kind of raw or truthful way. I am interested in those moments, whether in dramatic ones or highly introspective ones in which people reveal their innermost heart.

Longworth: So is there a consistent theme throughout your work?

ZWICK: I don't know—I'm just speculating.

Longworth: Well, let me try this from a different angle. How has your film style affected your television work, and vice versa?

ZWICK: You know, I honestly believe that it's all about the storytelling. I think you use different colors and the size of the brushes is different and the amount of money and time is different, and yet, what you learn about the beginnings, middles, and ends of things, and movements and the narrative movements and the juxtapositions is absolutely the same. I really try not to approach one any differently than I would approach the other, and that's not to suggest that one's camera work or one's rhythms might not be totally different, but the central conceits of "now I'm going to sit you down and tell you this story," this notion of talking to people one at a time in the dark, this idea of letting you inside of something that up to that moment you've been outside of, or take you some place that you've never been before—that's the same.

Longworth: Let's talk about racial diversity for a moment. Here you are a guy who helped make Denzel Washington a superstar and gave Andre Braugher a break. Fast forward to 1999, and you find yourself attending press functions where you and ABC are defending your record on diversity, so to speak. What's wrong with this picture?

ZWICK: Well, those questions, as best as I can judge them, were all asked of me by white, middle-class journalists. Television—well, let's talk about art. Art is a mirror, and I think when you see a lack of diversity on television, it reflects a lack of diversity in society, let's be really honest. And so there's no surprise in that. I think you can truthfully find a way to talk about all sorts of different ethnic combinations—the black middle class is woefully underrepresented by network television, except in sitcoms. That's a real omission and yet, finally, what will be determinant of these things is not any boycott or affir-matively active redress, but rather the economic bottom line, which fuels everything in television. And that's the truth. Steven Bochco is talking about a hospital show coming on in midseason about an inner-city hospital which is staffed, as I understand it, by blacks and Hispanics. That show, if it is a won-derful show, will be the way to address this issue because it's going to be telling a truth, and, I hope, telling that truth in an entertaining and artful way. That's the way to do it, not through tokenism, and not through some arbitrary, historical redress to try and serve the agendas of a bunch of squawking jour-nalists who, three weeks from now, will have forgotten about diversity and will be writing about something else.

Longworth: Turning from one issue that divides us as a nation to one that divides millions of homes every year. You're a child of divorce. Is doing *Once and Again* some kind of cathartic exercise for you?

ZWICK: This is not about my parents, just as it's not about Marshall's marriage. But I certainly have a particular sympathy for the kids in this dra-matic situation that we've created. I think that I have a privileged view based on some painful experience. All writing is catharsis, but there have been many other and more important means of catharsis in my life that have pre-ceded this. What you try to do is to take the base metal of your experience and spin it in some kind of alchemical process into the gold of your craft. And sometimes that's cathartic and sometimes it's just work.

Longworth: Would your mom have been surprised at all of the things you've accomplished from '83 onward?

ZWICK: Obviously, it's a great regret and lament of my life that my mom's not alive to have seen a lot of these things. I don't believe that she would be surprised—what I mean is by my willingness to talk about things that were personal.

Longworth: Because she encouraged that trait?

ZWICK: Yeah, I think that she understood that a lot of what art is is look-ing within, so as to make some kind of joyous noise. No, I don't think she would be surprised.

Longworth: Final question. You've won Emmys and Oscars and all sorts of awards. What's left for you to do, adapt *The Siege* into a musical so you can win a Tony?

ZWICK: (*Laughs.*) It's funny, but I really only want what I have, Jim, which is the privilege of making a living as an artist. It's something that I dreamed of for a very long time, and never imagined that I would have either the opportunities or the recompense. But the privilege just to surround myself with these unbelievably talented people, all of whom are as committed as I am and who are willing to recognize me as their peer, it's a blessing far beyond any imagining. And with it, comes a responsibility that is to do the best, work the hardest, try and earn what I've already been given. I happen to like work. I happen to be filled up by the process of creating. The notion that I'm paid to write stories—that is constantly astonishing to me, even while it is constantly difficult.

11

BARRY LEVINSON | Rebel with a cause

Barry Levinson. PHOTOGRAPHER, PHIL CARUSO.
COURTESY OF NEW LINE CINEMA.

TELEVISION CREDITS

1969	*The Lohman and Barkley Show* (KNBC)
1970	*The Tim Conway Comedy Hour* (CBS)

1972	*The Marty Feldman Comedy Machine* (ABC)
1972	*The John Byner Comedy Hour* (CBS)
1973	*Comedy News* (ABC)
1974–75	*The Carol Burnett Show* (CBS)
1975	*Hot L Baltimore* (ABC)
1976	*The Rich Little Show* (NBC)
1978	*Peeping Times* (NBC)
1983	*Diner* (CBS pilot)
1983	*Stopwatch: Thirty Minutes Investigative Ticking* (HBO)
1984	*The Investigators* (HBO)
1987	*Harry* (ABC)
1990	*Time Warner Presents the Earth Day Special* (Warner Bros.)
1992–98	*Homicide: Life on the Street* (NBC)
1997–	*Oz* (HBO)
1999–2000	*The Hoop Life* (Showtime)
2000	*The Beat* (UPN)

〰 〰 〰

On April 29, 1962, at a dinner honoring a group of Nobel Prize winners, President Kennedy observed, "I think it's truly the most extraordinary collection of talent . . . that has ever been gathered together at the White House, with the possible exception of when Thomas Jefferson dined alone." JFK's implication was that Jefferson was a "Renaissance man," whose knowledge and abilities extended to countless disciplines.

In entertainment, the same could be said of Barry Levinson. He is an Emmy Award–winning television director and an Academy Award winner for Best Direction. He has three Peabodys for TV drama, and one of his films received an Oscar for Best Motion Picture. He has been nominated for Oscars and has received Emmys for screenwriting. He has acted with Mel Brooks and Dustin Hoffman, and he has appeared in comedy and drama, on both the small and big screens.

To put it into perspective, if every major Hollywood trade association went on strike at the very same time, Barry would have to pull picket duty at about a dozen different sites. Not bad for a third-generation American who, after seeing *Rebel Without a Cause* for the first time, remembers "identifying with that feeling of, God, what am I going to do with my life."

Barry has done much with his life. Though there may be a bit of the rebel in him, he is not without a cause. His is a life of telling stories, but always truthfully and always thought-provokingly.

David Kalat, in his book *Homicide: Life on the Street—An Unofficial Companion*, writes, "Levinson has consistently chosen to engage in challenging, difficult, experimental projects instead of [the] play-it-safe approaches of his peers." Barry has also created challenges for himself as well as for those who view his work, in films or on television. It is perhaps ironic, though, that a man so well known for his film work has logged more time in television than any other active creator/producer except Aaron Spelling. It is also interesting that a man first known for his comedic genius is generally recognized for his serious work on television and in the movies. Tom Fontana comments: "Barry loves television. He loves television. It's great that a guy like Barry Levinson could embrace our medium as passionately as he does his films. . . . There are a lot of big-name movie directors who get into television sporadically, and I think they do it for the money, as opposed to Barry who seems to really do it because he wants to. He sees television as an opportunity to tell different kinds of stories than he can in films."

In Levinson's semiautobiographical film *Avalon,* (which follows the lives of first-generation Americans and their descendants), Sam, the family patriarch, watches as everyone stares in wonder at nothing but a test pattern on a new invention called television. Sam says, "You better hope they start getting some more interesting programs."

At times over the past decade, it may have seemed as though a test pattern would be better than many of the mindless comedies and homogenous magazine shows that we were left with, but, thanks to Barry Levinson, programs are more interesting and television is more compelling.

At the end of the twentieth century, America was obsessed with compiling lists. Who was the best baseball player of the past hundred years? What individual had the most impact on history? Some lists even speculated about imaginary match-ups: Who's better? Ali or Louis, Ruth or Aaron? Everywhere we turned, some columnist was making a big fuss over Orson Welles because he directed, wrote, and acted in several films. Well, annoying as such exercises in futility can be, I am compelled to enter the fray. Pardon the emotionalism, but in a head-to-head competition, Levinson kicks Welles's butt.

Levinson is a rebel who also works within the system. He holds traditions dear but breaks the rules whenever a story requires it. He is a creative talent who does one thing at the time well and several things all at once, spectacularly. Barry's versatility is born of passion and adaptability—he is a virtual melting pot of talent, and that comes as no accident.

Born in Baltimore, Maryland, in 1942, Barry lived amid first- and second-generation Jewish immigrants in an area known as Forest Park, where his grandparents had settled in the early part of the century. Barry's father owned an appliance store and a carpet store, and, as a result, the extended family lived comfortably.

In *Levinson on Levinson*, Barry says, "I lived with my parents and grandparents in the same house, so I think I saw a much wider spectrum of the adult world than most American kids of my generation."

Growing up, Barry's favorite "sports" were watching television and going to the movies. He was particularly taken with film comedy. After graduating from Forest Park High School, Barry eventually enrolled at Baltimore Junior Community College, then dropped out and attempted unsuccessfully to sell cars and encyclopedias. A viewing of *The Young Philadelphians* inspired him to pursue law at Mount Vernon College, but that was short-lived as well. Returning to junior college, Barry became serious about his study of broadcasting, and was able to transfer to American University's School of Broadcast Journalism.

In 1963 Barry got his first real job in television working at WTOP-TV in Washington, D.C. There, his duties ranged from anchoring the morning news to working hand puppets on *The Ranger Hal Show*. He also gained experience in station promotion and sales. Then, in 1967, he journeyed to California hoping to get a job at a Los Angeles TV station. But while he was job hunting, Barry decided to take acting classes at the Oxford Theater, where he met future TV star Craig T. Nelson (*Coach*). The two hams hit it off, dropped out, and tried their hand at the comedy club circuit. Before long, they were appearing on a local variety show that aired weekly on KNBC-TV. Levinson and Nelson's writing and performing of off-the-wall sketches landed Barry jobs with a number of network shows, including *The Tim Conway Comedy Hour, Peeping Times* (a *60 Minutes* spoof starring David Letterman), and *The Carol Burnett Show*, for which he won three Emmys.

In 1976 Levinson began an association with Mel Brooks, which yielded two comedy films, *Silent Movie* and *High Anxiety*. He wrote and acted in both, and in *High Anxiety* appeared as a crazed bellhop. After having been angered by a hotel guest's (Brooks) repeated request for a newspaper, the bellhop (in a send up of *Psycho*) attacks Brooks in the shower with a rolled up newspaper, shouting, "Here's your stupid newspaper. Happy now? Happy? Happy now?" Barry's comedic timing was impeccable. Tom Fontana admits, "The truth is, Barry is one of the funniest people that I've ever met."

Something serious came from those zany films. As David Kalat writes, "Brooks encouraged the young writer to make a film based on the stories he was always telling about the ten boys with whom he hung out in his childhood." The film became *Diner*, and overnight Barry's reputation as a Hollywood-caliber writer/director was made. He also collaborated with his first wife, Valerie Curtain, on the screenplay for *Best Friends*, a film starring Burt Reynolds and Goldie Hawn as a bickering, married writing team. The film was loosely based on the Levinsons themselves. In 1982 Barry and Valerie divorced. A year later, Barry pitched a TV series based on *Diner* to CBS, who promptly aired the pilot, then killed the project.

What they didn't kill, however, was Barry's spirits and his determination to write, direct, and produce films, including two more in his "Baltimore" series, *Tin Men* and *Avalon*. Taken as a trilogy, the three semiautobiographical movies told us much about the immigrant experience in America, and about how immigrants helped adapt to and shape American culture. Along the way, Levinson also directed a number of other films, including *The Natural* (with Robert Redford), *Good Morning, Vietnam* (with Robin Williams), *Bugsy* (with Warren Beatty), and *Rain Man*, the Dustin Hoffman/Tom Cruise classic that won Oscars for Best Picture, Best Direction, and Best Screenplay.

In 1992 it was back to television for Barry with an innovative cop show set in, where else, Baltimore. *Homicide: Life on the Street* broke new ground for TV police dramas, in part because of its lack of melodrama and violence and because of its stark, manic film style. Barry the "rebel" first approached John Masius (*St. Elsewhere, Touched by an Angel, Providence*) and John Tinker (*St. Elsewhere, Chicago Hope, Judging Amy*) about serving as executive producers and writers, but the pair declined and suggested that he talk to Tom Fontana. Fontana reveals that "my favorite thing about Barry is that he comes at the world from his own unique perspective. So what he's able to do with people that he works with is . . . with very few words . . . send you in a direction that you would have never thought of yourself. In terms of the shooting style [of *Homicide*], I remember once we had a conversation where he said, 'I don't understand why people take so long to light for television. It's not like every television set is the same all over the country. So here we are trying to get the exact lighting and somebody's watching it on a five-inch screen in their bathroom.' And so, that allowed us a certain kind of liberation on *Homicide* to just shoot it—that kind of guerilla style that we had, where it wasn't about being pretty, it was about being real."

Barry is a disciplined writer, but, rebel that he is, he never works from an outline—he just follows his instincts and those of his characters.

In *Levinson on Levinson*, Barry says, "I try to work as quickly as possible in a fairly regimented way, starting around ten-thirty in the morning and writing until one-thirty, breaking for lunch, and then I'll write until six or seven o'clock in the evening. I'll play music constantly until I get there, trying to go as fast as possible, because all these voices are talking and these events happening, and I'm just trying to keep up with it. In a sense, I'm just taking dictation."

Barry won an Emmy for best direction in the first season of *Homicide*, and he and Tom went on to form the Levinson/Fontana Company, whose next effort would be a prison drama. Barry the "rebel" was at it again—breaking new ground with *Oz* for HBO.

Chris Albrecht of HBO says, "Barry is one of those classic feature film directors who got their start in television, and I think that's a great asset for a director or a producer, because they learn their craft by actually doing it over and over again. . . . What he's bringing us is not only that skill, but a tremendous cache, which goes along with the additional skills that he's accumulated. Not even a handful of people have that."

And what is "Barry the Rebel's" assessment of *Oz?* "There is no hero. There's just all these people who are . . . flawed, and exceed our level of villainy. I think it's a combination of good storytelling, and very interesting characters. People say we don't know how to relate to (prisoners), but we don't always have to know how to relate to everyone. I think there's enough to be captivated in the storytelling" (*Oz* on-line, 1999).

Levinson continued his storytelling on the small and big screens, taking time out from his two series to make films such as *Sphere* (with Sharon Stone and Dustin Hoffman) and *Wag the Dog* (with Hoffman and Robert DeNiro). The Levinson/Fontana Company also produced *The Hoop Life* for Showtime, a drama about the fictional New England Knights pro basketball team, and *The Beat*, a police drama for UPN that follows the lives of two New York City cops. A *Homicide* movie also aired in February 2000.

Today, Barry lives with his wife, Diana, and two sons, Sam and Jack. At the time of our second interview, NBC had just announced the cancellation of *Homicide*, and the special two-hour movie was in the works for February 2000.

Longworth: I told my wife that in order to effectively write the chapter on you, I would need to go out to L.A. and spend some time with Sharon Stone for background. My wife informed me that this book didn't have to be published.

LEVINSON: (*Laughs.*)

Longworth: I noticed in the film *Avalon* that *The Cisco Kid* was playing on Jules's TV set, so it prompted me to ask you what TV shows you enjoyed in the fifties, and which ones influenced your career?

LEVINSON: There are different ones. I think *Naked City* was probably one of the best dramas—it was a cop drama—but one of the great dramas, period. I think it was extraordinary what they did on a weekly basis. Some nights they drifted into some of these very personal tales, and I remember some of the titles, *The Day the Man Who Killed the Ants Is Coming* (*Both laugh.*) and titles that were so unusual, like *The One Marked Hot Brings Cold.* And they were just some extraordinary pieces. I think that's what stands out in my mind.

Longworth: And there's maybe some of that in *Oz* and *Homicide* and some of your other works?

LEVINSON: Probably, probably. I mean, I think in the fact that we try to not just go straight down the line and deal with cops, or do *Oz* as a prison drama as we know it. So I look at *Naked City* as one of the first shows that broke a lot of the rules.

Longworth: While we were up at the Museum of Television and Radio in New York, Fontana, Dick Wolf, and the other guys talked a little bit about TV violence and violence in our society. The shootings at Littleton had recently occurred. Tom said NBC had made you change the order of a couple of episodes of *Homicide*. A *Buffy* episode was shelved for a while too. I was thinking, one of your sons is a teenager, the other a preteen. What if Tom had told NBC "Screw you, we're playing the shows in order," or the folks at Buffy told WB that the violent prom scene was going forward. Would your boys have been in some way adversely affected or influenced by that? What's your view on this issue in particular and censorship in general?

LEVINSON: Well, the episode—the one that we had—I believe had really almost nothing to do with Littleton. So, in that case, I don't think it was pertinent to the situation. Sometimes you may be doing an episode where real life cross paths and sometimes—I mean, if your show has something to do with airplane crashes, and there happens to be a plane crash that week, you don't really need to have this episode running while this whole thing is taking place. There's validity to it, the mood at that particular moment, and the effects that it has on the population. So, sometimes I think it makes sense. I don't see any great harm in that.

Longworth: What about the effect on your kids?

LEVINSON: From our episode?

Longworth: Maybe not that show specifically, but also the dangers we might face from Congress getting involved.

LEVINSON: Well, I think the entire thing is a little bit like there's this giant mountain that needs to be dealt with, and we're still panning for the little stones at the bottom of the hill. I mean, it's a much greater, much more complex issue. Congressmen basically don't really want to get to the problem. They basically just want to get the attention and ultimately to stir up something that, you know, builds their image in their community. And that's why you see so little relevant legislation that's done. They can carry on and talk all they want about trying to resolve things, but they do very little. All they do periodically is poke their heads out when an issue takes place. And all of the sudden they begin to spout because the thirty-second sound bite is there and that's what they do. Because they don't deal with these issues in a real comprehensive fashion. You know, in twenty-some days the Congress at the beginning of our country in the 1780s ultimately came up with a concept of the branches of government and how the representation would work, and the Supreme Court. They did that in twenty-some days. You know, these people [today's congressmen], what they do, most of the time, is nonsense—it's words to get attention and very little substance. So every so often things flare up and they just stick their heads out and try and catch a little wave of support, and then they go about their business of fund raising again.

Longworth: Not that this is a book about film, but I keep wanting to tie in television references from *Avalon*. We've been speaking of violence and violence on TV and television as a disruptive force. I can't help but think back when Jules was talking about TV advertising, and it seemed to have a real influence over the entire movie. Indirectly, it was the fact that they bought TV ads that sunk the store, because they then didn't have enough money for fire insurance. And later, at the cemetery, Sam says something like, "It's not a family anymore," and you immediately dissolve to Jules's house, where nobody is talking or communicating—they're all eating dinner by the television set. I guess in a protracted way, I'm trying to tie all this together, and ask you were you telling us then, ahead of time, and do you believe now, that television is indeed an inherently disruptive force in the family and in society, whether for good or bad?

LEVINSON: You know, I don't like to talk too much about a movie when it's first put out. You put your movie out and that's it, and it speaks to what it is. I used to read things about "it's the story of the immigrant experience in America," which I never thought it was. The point of *Avalon*, I thought, was about the death of the storyteller. And the storyteller was really the head of the family, who told the tales and passed on the traditions, etc., and he was replaced by a new storyteller that was in a box, and its stories were different. And what it did was it ultimately dismantled many of the foundation pieces of the family. That's what I thought the piece was about. And very early in the movie the box came in a package with a nice bow, and by the end of the movie, it had changed everything in its path.

Longworth: And yet, you've been successful in television, and that's why I had to come right out and ask you—

LEVINSON: Yeah. Because it has to do with—it's not like "gee, TV's terrible, let's get rid of it." You have to deal with the issues of all of the things that ultimately influence us in the inventions of the twentieth century. I mean, when the automobile was invented, we said, "Gosh, it gets us from one place to another and it's cheap transportation." And, in one of the earliest ads, if you've ever seen them, it says "The horseless carriage—the end of pollution"—(*Laughs.*) the irony of that. So the automobile was a terrific invention; however, millions of people have died because of it. It has changed the landscape of the world. It has also created enormous environmental problems on land and in air. There's the good and the bad, that's the nature of things. But what you have to do is say, "No, no, no, you just can't have the road here if it's going to completely destroy this community. It'll go right through the center of it, we have to find something that makes better sense." So you begin now to realize cause and effect. There's cause and there's effect all of the time. Television is more difficult to see because it's much more subtle, it's dealing with our heads. There are great things that come from television, and there's a negative side of television. What is it like when you put a three-year-old on the floor and at every seven minutes in one of these kiddy shows, they get a barrage of about eight different things they should have? And they keep coming [to you], "I'd like to buy this, Daddy. Can we get that?" And you have to explain you just can't get everything you want.

Longworth: Yeah, *Ranger Hal* says to buy this.

LEVINSON: Right. You have to ultimately put it into a context and you have to explain to the kids. And if you don't explain to the children, what happens? What happens when all of a sudden "I want this, I want this and if I can't have it, I'll take it!"

Longworth: Speaking of kids shows and *Ranger Hal*, I worked on a similar show called *The Old Rebel Show* down in North Carolina and one day I got out from behind the camera and tried to help with the puppets. It was a disaster. I don't have hand/eye coordination—I was trying to watch the monitor and I knocked down the wall and the kids saw everything and it ruined it for them. So I was banned from doing puppets after that.

LEVINSON: We had that happen on *The Ranger Hal* show.

Longworth: Actually, my main job was to mop up under the bleachers after the show from where the kids got excited and peed all over the floor.

LEVINSON: (*Laughs.*)

Longworth: Fontana said to me that everybody has a story to tell, so when did you first know that you had stories to tell? I mean, I get this sense that you were always a funny guy, but in terms of having dramatic stories to tell, at what point did you know you had *that* in you?

LEVINSON: Well, I never really thought of ever being a writer, because I never knew any writer. I never knew anyone who worked in television and movies or any of that. So I didn't think about that. I used to write some stuff, for papers at school. And I guess if you were to try and trace it in a way, I guess that's the first time that I began to understand this connection that you have with an audience in terms of what you write and how they react. And so we used to have this professor in college, and he would read your paper in this creative writing class. And up to that point I never did particularly well in school because I never really cared about the grade, you know, if you got an A or a B or a C, it doesn't matter to me. And you just had to pass, that was all. So he was going to read *my* paper. The idea that I would write something and afterwards someone would say to me, "Gee, that was really boring, I could hardly stay awake," but I felt this obligation, so therefore, I worked on this paper in a way so that the other students wouldn't be bored. And, then, later, I began to think, Oh, if you write this, you can get them involved. They can laugh or they can wonder what's going to happen. But I didn't think of that up front, I just was trying not to be boring in the classroom.

Longworth: Let me skip ahead to *Homicide*, which was never boring. I remember when you guys brought in Robin Williams for a guest shot. The media says, "Williams comes on show. Friend of Levinson's to boost ratings." And the show did well. So I have to ask in retrospect, why wouldn't you have called in favors every week during sweeps—Robert Redford, Dustin Hoffman, Sharon Stone—so that in February you get a four million rating every time out?

LEVINSON: Well, there's a lot of different kind of reasons. I mean, the nature of the show is such that it's not always a real star vehicle program. I mean, Robin happened to mesh nicely, it happened to be that kind of a role. You could say it was a star turn, but it wasn't forcing the show out of its normal orbit. Therefore, to start to do that would ultimately be to change the show. And ultimately, *Homicide* had to live or die based on its own vision.

Longworth: It would have become *Burke's Law* with guest celebrities.

LEVINSON: Yeah.

Longworth: When Giancarlo was hired for *Homicide,* he said he was attracted to the show because it was the most "film like television show" he had ever seen. Was that a compliment to your experiences both in film and television, particularly film, and how you brought that over to television? Or was that a compliment in general to the overall team effort? What was he talking about?

LEVINSON: Well, I never asked him. I think it applies to—there are two parts to it—I think it applies to the visual style that goes back to how we established the show in the pilot. And the other is the nature of the writing. Because the writing is much more complex, films of today are becoming more simplistic. I think that the way that we did it in terms of the writing and the way we shoot it, it became a unique acting experience.

Longworth: Is it true that of the two of you guys [Fontana and Levinson] that it was you who wanted to shop *Homicide* around after NBC canceled it, but Tom was burned out? Any truth to that?

LEVINSON: Well, I'm happy on one hand. Look, we had seven years of 120-some episodes, whatever. And we had an effect on television—doing a show that really makes a mark. We did that—we accomplished all that. And I think you can be satisfied with that. I was frustrated in a sense with what NBC was doing with the show in the final year by never advertising it, and then replacing us with reruns of *Law & Order,* and not even saying "*Homicide* returns next week," so that they would completely confuse our audience all the time. *I* didn't know when we were on! Now, if I don't know when we're on, I don't know what the regular viewer's thinking. I was confused: Were we on last night? No, that's the *Law & Order* rerun this week. Not even our *own* reruns, but another show, which I've never heard of [doing] before. So I was very frustrated. One time they ran a spot on *Providence,* saying that we were going to be on that evening, and that particular week we almost beat *20/20.* We beat *Nash Bridges.*

Longworth: Because people were looking for the show.

LEVINSON: Because they knew we were there. NBC, I think, confused the audience so, it didn't know when the hell we were on. And so, I was frustrated by that.

Longworth: And it never seems to change. Fred Silverman once talked about television being taken over by bean counters. In Baker and Dessart's book *Down the Tube,* they talked about how network executives are creating an industry of "imitative mediocrity." And by playing the shell game, and by only broadcasting programs that will be popular right now, do you have a fear that network television (not HBO or Showtime) is moving toward what Baker and Dessart were talking about? In other words, imitative mediocrity is "in" because that's what's going to sell?

LEVINSON: Well, I don't know that it sells. They're losing a share of their audience every year. So I don't know that what they're doing sells, in the final analysis.

Longworth: Describe your collaboration with Tom Fontana and how the creative process works, given that he's always in New York and you're usually in Los Angeles.

LEVINSON: We kind of talk during the week. There are two parts to it. One is we talk at the end of the year for a while about what we're going to do for the coming season—what changes are we going to make, casting, storytelling, etc., and we kind of lay out a general direction of things that we want to explore during the course of the year. And then, that gets broken down more specifically, and we talk on and off during the course of the week about different things. One of the great things in us getting together is I think we have a very similar sensibility . . . I can't even tell you a situation where I think we differed about what we should be going for. I can't remember any creative time when we were at odds about any given situation. So I think that we are very connected in that respect. We also feel that, say, if you apply it to *St. Elsewhere* [and *Homicide*], you know, all shows are not going to be in the top ten, certain types of work you do isn't going to fit that sensibility. Not that there's anything wrong with that, but sometimes you can say, "Look, we can work over in this area here, and artistically it's satisfying and economically it makes sense for the network." And that's fine. And I think we're both comfortable in that respect. Now I think that somehow [if] you turn out a show and it becomes a big hit, it is that kind of a wonderful accident.

Longworth: How do two funny guys apply their sense of humor to television drama?

LEVINSON: I think what you do is—it's the honesty of it. The humor that does emerge in *Homicide* is very honest. We're not looking for the joke, we're not looking to make a situation funny, but some situations in life, in dramatic terms, are humorous. Now, you make a decision—do you back away from it, and make it melodramatic, or do you say, "Look, these aspects of humor are relevant, and sometimes very insightful." And so, I think that we take that on and allow it to be part of a particular subject matter that we're exploring.

Longworth: Why haven't you and Tom teamed up to do a movie?

LEVINSON: Well, that would be great if we were able to find time to where that connected. Because a writer's a writer. Sometimes things get categorized when they really shouldn't—but if you write, you write [whether it's TV or films]. One more thing about TV. Television is in an interesting phase right now, because the funny thing is you always say to yourself, "Why wouldn't a network want to try something that was really different?" Because the worst thing that would happen is that it won't get a good rating. Now, they do that with these mediocre shows that they think are going to do well, and they get a bad rating anyway. So if you try something that is really innovative, you won't do any worse than the shows that you're putting on that don't do well. I don't understand what the big scare is, because it's not like you're going to fall off the earth. You'll see them try a show that goes completely into the toilet and that was the most mediocre piece of garbage they could put on television, and you say, "Well, then, why not try to be innovative? Maybe that may work some time." Very seldom do they want to step up to that.

Longworth: *Hoop Life* and *The Beat* . . . did you consider going to the networks with them?

LEVINSON: We didn't go to the network with them. It just sort of evolved out of discussions that we had, and we went our own course. And you also get to the point where the networks don't do this kind of stuff, so why even bother to have a phone call with them.

Longworth: So give me a one-liner on *The Beat*.

LEVINSON: *The Beat* is a cross between a cop show and *Diner*. Because it's just dealing with their personal lives and problems and dating, whether they should be married, or that kind of thing. And they happen to be police-men. You know, policemen aren't bred on a farm somewhere. (*Laughs.*) They're like people with all of the same characteristics of everyone else.

Longworth: They're like people—what a great line.

LEVINSON (*Laughs.*)

Longworth: Are these new shows going to have sort of a Levinson-type edge to them in terms of humor, or will they be edgier like *Oz?*

LEVINSON: I can't speak as much to *The Hoop Life,* because ultimately Showtime wanted to shoot it in Canada because of the economics of it, and both Tom and I said we can't really supervise this show that's up in Canada. We thought it should have been done in Baltimore or New York. So we are going to do it, but we're not going to be directly involved on a weekly basis in that way.

Longworth: Since you and I came up in local television, let's talk about technology for a moment, HDTV specifically. When color TV hit the market, it was years before most people could afford a set, and about a decade before the price was reasonable. But with HDTV, you're talking five thousand to ten thousand dollars for a TV, and yet the network guys are putting pressure on local affiliates to convert, and they're saying within two years everyone in America will have an HDTV set. Is this something the public is really going to invest in? And is it going to increase production costs for producers like you? Will it have any effect on what you're doing, since you're going through nontraditional routes anyway? Will it just affect network affiliates?

LEVINSON: Well, ultimately, there's going to be new technology. It's not going to stay away, so eventually the technology will change. Things eventually won't be shot on film, it'll all be on digital, and you'll create it and make it look like videotape, or gritty like some kind of movies. You'll make those decisions digitally. So all of this technology will come into play, and eventually high definition will basically be the format, I would assume. And its cost will ultimately become manageable. It's not going to stay up there or it'll never happen.

Longworth: Are you one of these guys that pines for the days of live TV, and asks, Can we ever go back to that?

LEVINSON: I doubt it. It's not the fact that it was just live TV that I would lament losing, because, you know, things continue to evolve. It was the fact that we told better stories. I mean, if you think about it, too much of story-telling today is about somebody has a gun and they're coming to kill you.

That's like a form for everywhere. And we tell too many of our stories that way. If you go back to live television, you know, *Requiem for a Heavyweight*, some of the ones that are famous, they were like stories. That one was about a failing fighter. This one [*Marty*] was about a guy who was a butcher and had a hard time dating. Can you imagine trying to do that today? So what's the big hook? Well, here's this guy, and he's not a particularly attractive guy and he wants to date and he's having a hard time. We used to tell a wider range of human stories than we do today. We've kind of gimmicked it up, and we've added all kinds of like bells and whistles to it, and we don't really tell stories as good as we used to about the common man.

Longworth: When *ER* did their live broadcast, people sort of looked at it and were disappointed because, ironically, they had already gotten used to great postproduction, quick editing. And then you take them back to something live and they think there's something wrong with it.

LEVINSON: Yeah, well, that didn't really make sense. Sometimes there will be live shows and they'll be live because there's a reason for it to be live, you know what I mean? And so, certain events will be handled that way, and if there's a story that needs to be told live and that's the best way to tell the story, then that will happen. But it's the nature of the story that is in jeopardy.

Longworth: With this great sense of humor you have, and your history in TV and films with Mel Brooks and Letterman, why is it, with all your clout, that you haven't developed some television comedies for network or cable? You've produced so many great dramas on film and for television, and yet you have so much comedy in you. Has that part of you disappeared? Will you never do another comedy TV show?

LEVINSON: I would if I were able to do one that's not like some of these sitcoms. If it were different, I would. But too much of it wants to be in a style that I don't particularly care for. I find that the sitcom today is a very kind of tired form. It looks boring to me. It just seems tired. And so I think the sitcom has to evolve from where it is today, just sort of catch up to changing life.

Longworth: But you're not ruling it out?

LEVINSON: No, I would love to do a half hour that had some humor to it if it's done in a way that I felt comfortable with it. I'm just tired of the form. So it hasn't evolved much and so I think that's the reason that holds me up— I wouldn't mind doing it, but I wouldn't want to.

Longworth: But you're also staying so busy. When do you ever have a moment alone to sit down and think of some funny stuff?

LEVINSON: Well, I mean, I do. You sometimes put that into the work that you do. *Wag the Dog* was a piece that emerged out of one of these ideas that came about. So that kind of humor works, but you would probably never get to do that kind of humor on television, you know, 'cause they don't do much of that. So sometimes you have to go away from the form. Sometimes you have to go away from television and say, "OK, look, I can't really do a half-hour form at this point because you're so locked into this tired format that—what am I going to do? Am I going to hit my head against the wall and keep trying to do something?" Look, I tried to do—the network was interested in 1982 or '83 when I did *Diner*—and they said we'd like to do *Diner* as a television series. I said OK, but I'd like to do it the way the movie is, in that kind of humor. And they said, "No, that's fine." And I said, "But you know, if you test this thing, it's not going to test well because the movie didn't even test well initially." And they said, "No, no, we understand." So I did the pilot, shot it, and they said, "You know, it doesn't test too well." (*Both laugh.*) "And because it's so different, it's incompatible with the other shows we have." And I said, "Well, is that *my* problem? I was supposed to, what, make it like the other shows you have? Or why don't you have different kinds of shows, what's wrong with that?" So that was the end of that. We had a terrific cast.

Longworth: And you only shot the pilot, and that was it, right?

LEVINSON: Yeah.

Longworth: Who was in that?

LEVINSON: Michael Madsen, James Spader, Paul Reiser, and the guy who was in *Murphy Brown*, the painter, Robert Pastorali. We had all these young people in the show. But it was quite good, it wasn't bad.

Longworth: Are we going to see you doing any cameos in any TV shows in the future?

LEVINSON: I did a documentary for Showtime about dealing with the millennium; it deals with the future as seen from the twentieth century—kind of interesting piece. And I mean, we're doing these two other shows, so we continue to try to work in our own way.

Longworth: Well, thanks for doing the interview. Basically, I admire you because you could do puppets and I couldn't.

LEVINSON: (*Laughs.*) I did *Marvin Monkey*.

Longworth: *Marvin the Monkey.* You did the voice for him too?

LEVINSON: No, he didn't have a voice.

Longworth: So he was a network executive?

LEVINSON: Yeah, he was just a monkey who did mime.

Longworth: You should have called him Marcel Monkey.

LEVINSON: Yeah. (*Laughs.*)

Longworth: Forgive me, but I have to ask. When you're directing and you're really riding the actors pretty hard, trying to get the most out of them, you badger them and badger them until, finally, they nail it. Have they ever turned to you with a rolled up script and yelled, "Happy? Happy now? Happy?"

LEVINSON: (*Laughs.*) It hasn't happened yet. (*Laughs.*)

MM **12** MM

STEVEN BOCHCO | Legend of the Fall

Steven Bochco. PHOTOGRAPHER, MURRAY D'ATLEY.
COURTESY OF THE PHOTOGRAPHER.

TELEVISION CREDITS

1968–71	*The Name of the Game* (NBC)
1971–77	*Columbo* (NBC)
1971–77	*McMillan and Wife* (NBC)

1972–74	*Banacek* (NBC)
1972	*Lieutenant Shuster's Wife* (ABC movie)
1973	*Double Indemnity* (ABC movie)
1973–74	*Griff* (ABC)
1976–77	*Delvecchio* (CBS)
1975	*The Invisible Man* (NBC)
1978–81	*The White Shadow* (CBS)
1978	*Richie Brockelman, Private Eye* (NBC)
1979–80	*Paris* (NBC)
1979	*Vampire* (ABC movie)
1981–87	*Hill Street Blues* (NBC)
1983	*Bay City Blues* (NBC)
1986–94	*L.A. Law* (NBC)
1987–89	*Hooperman* (ABC)
1989–93	*Doogie Howser, M.D.* (ABC)
1990	*Cop Rock* (ABC)
1991–93	*Civil Wars* (ABC)
1993–	*NYPD Blue* (ABC)
1997	*Brooklyn South* (CBS)
1995–96	*Murder One* (ABC)
2000–	*City of Angels* (CBS)

MW MW MW

In an industry where fame is reserved for actors, Steven Bochco is that rarest of commodities—he is a producer who has achieved celebrity status. To do so, Bochco has evolved into a composite man. He is part Andrew Jackson, part P.T. Barnum, and part John Wooden.

Like Jackson, Bochco has created programs that have appealed to many groups on multiple levels. During his first inaugural, Jackson's White House was overrun by rural rabble who believed that the slang-talking hero was one of their own. But in related fetes, Jackson impressed the social elite with his polished manner and impeccable grammar. His ability to please diverse groups with a quality "program" led to two terms in office, or, as we say in television, a long run.

For better or worse, America has, over the past two decades become a nation of niches, and now, with the five hundred channel universe within our grasp, television has taken the art of shrinking demographics and fragmented audiences to new heights (and lows). Well, thank goodness for Old Hickory, I mean, Old Bochco, a producer who continues to redefine quality programming as something that can have relevance to everyone—not just teenagers to the exclusion of adults. Not just women to the exclusion of men, or whites to the exclusion of blacks.

Like P.T. Barnum, Bochco has become more famous and enduring than have most of his creations, and, like UCLA's John Wooden, he has been able to consistently build dynasties. As a "head coach," Bochco has recruited and nurtured winning teams or ensembles, and he has done so across three decades, first with *Hill Street Blues*, then *L.A. Law*, and now, *NYPD Blue*. Yes, he has had some losing seasons, but they have been rare. Moreover, those losses have still contributed to the industry and to our culture.

In his book *The Last Great Ride*, the late Brandon Tartikoff writes of Bochco, "Even when he failed, his failures were always interesting. He explored characters in a depth not usually seen on TV. He had a great ear for dialogue, and a great eye for the absurd. He took risks." Those risks led to great successes, programs that worked well on multiple levels for a diverse viewership, and which comprised Ivy League writing, world-class acting, and lots of blue-collar appeal. Bochco's programs are "steak dinners" that taste like filet mignon to one person, and hamburger to another, with both palates being satisfied simultaneously.

Bochco is a man of "Peabodys and naked bodies," and that's why we keep "reelecting" him every year, and why everyone turns out to his "inaugurals" every fall.

Jacksonian in his democratic approach to programming, Bochco's face may never grace a twenty-dollar bill, but he has changed the face of television drama forever, and, for that, he is an American legend.

Steven Bochco was born in 1943 in New York City. His mother was a housewife, painter, and designer. There was creativity on the paternal side as well. Steven's father, Rudolph, was an accomplished violinist. In fact, if you watch and listen carefully to the end credits of any Bochco show, you'll see a computer-animated photo of the elder Bochco, and you'll hear a few bars of Vivaldi's "Four Seasons." According to Steven, though, one violinist in the family was enough. "I took one lesson at the hands of my father, and we sort of agreed to disagree. (*Laughs.*) I had no aptitude for it, or no interest in it. And truth be known, he had no interest in me being a musician, because he hated it. He thought being a musician was blood money. He just didn't believe that artists could make a buck, 'cause *he* never did. My dad wanted me to be an engineer."

Steven did inherit a talent for music, and a baritone voice was his instrument of choice, which he developed while attending the High School of Music and Art in New York City. "They had me singing bass in the chorus 'cause I could hit those [low] notes, but I never really had a true bass voice. I had no interest in being a singer, but it was the only way I knew I could get into that school, which is where I wanted to go."

Once accepted into the prestigious school, Bochco began working at his first love—writing. "Well, I always wanted to be a writer. I could always write. My teachers always told me I could write, and so it just sort of seemed clear to me at a very early age that that's what I did better than anything else . . . I just wrote a lot. I wrote short stories, I'd write poems. I always enjoyed the actual act of writing. I enjoyed expressing myself on paper."

Steven tried one year at NYU, then transferred to Carnegie Tech's theater department (now Carnegie Mellon), where he majored in playwriting. "In those days I never thought in terms of film and television. I really did think in terms of theater. I just had no frame of reference for film and television particularly. . . . Oh, I watched everything, but I always translated it into theater terms. When I was a boy, there were all these wonderful anthological dramas on television, *Playhouse 90, Studio One, Chrysler Theatre*. I never really thought of them as TV. I always sort of thought of them as theater—I mean, to the extent that I thought of them at all. And so, I sort of gravitated towards that, and it never occurred to me to think in terms of writing for the screen."

Just three days after graduation from Carnegie, Bochco found himself on the staff at Universal television, and, from that day forward, he would confine his writing exclusively to the small screen. His first assignment was to sweeten a script for *Bob Hope Presents the Chrysler Theatre*, but with *The Name of the Game*, he established his talent for the crime and mystery genre. Bochco also wrote for Universal's *Columbo, McMillan and Wife*, and *Banacek*, and was then promoted to producer of such shows as *Griff* (with Lorne Greene), *Delvecchio* (with Judd Hirsch, Michael Conrad, and Charles Haid), *Richie Brockelman, Private Eye* (a *Rockford* spin-off), and *Paris* (starring James Earl Jones). Then it was on to MTM, where he wrote for *The White Shadow*, and later teamed with the show's producer, Bruce Paltrow, to shoot a pilot for *Operating Room*, a proposed medical drama.

Grant Tinker, in his book *Tinker on Television*, says, "Although each would go on to individual success with dramatic shows that incorporated considerable comedy, this joint Paltrow/Bochco effort just didn't work. Perhaps it was because *Operating Room* was lopsided in favor of comedy; their subsequent landmark shows were built on more substantial dramatic foundations."

Paltrow, Mark Tinker, and *White Shadow* writers John Masius, Josh Brand, and John Falsey would later develop their own medical drama, *St. Elsewhere*, but not before Bochco and partner Michael Kozoll had beaten them to the punch with *Hill Street Blues,* a groundbreaking police ensemble show known for its multiple, often unresolved story lines—something that bothered NBC brass and amused *Mad* magazine. In their parody "Swill Street Blues," *Mad* showed a viewer being hauled off in a straitjacket, yelling, "They didn't finish the story. They almost got to the end and stopped! Two years I watched it, and I never understood a thing! I can't stand it anymore!" One of the cops replies, "It's very interesting to observe how the human mind reacts when its limits of disorientation are exceeded . . . insanity wise!"

Bochco and his "insanity" prevailed, however, thanks in no small part to MTM chief Grant Tinker, who writes in *Tinker on Television*, "Steven had succeeded in bringing a new form to television. . . . [He] calls the knowledge that he had our total support on all creative matters, 'A really profound difference between MTM and a place like Universal.' That kind of support made it possible for our producers to stand up to the network."

Hill Street Blues racked up twenty-six Emmys and ninety-eight nominations, but it also gained respect outside traditional industry circles. Bob Thompson, in his book *Television's Second Golden Age*, notes that novelist Joyce Carol Oates told *TV Guide* (1985) that *Hill Street Blues* "is as intellectually and emotionally provocative as a good book." Quite a step up from FCC commissioner Newton Minnow's declaration two decades before that television was a "vast wasteland."

Besides growing critical acclaim for its pioneering format and riveting scripts, Hill Street, despite its relatively low ratings, was also attractive to advertisers. In *The Last Great Ride*, Brandon Tartikoff writes, "Why did we renew it? Research [was that] *Hill Street* was getting a higher rating in homes that had pay cable than in homes that didn't. That meant people who could choose from a twenty-channel cable universe . . . were seeking out our show to watch."

Yet, despite *Hill Street*'s success, Bochco and Arthur Price (Tinker's successor at MTM when Grant left to run NBC) parted company after five seasons (the show continued for two more). Meantime, the man with a flair for theater was getting ready to "stage" another innovation—an ensemble legal drama titled *L.A. Law*. Tartikoff says, "That show came out of a very brief meeting with Steven Bochco in 1985, and it proves that simple ideas are often the most powerful ones. '*Hill Street* is about eighty-five percent cops and fifteen percent lawyers,' I said. 'Why don't we flip flop the proportions, and see what happens'?" (*The Last Great Ride*).

What happened was eight seasons, four Emmys as best drama, and a new way of looking at the legal profession on television.

In 1990, while riding high on *L.A. Law,* Bochco returned to his musical roots with *Cop Rock,* a sort of *Hill Street* set to music, and featuring everything from singing juries to rapping protestors. Some critics called it "bold," others, "insane," but it was innovative. It was also a lot of work. Longtime Bochco music composer Mike Post told *TV Guide's* Timothy Carlson (October 1990) "[I]t's like writing the first act of a Broadway show every week."

Cop Rock starred future *NYPD Blue's* James McDaniel and *Hill Street's* Barbara Bosson, Bochco's wife at the time. *Cop Rock* lasted only one season, and several years later Steven's twenty-eight-year marriage to Barbara ended. In between those two breakups, Bochco, David Milch, and Detective Bill Clark hit pay dirt with *NYPD Blue*. This time, there were no singing cops, just naked ones.

In 2000 *NYPD Blue* entered in its seventh season, but not without some controversy. After *Once and Again's* strong performance in the Tuesday night ten o'clock time slot, ABC made noises about moving *NYPD Blue* to another night. A flood of protest from Bochco and fans, coupled with NBC's offer to take *NYPD Blue,* caused ABC to reconsider its decision. Today, *Blue* is stronger than ever in it story lines, and Bochco is at ease with his legacy, and buoyed by a new long-term deal with Paramount.

In the 1830s, Andrew Jackson understood the value of political theater and how the message worked best when it worked on all levels. As we settle into a new millennium, Steven Bochco knows that television-as-theater is not a lost art. He knows how important it is to continue to make quality drama more accessible and palatable.

I caught up with Steven on two occasions, in June and in September of 1999.

Longworth: What was the first real play you remember writing that was actually performed?

Was it in high school?

BOCHCO: Well, Carnegie Tech actually accepted me based on other writing. I had never written a play when I went there, so the first play that I ever wrote was produced in their studio theater, and it was purely a student production. It was pretty much universally panned. (*Laughs.*) Everybody thought it was a piece of shit. And there's nothing more vicious than a group of your writing peers or acting peers if you're an actor. I've been in enough acting classes and theater groups to know that they're sort of like jackals. When you're vulnerable, they'll just rip your tits off. (*Laughs.*)

Longworth: Well, was it actually bad, or were they just not getting what you wrote?

BOCHCO: Uh, I think it was probably actually bad. (*Laughs.*) In fact, probably most of what I did for the first ten or twelve years of my writing career was kind of bad.

Longworth: Today, if you write something or come up with an idea for a show, is there some sort of gauge in your head, so that you know before you get too far into it that you can say, "God, I remember what the jackals at school would say, so I'm not going to go through with this"?

BOCHCO: No, I've never done that in my life. I don't know if it's because I'm stupid or I'm just sort of blessed with an internal sort of optimism about things. I'm just sort of arrogant in believing that "well, shit, if I thought about it, it must be great."

Longworth: Speaking of something great that didn't last, and I hope this doesn't offend your sensibilities about *Hill Street* or *NYPD*, but do you know what my favorite Steven Bochco show is?

BOCHCO: What?

Longworth: *Delvecchio.*

BOCHCO: (*In a smiling tone.*) Really? Cool.

Longworth: And it just bummed me out when it went off the air. Lucky for CBS I wasn't a member of a radical militia group at the time.

BOCHCO: Yeah, I was disappointed too. For me, the year I spent working on that show sort of changed my internal process.

Longworth: How?

BOCHCO: Well, first of all, I had a great teacher . . . Billy Sackheim. [He] was a truly wonderful mentor, both as a writer and as a producer. He taught me the most valuable lessons probably I ever learned as a writer, and he also gave me a lot of room on that show to create, and I took it.

Longworth: It was great.

BOCHCO: It was a good show. It was certainly a show that was growing and evolving. And to be able to write for actors like Judd Hirsch and Michael

Conrad and Charlie Haid, it was really thrilling. Because for me, it was a little like coming home, in the sense that that show was theater to me. That show really celebrated words more than actions. God, I wrote a ton of those shows.

Longworth: Was that your first big gig in television?

BOCHCO: No. Not at all. My first real success on television was on *Columbo*.

Longworth: But you didn't have complete control over that?

BOCHCO: I didn't have any control. But I got a lot of recognition for that, and God knows I didn't have complete control over *Delveccio* by any stretch of the imagination. But I did have—what's the word?

Longworth: Latitude.

BOCHCO: Yeah, a lot of latitude, and an enormous amount of support.

Longworth: So *Columbo* gave you a chance to explore your ability to write for television.

BOCHCO: Yeah. Now, my first real television writing—I had been a story editor on *The Name of the Game* [1969–70].

Longworth: With Tony Franciosa.

BOCHCO: Franciosa, Bob Stack, Gene Barry. And then I went over to *Columbo* in 1971.

Longworth: But how did you just walk in and get your first writing job in TV?

BOCHCO: I was under contract to Universal, and I was sort of a "cork," and they would plug me into wherever there was a hole.

Longworth: Sort of a utility infielder.

BOCHCO: Yeah, I really was a kid, and I didn't cost them anything. I was making three hundred bucks a week.

Longworth: At what point, then, did you go to work for the Grant Tinker college of television?

BOCHCO: I went to MTM in 1978, and I was there from 1978 to 1985.

Longworth: Did you feel that you had the kind of latitude on *Hill Street* that—

BOCHCO: That was the most creative control I had ever had. I had creative autonomy on that show, for the first time, I had creative autonomy.

Longworth: I can't get anyone to say anything remotely negative about Grant, and then, when I talk to him, it's like he takes no credit for anything. He says, "Well, I just had good people."

BOCHCO: I know. He would protect you. He created an environment in which you could function. He adored writers. He was just a remarkable man. And he created an amazing company, and the environment in that company was truly unique for its time in much the same way I hope that the environment of my company is unique and certainly a reflection of, or an attempt to some degree of re-creating, the environment that existed in those days at that company.

Longworth: And it was competitive among the MTM shows, but a friendly kind of competitiveness.

BOCHCO: Oh, yeah, oh, yeah. You know, Bruce Paltrow and I had been friends even before we wound up inhabiting that building over there. And so he was doing *St. Elsewhere* downstairs and we were doing *Hill Street* upstairs, and it was really great. It was a building full of wonderful writers and directors and producers.

Longworth: Did Dick Wolf work for you?

BOCHCO: I was already gone.

Longworth: So you didn't hire him?

BOCHCO: No.   I was fired in 1985, and Dick came on for the sixth season of *Hill Street*.

Longworth: What was the real reason behind the firing?

BOCHCO: Well, the ostensible reason for firing me was that I was a profligate producer, you know, I was spending too much money, I wasn't responsive to the company. But in fact, I think the real reasons were much more complicated and much more personal.

Longworth: And yet, you still have good things to say about them?

BOCHCO: About the company? I have great things to say about my time making that show, and I have great things to say about that company in the years that Grant was there.

Longworth: It seems that a lot of *Above the Line* folks I talk with have either fired somebody or they've been fired themselves. How important is chemistry between the executive producer, the writers, and management?

BOCHCO: It's everything, it's everything. What we do is magic.

Longworth: But just because you were fired doesn't mean that you were a bad producer.

BOCHCO: No, I was a great producer on *Hill Street*, and I think what happened to that show subsequent to my leaving proved it. Their budgets doubled after I left. I always maintained that we were producing the most economical show on television relative to what was going on the screen.

Longworth: So obviously, then, you've taken a lot of that MTM experience into making your operation what it is today. In other words, it's not just a matter of copying the good things, but rather avoiding the bad things.

BOCHCO: Almost more importantly that. And I've always said that the twelve years that I spent at Universal, for me, was much more valuable in the context of learning how *not* to behave than how to behave.

Longworth: Universal seemed to have a lot of conflicts, like with James Garner over payments from syndication profits of *Rockford.*

BOCHCO: Studios were always in the business of cheating you. And they did. (*Laughs.*) They robbed you blind.

Longworth: But even as big as you are, it could still happen today?

BOCHCO: I think it continues to be more the norm probably than not. But I don't think it's as prevalent now as it was then, because it's just not as orderly a universe, where you had three studios and three networks and they're controlling everything. It's so competitive out there, and people become so sophisticated in their deal making, and everybody understands the economics of television so much better than they once did. [Shortly after completing our interview, Bochco sued Fox, alleging that he had been cheated out of millions of dollars in profits from the sale of *NYPD Blue* into reruns on the FX cable network.]

Longworth: Well, if the economics have always been so important, and you were so good at making an economical show, it seems that, by now, you would have thrown up your hands, and said, "I'm going over and make some deals with cable . . . maybe there'll be less money in it for me, but there'll be more latitude, and I'll trust them more."

BOCHCO: Well, you do and you don't. You know, I've had contractual, creative control over what I do for a very long time. I may go over to do something with HBO, where in theory you have a lot more creative latitude than you do in broadcast television, which is true. On the other hand, HBO retains creative rights, creative controls.

Longworth: I didn't realize that.

BOCHCO: Yeah, you bet. They won't give them up.

Longworth: Give me an example of how that could hang you up.

BOCHCO: Anytime you're in business with an entity that has "above the line" creative controls, it means, in theory at least, you cannot hire an actor without their approval. You cannot hire a director without their approval. You cannot hire a writer without their approval. They have control over final cuts of all your product. So, on the one hand you're gaining tremendous latitude on the page, but you're giving up a tremendous amount of creative control on the other side of it. So, you know, I'm not sure that's such a great bargain, quite honestly.

Longworth: So then, you have a good relationship with the networks you now work with in terms of latitude and creativity?

BOCHCO: I have complete creative control, and have had for many many years, yes.

Longworth: Over the years, have there been times when a network person has come in and said, "I don't want you to use this word" or "You have to take out this scene"?

BOCHCO: Oh, I've had horrible fights, because even though you may have creative control, you still have to deal with broadcast standards. Shit, I've been at war with those turkeys ever since I've been in television. But I've never lost an episode to it. I've never had to fundamentally alter an episode.

Longworth: I remember they wouldn't let Paltrow use the word *condom* on *St. Elsewhere*.

BOCHCO: I know.

Longworth: And that was in 1983.

BOCHCO: Oh, I know. The world has changed.

Longworth: You're sort of a devilish person, though. Do you try to push the envelope just to . . .

BOCHCO: Fuck with them? No. No, I think that's childish. My big beef with broadcast standards has always been that they treat us as if we're precocious children that have to be constantly watched and monitored, or we will get into trouble. Well, I'm fifty-five years old. I'm not a child, and I don't want to be treated like a child. And, by the same token, I don't want to play childish games with them. You can't have it both ways.

Longworth: In Gitlin's *Inside Prime Time*, you said, "I have been put on earth to torment Standards people." I can't help but think back to the "Ewe and Me Baby" episode from *Hill Street Blues*. Can you relate how that was finally resolved? And do you in fact live to torment these people?

BOCHCO: Well, there's a difference between playing with them and tormenting them. (*Laughs.*) You torment them simply by presenting them with the kinds of material that you know you're going to end up getting in a fight over. And then, fighting them "till you drop," which is just what I've always done. When you were talking about playing with them, you either suggested or implied that I would put things in there just to fuck with them, or put things in that you could trade off later, or whatever. And I don't do that. When something goes in a script, it goes in because that's the story we want to tell in the way we want to tell it. And you just know certain kinds of stories, and the way you treat certain kinds of things *is* going to make 'em nuts. My attitude essentially is (*pause.*) fuck 'em. (*Laughs.*)

Longworth: (*Laughs.*) Now, tell me again how the sheep thing got resolved. In the episode, a man is found dead in a hotel room with a sheep.

BOCHCO: Well, we won it. First they said you can't do it. And we fought about that for a while. And then finally they said, "All right, you can do it," but (*Laughs.*) this is pretty funny. Then they got really concerned that people would assume this guy was "plugging" this sheep in the ass or something. (*Longworth laughs.*) So I think we finally agreed to put a bow on it to let people know that it was a female sheep. (*Both laugh.*)

Longworth: Now, on a similar theme of controversy, let's skip ahead to *N.Y.P.D. Blue.* There were more than fifty ABC affiliates that refused to air the premiere episode because of nudity and language. You had to know the kind of shit storm you were going to generate, before you ever shot the episode?

BOCHO: Uh-huh.

Longworth: Then why did you do it? Did you just figure that the back end would pay off because of all the publicity?

BOCHCO: No. No. I did it because it was time to do it. That's why. I did it because there was simply no reason to do another cop show, or another "this" show or another "that" show, the same old way we'd been doing every other goddamned show, and getting our brains beat out, 'cause people weren't watching. We were being deserted in droves for cable [and] movies. And I felt if we didn't make this kind of a show, and get people back in our tent by being more adult, and more contemporary in our use of language, then we were going to be out of business; it's just as simple as that. And as with everything else in life, people resist change, and you have to overcome that. If you're going to do it, you got to be prepared to fight the battles. If you fold your cards, why do it to begin with?

Longworth: Obviously, then, control is important, both creative and otherwise. I was fascinated to learn that you were once offered the top job at CBS. Why was the offer made, how much control would you have had over program development, and why did you turn them down?

BOCHCO: I think the offer was made because they needed to make a change, they wanted to make a change. They, through various circuitous means, heard that I had always been interested in running a network, and—

Longworth: Which you had?

BOCHCO: Which I had been. And they contacted me. I went back to New York, and I spent a day with William Paley, and had dinner that night with Larry Tisch, and they offered me the job.

Longworth: Even as successful as you were then, and you were already a household name, that had to feel pretty unreal to you.

BOCHCO: I didn't feel unreal. I knew I probably wouldn't take the job if they offered it to me because the timing was just lousy. I was deep into negotiations with ABC already for that ten-series commitment. This is in late-1987. Then I thought, shit, why should I go back at all? And my attorney, who used to be head of business affairs at CBS many years ago, said, "You have to go back, and you have to spend time with William Paley because he's the founder of your industry, for Christ's sakes." And I thought, Well, you know, if I'm going to go back and do this, then damn it, I want them to ask me to do the job—whether I take it or not. I don't want to get turned down, you know what I mean?

Longworth: Exactly. So he did ask you?

BOCHCO: Oh, yeah. They offered it to me. And I ultimately turned them down.

Longworth: Well, not to belabor the point, but—

BOCHCO: I don't know how—we never got specific to the point about how much control I'd have over programming, but given my nature, it would have been a deal breaker if I couldn't have had it.

Longworth: In your case, I know you had a lot of employees, a lot of people depending on you, but there's always a way to do something if you absolutely want to do it. So here's this great job offer and—

BOCHCO: I'm not sure it *was* a great job offer. It was a job offer.

Longworth: It's just that most people can't relate to what it would be like to be offered a job as the head of a network.

BOCHCO: Well, you know, CBS was in real disarray. It would have needed and did need, in fact, a massive, massive overhaul. It was then a very conservative, Eastern, political kind of company. It would have been a real, real, real uphill battle, which, that said, if they'd asked me two years earlier, I probably would have taken the job.

Longworth: So perhaps that was a mistake you didn't make, but let's talk about the ones you did. You told me that the biggest mistake you ever made in television was to produce *Bay City Blues,* a show about a minor-league baseball team. There are critics who beg to differ, saying *Cop Rock,* a police drama set to music, was a bigger mistake. Marsh and Brooks even seemed to question your sanity for attempting it. But other critics say *Cop Rock* was great, that even your failures are great. Now, the question is, Do you even consider shows like *Bay City Blues* and *Cop Rock* as failures?

BOCHCO: *Bay City Blues* was a failure. *Cop Rock* didn't succeed.

Longworth: Explain to me the difference.

BOCHCO: The difference is that I accomplished a great deal of what I was looking to accomplish in *Cop Rock.* So that, for me, from a creative point of view, I didn't fail at it. It didn't succeed commercially. *Bay City Blues* simply wasn't good enough at every level. It wasn't good enough at conception. It wasn't good enough at execution, on any level. It was just a failed show. I felt profoundly distressed by the mistake of it. I wasn't happy with any part of it, you know, looking back on it, it just was a wrong show.

Longworth: You said during the Museum of Television and Radio seminar that one of the most fun times in your career was what I call the "Team Bochco" years on *L.A. Law,* where you had such synergy with the guys that worked with you, going in each day, brainstorming ideas. One of the young writers you brought in was David Kelley. Why was that so much fun for you, and how was it you came to discover Kelley?

BOCHCO: I discovered David Kelley by reading a script. He was a practicing attorney in Boston, and he had written a screenplay that was in the hands of an agent down here, and I was looking for writers with a law background, so they sent the script over, and I read ten pages of it, and I said, "Boy, get this guy on an airplane and get him out here." And that was that. I had a ball on that show.

Longworth: But he was just one of the team members. So what was so good about that group?

BOCHCO: It was a great group, you know? I mean, we were doing a show that we believed in and were having a real good time with. It was kind of a fresh way to do a law show, and I was having a good time. I felt sort of liberated from MTM and my time there (and years doing *Hill Street* and everything), and I felt like I had something to prove, so I was highly motivated. So it was just a great time.

Longworth: *Hill Street* was innovative because it was the first ensemble cop show. Same with *L.A. Law* and the legal profession. And while *NYPD Blue* broke the language and nudity barriers, you also innovated the subtle use of dead air. Someone at the Museum of Television and Radio in New York asked if you considered commercials to be an intrusion, and you talked of devising a solution that involved stealing a couple of seconds of program time.

BOCHCO: I don't even know if it was that long—yeah, it was probably a couple of seconds.

Longworth: So how did you come up with that innovation?

BOCHCO: On *Hill Street,* so often, you'd end an act on a terrifically emotional moment, and then, bang! That hard cut right into some sort of a soap commercial. It was always very, very emotionally jarred. And so Greg (Hoblit) and I just—I don't remember if it was his idea or my idea, or how it came up—but we decided to just use like a second or two of our own program time to go to black, so that we delivered to the network format a show that had just a second or two of black at the end of each act. It was this tiny, almost subliminal buffer between the show and the commercial.

Longworth: Now, that's something that had quite an impact on the audience, even though they probably didn't realize what you had done, and that brings me to a question about the audience. You were once quoted as saying that your fundamental responsibility is to yourself, and not to your audience. What exactly did you mean? Because at first glance, that sounds a bit arrogant.

BOCHCO: Well, it's not arrogant, I don't think. What it is is that in my experience, what I realize is that when you have an audience watching what you do, numbering in the millions and millions of people, there's no way you can please everybody. You just can't, and if you start thinking that way, you're going to wind up manufacturing—what's that old cliché—a camel is a horse designed by committee? (*Both laugh.*) If you start listening to everybody who's telling you what's wrong with what you're doing, and why it's not appropriate, and why it's this, and shouldn't be that, and blah, blah, blah, or why this won't work, you've got a "horse" designed by committee. So when I say my responsibility is to myself, I trust my judgment. I can work out my own conflicts about something internally, and come to my own conclusions about it. When you say "the audience," the audience is a hundred different points of view, you know, based on age, region of the country, religion, philosophy, and gee whiz, how can you look to your fundamental responsibility outside yourself? You have to trust your own artistry, you have to trust your own sense of ethics, your own sense of right and wrong, and your own sense of balance about things, and then proceed with your work accordingly. Imagine as a painter or as a novelist sitting down to try to figure out whether the story you wanted to tell, or the picture you wanted to paint, might offend somebody. And you've got to be true to your own vision. So that's not arrogant, I don't think. That's trying to stay true to your art, your vision.

Longworth: Final question about audience. Have you had any feedback over the years from shows you've done where you know you really made a difference in somebody's life, that you've touched something in them?

BOCHCO: Of course. I remember getting a letter from a guy written on motel stationery, having just seen the episode of *Hill Street Blues* where Frank Furillo reveals himself as an alcoholic. And in the letter, he said he was in this motel room thinking of killing himself. And then that episode inspired him to get sober and change his life. I've had all kinds of experiences like that.

Longworth: Would you rather have one of those letters a week, or an Emmy each year?

BOCHCO: (*Laughs.*) I'd like to have them both. (*Laughs.*)

Longworth: Well, you get them anyway, so it's a moot point. But anyway, you clearly have a gift for being able to motivate and impact viewers with your hour dramas, so that leads me to revisit something that you and I talked about in New York, which is why don't we see more half-hour dramas on television anymore? I think back to *Wonder Years, Frank's Place,* and your show *Doogie Howser.* First of all, they'd be cheaper to produce and—

BOCHCO: Not much.

Longworth: Why do you say that?

BOCHCO: Because they're not. You don't pay your actors less. You don't pay your crew less. The film doesn't cost less. The stage doesn't cost less. The sets don't cost less. The only reduction in cost is in the number of days you shoot a half-hour show. You used to shoot them in five days, and now an hour drama might be seven and a half or eight days. So that's where your cost savings comes in. But a half-hour show does not cost half of what an hour show costs. It's really more like three-quarters of what an hour show costs.

Longworth: But aren't half hours easier to sell in syndication? For example, what if *NYPD Blue* was a thirty-minute drama?

BOCHCO: I doubt it. Certainly there's no history that would indicate that half-hour filmed shows of a dramatic nature do well in syndication.

Longworth: You mentioned paying the casts. Now, with modern-day ensembles like yours, there's more demand on the writers because you have so many story lines going on, and involving all of the cast members. What's good about ensembles from your standpoint, and what's bad about ensembles?

BOCHCO: I don't think there's anything bad about ensembles. And what's good about them is you have many, many more characters to work with. More stories to tell. There's more combinations of relationships you can work with. And ultimately, it's a situation in which the show remains the star. In a real ensemble, you can always replace somebody. Not always with impunity. I mean, when Michael Conrad died, I don't feel we were ever adequately able to replace him [on *Hill Street Blues*]. I mean, that's not to say that Bob Prosky isn't a wonderful, wonderful actor, but Michael Conrad was so unique in that role and so special to that show that I think we lost something irreplaceable when he died. But because it was an ensemble, we were able to survive it and go on. If it had been "The Michael Conrad Show," we were fucked.

Longworth: You've always featured diverse casts in your shows, but I'm going to ask you about on-screen racial diversity anyway, because, at least where Hollywood and television is concerned, it's an issue that's not going to go away anytime soon. A newspaper article reported that it took "all of twenty minutes" for Leslie Moonves to green light *City of Angels*, the new show you, Nicholas Wootton, and Paris Barclay have created. Do you think that's because Les could feel the pressure coming down on him, or just because it was a damn good idea?

BOCHCO: I don't think it had anything to do with pressure. This was long before schedules are set for the fall. This was like in March, maybe February, fully two to three months before pilots were finished and schedules are set, so no, it had nothing to do with that. It had to do with the fact that it's what I wanted to do. I think he sensed my passion about it. I think I had some really good answers to some questions that he had. And I think both of us agreed that if I had one more show to do for CBS, I think we both wanted it to be something that I felt deeply committed to. I think it also made sense. It was smart programming.

Longworth: And since you and Paris pioneered this for the right reasons, meaning that it preceded and predated the political pressures, and we've gotten past that, do you then think that there's going to be added pressure on you and him to make sure that people tune in to this show?

BOCHCO: You can't make sure that people tune in. All you can do is make a good show and hope that you get sampled, and then hope that people like what you do and that they're watching in sufficient numbers for you to survive.

Longworth: But it's not like you haven't tried to do good programs with black characters, for example, the show *Paris*, starring James Earl Jones.

BOCHCO: Well, it's twenty years later, and this [*City of Angels*] is a better show because I'm a better writer and I'm a better producer than I was twenty years ago.

Longworth: How much better are you?

BOCHCO: A lot better, about twenty years better. (*Laughs.*)

Longworth: You were quoted as having said, "Once you're a known quantity, you don't surprise." So I have to state the obvious. Everyone knows your name. You could probably walk into a cornfield somewhere and the farmer would say, "Hey, it's the TV guy." So you're known everywhere.

BOCHCO: I don't know that I was talking about myself.

Longworth: But I am.

BOCHCO: No, but the quote that you're offering I think was in reference to a show. That once a show succeeds, no matter how different it was perceived to be, once it succeeds, it no longer retains the ability to surprise.

Longworth: Exactly, but I've adapted this into a Bochco question. So, in other words, you're a known quantity and you're still surprising people.

BOCHCO: Well, good!

Longworth: And obviously, you're still out there thinking of ways to take us in a different direction. So do you have other surprises planned for us?

BOCHCO: I hope so.

Longworth: I don't mean just an idea for a new show, but a different direction. Do you know where that direction is?

BOCHCO: Yeah, if someone will let me do it.

Longworth: But you're not going to tell me?

BOCHCO: Of course not. (*Both laugh.*)

Longworth: How do I know you're telling me the truth?

BOCHCO: 'Cause I'm not lying, cause I don't lie. If I don't want to answer a question, I won't answer it, but if I answer it, I'm telling you the truth.

Longworth: But how will I know when you've taken us in this new direction?

BOCHCO: Again, as I say, if somebody will let me do it.

Longworth: Will there be a sign from God? How am I going to know when this new direction starts?

BOCHCO: You'll know. (*Laughter.*)

Longworth: All right then, I'm hanging up the phone and I'm going to go wait for it.

BOCHCO: Well, you may wait for a while. I'm not sure anyone's about to let me go off and do this thing that I'd like to be doing.

Longworth: Nevertheless, I'll go turn on the TV right now and just sit there until it happens.

BOCHCO: OK. (*Laughs.*) But you'll have to have somebody come in and clip your toenails for you. (*Both laugh.*)

Longworth: Thanks.

BOCHCO: All right, my friend.

ᙢᙢ 13 ᙢᙢ

AFTERWORD | TV Drama— A case for proper Recognition

AS early as January 1999, when *Providence* proved to be a strong midseason starter for NBC, it became clear that viewers were willing to give dramas a second look, and, by September, a new trend had emerged. Dramas were beginning to replace sitcoms as the dominant genre.

When the new millennium arrived, there were no fewer than sixty hour dramas on television (including syndication and cable), and the "Age of Drama" had officially begun. Given the reemergence and popularity of dramas, and the fact that their individual natures were quite diverse, I asked my friend John Leverence of the Academy of Television Arts and Sciences why Emmys couldn't be awarded according to "subcategories," rather than by grouping all dramas together. What follows is a portion of the interview I conducted in October of 1999.

ᙢᙢ   ᙢᙢ   ᙢᙢ

Longworth: I'm going to identify five different dramas to you off the top of my head: *JAG, The X-Files, The Practice, NYPD Blue,* and *Once and Again.* Now, I've just listed five different genres within the drama category. So with the reemergence of television drama, why shouldn't we move toward the awarding of Emmys in subcategories of drama?

LEVERENCE: The Board of Governors of the Academy have approved for the 2000 competition a new rule that states that for two consecutive years,

210

if a peer group identifies that there would have been (had the category been in place) fourteen or more entries that define such a specialized and distinct achievement that they are no longer represented adequately *within* an existing category, they should be separated into a *new* category. I think that that is a mandate for the awards committee, and for the Board of Governors to take a look at exactly the question that you have raised as to whether or not there are subgroups within the drama series category that would compel them to attend to this rule.

Longworth: But why fourteen?

LEVERENCE: They just felt that fourteen was a number that gained critical mass. In order to get five nominations (per another rule that we have that's referred to as the "one-third rule") you can have no more than one-third the number of nominations that you have entries. So, in order to get five entries, you would have to have, rounding out, a total of fourteen entries.

Longworth: But you'd be hard-pressed to identify fourteen police dramas or fourteen medical dramas. So isn't the new rule moot?

LEVERENCE: Well, they feel that without that critical mass, there's no compelling argument for splitting out. They're not going to do it for a handful. Say you have six medical shows. The maximum number of nominations you could get using the one-third rule would be two. They're not going to set up a new medical drama series category and have two nominations.

Longworth: But most of today's dramas have nothing in common except that they are an hour long.

LEVERENCE: And so, therefore, we are unfairly asking people to vote their preference on profoundly disparate nominations?

Longworth: Right.

LEVERENCE: Well, that *is* an argument on one side. The argument on the other side is that despite the fact that these might be generically different, there are certain common elements of dramatic production that are constant to all of them. And the professionals in the field can sort through the differences to get to the similarities, and based on those can cast their vote in a preferential manner.

MW   MW   MW

Clearly, the Board of Governors is making a step in the right direction, but the best solution is to change the one-third rule. After all, what's wrong with having *ER, Chicago Hope, Third Watch,* and *City of Angels* compete in a subcategory for best medical drama? So what if there aren't fourteen medical dramas on the air. Let those that *are* broadcast be recognized for excellence within a specific genre.

What appears in appendix A is my recommendation for the establishment of new Emmy subcategories in the drama genre.

Appendixes
selected Bibliography
Index

Appendix A

Dramas of the 1999–2000 Television season by category

MEDICAL

Chicago Hope	Third Watch
City of Angels	Wonderland
ER	

CRIME/POLICE

Beat, The	Oz
Cover Me	Profiler
Diagnosis Murder	Secret Agent Man
Law & Order: Special Victims Unit	Snoops
Nash Bridges	Sopranos, The
NYPD Blue	Strip, The

FAMILY

Chicken Soup for the Soul	Safe Harbor
Destination Stardom	7th Heaven
Hope Island	Touched by an Angel

LEGAL

Family Law	Law & Order
JAG	Practice, The

ACTION/ADVENTURE

Badland, The	Pensacola, Wings of Gold
G vs E	Walker, Texas Ranger
Martial Law	

SCI-FI/FANTASY

Angel	Others, The
Buffy	Pretender, The
Charmed	Roswell
Early Edition	Seven Days
Earth: Final Conflict	Stargate SG-1
First Wave	Star Trek: Voyager
Harsh Realm	Twice in a Lifetime
Hercules	Xena: Warrior Princess
Now and Again	X-Files, The

ADULT

Any Day Now	Once and Again
Beggars and Choosers	Providence
Beyond Chance	VIP
Hoop Life, The	West Wing, The
Judging Amy	

YOUNG ADULT

Beverly Hills 90210	Party of Five
Dawson's Creek	Popular
Felicity	Ryan Caufield
Get Real	Time of Your Life
Manchester Prep	Wasteland

Appendix B

Dramas of the 1999–2000 Television season by Time slot

SATURDAY

	6:00 P.M.	7:00 P.M.	8:00 P.M.	9:00 P.M.	10:00 P.M.
CBS			Early Edition	Martial Law	Walker, Texas Ranger
NBC			The Pretender	The Others	Profiler
UPN		Star Trek Voyager	Stargate	Earth: Final Conflict	
Sci-Fi	First Wave				

SUNDAY

	7:00 P.M.	8:00 P.M.	9:00 P.M.	10:00 P.M.
ABC		Snoops	The Practice	
CBS		Touched by an Angel		
FOX			The X-Files	

Major networks and pay cable only. Show times may vary on cable.

	7:00 P.M.	8:00 P.M.	9:00 P.M.	10:00 P.M.
NBC		*Third Watch*		
PAX			*Hope Island*	
WB	*7th Heaven Beginnings*	*Felicity*		
UPN	*VIP*			
Liftime				*Any Day Now*
HBO				*The Sopranos* (various times)
Showtime				*The Hoop Life*
USA		*G vs E* *Cover Me*		

MONDAY

	7:00 P.M.	8:00 P.M.	9:00 P.M.	10:00 P.M.
ABC				*Once and Again* (2000)
CBS				*Family Law*
FOX		*Time of Your Life*		
PAX		*Destination Stardom*		
WB	*7th Heaven*	*Safe Harbor*		
Lifetime		*Beyond Chance*		

TUESDAY

	8:00 P.M.	9:00 P.M.	10:00 P.M.
ABC			*Once and Again* (1999) *NYPD Blue* (2000)
CBS	*JAG*		*Judging Amy*
FOX		*Party of Five*	
PAX	*Chicken Soup for the Soul*		
WB	*Buffy*	*Angel*	
UPN	*Secret Agent Man*	*The Strip*	
Showtime	*The Hoop Life*	*Beggars & Choosers*	

WEDNESDAY

	8:00 P.M.	9:00 P.M.	10:00 P.M.
CBS	*City of Angels*		
FOX	*Beverly Hills 90210*	*Get Real*	
NBC		*The West Wing*	*Law & Order*
PAX	*Twice in a Lifetime*		
WB	*Dawson's Creek*	*Roswell*	
UPN	*Seven Days*	*Star Trek Voyager*	
HBO			*Oz*

THURSDAY

	8:00 P.M.	9:00 P.M.	10:00 P.M.
ABC		*Wasteland*	
CBS	*Diagnosis Murder*	*Chicago Hope*	

THURSDAY (continued)

	8:00 P.M.	9:00 P.M.	10:00 P.M.
FOX	*Manchester Prep*		
NBC			*ER*
WB	*Popular*	*Charmed*	

FRIDAY

	8:00 P.M.	9:00 P.M.	10:00 P.M.
CBS		*Now and Again*	*Nash Bridges*
FOX	*Ryan Caufield/* *The Badland*	*Harsh* *Realm*	
NBC	*Providence*		*Law & Order:* *Special Victims* *Unit* (2000)

selected Bibliography

Altschuler, Glen C., and David I. Grossvogel. *Changing Channels: America in TV Guide.* Chicago: Univ. of Illinois Press, 1992.

Baker, William F., and George Dessart. *Down the Tube: An Inside Account of the Failure of American Television.* New York: Basic Books, 1998.

Bianculli, David. *Teleliteracy—Taking Television Seriously.* New York: Touchstone, 1992.

Brinkley, Joel. *Defining Vision: The Battle for the Future of Television.* Orlando, Fla.: Harcourt Brace, 1997.

Brooks, Tim, and Earle Marsh. *The Complete Directory to Prime Time Network and Cable TV Shows, 1946–Present.* 7th ed. New York: Ballantine Books, 1999.

Courrier, Kevin, and Susan Green. *Law & Order: The Unofficial Companion.* Los Angeles: Renaissance Books, 1998.

Feuer, Jane. *Seeing Through the Eighties.* Durham, N.C.: Duke Univ. Press, 1995.

Feuer, Jane, Paul Kerr, and Tise Vahimagi. *MTM: Quality Television.* London: British Film Institute, 1984.

Gitlin, Todd. *Inside Prime Time.* New York: Pantheon, 1983.

Goldberg, Lee. *Unsold Television Pilots.* Jefferson, N.C.: McFarland, 1990.

Hill, George H., and Sylvia Saverson Hill. *Blacks on Television—A Selectively Annotated Bibliography.* Metuchen, N.J.: Scarecrow Press, 1985.

Kalat, David P. *Homicide: Life on the Street—The Unofficial Companion.* Los Angeles: Renaissance Books, 1998.

Levinson, Barry. *Avalon, Tin Men, and Diner. Three Screenplays by Barry Levinson.* New York: Atlantic Monthly Press, 1990.

———. *Levinson on Levinson.* Edited by David Thompson. Boston: Faber and Faber, 1992.

Marc, David, and Robert J. Thompson. *Prime Time, Prime Movers.* Syracuse, N.Y.: Syracuse Univ. Press, 1995.

Marill, Alvin H. *Movies Made for Television, 1964–1986.* New York: Baseline, 1987.

Martindale, David. *Television Detective Shows of the 1970s.* Jefferson, N.C.: McFarland, 1991.

Milch, David, and Detective Bill Clark. *True Blue: The Real Stories Behind N.Y.P.D. Blue.* New York: William Morrow & Co., 1995.

Nelson, Robin. *TV Drama in Transition: Forms, Values, and Cultural Change.* New York: St. Martin's Press, 1997.

O'Neil, Thomas. *The Emmys.* New York: Perigee, 1998.

Pourroy, Janine. *Behind, the Scenes at ER.* New York: Ballantine Books, 1995.

Skutch, Ira. *The Days of Live: Television's Golden Age As Seen by Twenty-one Directors Guild of America Members.* Metuchen, N.J.: Scarecrow Press, 1998.

Spigel, Lynn. *Make Room for TV: Television and Family Ideas in Postwar America*. Chicago: Univ. of Chicago Press, 1992.

Stark, Steven D. *Glued to the Set*. New York: Delta, 1997.

Stempel, Tom. *Storytellers to the Nation: A History of American Television Writing*. Syracuse, N.Y.: Syracuse Univ. Press, 1992.

Sumser, John. *Morality and Social Order in Television Crime Drama*. Jefferson, N.C.: McFarland, 1996.

Tartikoff, Brandon, and Charles Leerhsen. *The Last Great Ride*. New York: Turtle Bay Books, 1992.

Terrace, Vincent. *Experimental Television, Test Films, Pilots, and Trial Series*. Jefferson, N.C.: McFarland, 1997.

Thompson, Robert J. *Television's Second Golden Age*. New York: Continuum, 1996.

Tinker, Grant, and Bud Rukeyser. *Tinker in Television: From General Sarnoff to General Electric*. New York: Simon and Schuster, 1994.

Wild, David. *The Showrunners*. New York: Harper Collins, 1999.

Wilk, Max. *The Golden Age of Television: Notes from the Survivors*. Chicago: Silver Spring Press, 1999.

Index

Index | 229